THE CAUCASUS

ie Caucasus is one of the most complicated regions in the world: with many dif-
rent peoples and political units, differing religious allegiances, frequent conflicts,
d where historically major world powers have clashed with each other on many
.ccasions. Until now there has been no comprehensive introductory book for those
wishing to learn about this complex region. This book fills the gap, providing a
clear, comprehensive introduction to the Caucasus, which is suitable for all readers.
covers the geography; the historical development of the region; economics; politics and government; population; religion and society; culture and traditions; alongside its conflicts and international relations. Written throughout in an accessible
style, it requires no prior knowledge of the Caucasus. The book will be invaluable
for those researching specific issues, as well as for readers needing a thorough
introduction to the region.

Frederik Coene is currently Attaché dealing with post-conflict assistance in the
Delegation of the European Commission to Georgia. His research on the Caucasus
began in 1999 during his internship in the Private Office of the Secretary-General
at NATO Headquarters. Since then he has researched, worked and travelled in all
parts of the Caucasus.

ROUTLEDGE CONTEMPORARY RUSSIA AND EASTERN EUROPE SERIES

THE CAUCASUS

An introduction

Frederik Coene

Routledge
Taylor & Francis Group

LONDON AND NEW YORK

First published 2010
by Routledge
2 Park Square, Milton Park, Abingdon, Oxon, OX14 4RN

Simultaneously published in the USA and Canada
by Routledge
711 Third Avenue, New York, NY 10017

*Routledge is an imprint of the Taylor & Francis Group,
an informa business*

First issued in paperback 2011

© 2010 Frederik Coene

Typeset in Times by
Book Now Ltd, London

British Library Cataloguing in Publication Data
A catalogue record for this book is available from the British Library

Library of Congress Cataloging in Publication Data
Coene, Frederik.
The Caucasus: an introduction / Frederik Coene.
p. cm.
Includes bibliographical references and index.
1. Caucasus—Description and travel. I. Title.
DK509.C64 2009
947.5—dc22
2009010323

ISBN10: 0–415–48660–2 (hbk)
ISBN10: 0–415–66683–X (pbk)
ISBN10: 0–203–87071–9 (ebk)

ISBN13: 978–0–415–48660–6 (hbk)
ISBN13: 978–0–415–66683–1 (pbk)
ISBN13: 978–0–203–87071–6 (ebk)

CONTENTS

ILLUSTRATIONS

Figures

Maps

Tables

FOREWORD

The recent fighting between Russia and Georgia, which broke out in the summer of 2008, reminded the world that this region remains a potential area of dispute and conflict in the twenty-first century. Yet it is a sad fact that the world needed this reminder. Standing, as it does, at the junction of great land masses and historic empires, the Caucasus has for centuries been a contested land. The astonishing racial and linguistic diversity that characterizes the region, coupled with the Soviet legacy of ethnic displacement and highly divisive artificial borders, has made the Caucasus even more volatile and vulnerable to internal tensions and outside interference alike.

Today the Caucasus is one of the most important and sensitive regions of the world, with the potential to spark conflict between the great nations that border it. Its increasing significance as a producer of, and particularly as a transit route for, oil and gas adds an extra, and highly significant, dimension to the historic great-power territorial rivalry and local ethnic tensions. It guarantees, alas, that the conflicts in the region will continue to be of global significance. They will attract outside attention because they will have ramifications far beyond the borders of the states concerned.

But the region and its history are so complex that outsiders have always found it difficult to establish and comprehend the essential details. This has led in the past to seriously flawed analyses and, as a result, poorly informed policy decisions. Consequently, this excellent volume by Frederik Coene is most timely and welcome. Its wealth of relevant data, its great attention to detail, its balanced and straightforward description of events, and its clear and dispassionate analysis provide the scholar and policy-maker with a most valuable source of information and understanding. The work will allow current and future events in the region to be placed firmly in context, to the benefit of all concerned.

Christopher N. Donnelly
Director, Atlantic Council of the UK

PREFACE

Dedicated to my dear friend
Kureysh Nalgiyev
(23.02.1972–23.09.2005)

In 1999 I became involved with the Caucasus for the first time in my life. It would not only lead to a major change in my career path, it would also inflict a change on my way of thinking and my view of the world. In the following years, several visits to the region and research initiatives followed each other at a great pace. During my trips I experienced both positive moments, such as friendship and the beauty of the culture and the environment, as well as shocking events, such as the brutal assassination of Kureysh Nalgiyev, my guard and more importantly my close friend in Ingushetia.

My biggest disappointment in those initial years was the absence of any book that could give a basic introduction to newcomers to the region in a structured manner. There are definitely many books on the history, conflicts, population and economy of the Caucasus, but none combine and link the fundamental knowledge into a whole without confusing its reader even more. It is my strongest belief that, in order to come up with credible and valuable theories and conceptual frameworks, one should always be able to back this up with data and concrete knowledge of the real situation. Those who are looking for analysis or results of new research will be disappointed, as this is not my aim at all.

Based on my frustration and on the words of one of my lecturers – 'If there is no such book, then why don't you just write it yourself?' – I embarked in early 2001 on a task which for the following eight years would be one of my hobbies and personal challenges.

I hope this book will not just provide factual information, but will help the reader to understand the Caucasus a bit better so that they can experience the same fascination for the region as I do.

Frederik Coene
Veurne, 25 January 2009

ACKNOWLEDGEMENTS

Writing a book of this kind takes not only a lot of effort by its author; it would be impossible without the help and assistance of colleagues and friends, and I have been fortunate to be surrounded by many.

First of all, I would like to thank Chris Donnelly and the late Col. Leif Sponbeck for giving me the chance to take my first steps – both intellectually and physically – in the Caucasus. Thanks to them, my professional life took a completely new direction and I would not currently be where I am without them.

During the course of writing, many other people have helped improve this book by giving their valuable advice and recommendations or contributed with information, suggestions and comments: Dr Andrew Andersen, Dr Donnacha Ó Beacháin, Dr Daniel Lachat, Dr Zalina Pliyeva, Donald Bowser, Timm Büchner, Bruno De Cordier, Nicolai Hengeveld, Namik Heydarov, Kristin Höltge, Gerald Hübner, Levan Kvatchadze, Kureysh Nalgiyev, Maia Maisaia, Gayane Martirosyan, Alina Makeyeva, Giorgi Robakidze and Ineke van Nugteren. Without the support of Dr Valentin Kotzev, who helped me understand basic cartography, this book would not have had maps, and I owe my sincerest gratitude to Dr John Stopford, who spent several days correcting the language errors.

ABBREVIATIONS AND ACRONYMS

AD	anno Domini
ASSR	Autonomous Soviet Socialist Republic
BC	before Christ
CIS	Commonwealth of Independent States
CSCE	Conference on Security and Cooperation in Europe
CST	Collective Security Treaty
CSTO	Collective Security Treaty Organization
EU	European Union
EUSR	EU special representative
ENP	European Neighbourhood Policy (EU)
ENPI	European Neighbourhood Policy Instrument (EU)
FSB	Federalnaya Sluzhba Bezopasnosti (Federal Security Services)
GDP	gross domestic product
GMT	Greenwich Mean Time
GUAM	Georgia–Ukraine–Azerbaijan–Moldova group
GUUAM	Georgia–Ukraine–Uzbekistan–Azerbaijan–Moldova group
IDP	internally displaced person
IMF	International Monetary Fund
KFOR	Kosovo force
MPASSR	Mountain People's Autonomous Socialist Soviet Republic
MVD	Ministerstvo Vnutrennykh Del (Ministry of the Interior)
NACC	North Atlantic Cooperation Council
NATO	North Atlantic Treaty Organization
NGO	Non-governmental Organization
NRC	NATO–Russia Council (NATO)
OSCE	Organization for Security and Cooperation in Europe
PCA	Partnership and Cooperation Agreement (EU)
PfP	Partnership for Peace (NATO)
PJC	Permanent Joint Council (NATO)
PPP	purchasing power parity
SSR	Soviet Socialist Republic
TSFSR	Transcaucasian Soviet Federative Socialist Republic

UK	United Kingdom
UN	United Nations
US	United States of America
USSR	Union of Soviet Socialist Republics
UTC	Coordinated Universal Time
WTO	World Trade Organization

INTRODUCTION

This book provides an introduction to the discipline of Caucasian studies, i.e. the multi-disciplinary study on all issues relating to the Caucasus (the term should not be confused with Caucasiology, which deals only with the Caucasian language family). It does not look at countries separately, because state borders do not coincide with ethnic or geographical borders. Furthermore, North and South Caucasus, which are often falsely perceived as separate regions when it comes to geography, history, politics or economy, should be considered as one single entity. The main Caucasus mountain range is the centrepiece of the Caucasus and not a dividing line. The region can truly be called a paradise for academics and researchers, as it is complex in every possible aspect. Not only do the ethnolinguistic variations and many conflicts make it difficult to get a general overview, but also the history and geography are extremely diverse. On account of this complexity, especially in terms of ethnolinguistics, the Arabs in the Middle Ages called the Caucasus *jabal al-sun*, or the Mountain of Tongues.

In writing this book, several problems arose which anyone doing research on the Caucasus may encounter. This is especially the case in the field of data collection: data are often incomplete or absent (e.g. because of destruction in conflicts, such as in Chechnya, Abkhazia or Nagorno Karabakh); sometimes official data are classified; and methods of data collection vary in the different countries and so the results are not easily comparable – and even in some cases may have been purposely falsified. Another problem is the true academic value and the trustworthiness of sources. Literature may be biased in an ethnocentric or nationalistic way or simply be a source of propaganda. This is definitely true for Caucasian historiography, which is frequently used as a battlefield by academics.

An even harder task after having gathered all the necessary information is the actual writing process. A lot of issues covered in this book are highly controversial and some are disputed, especially where violent conflict is involved. Even when one tries to be objective, neutral and factually accurate, it will often be perceived as biased. The issue of national pride, which in itself is often based on incorrect historical information, should be carefully considered by anyone dealing with the Caucasus. The information provided in this book should not be accepted blindly as the truth and nothing but the truth. It tries merely to give the latest factual stance as far as academic research is concerned and follows the internationally accepted political situation, e.g. Abkhazia and Nagorno Karabakh are not considered as sovereign states by the UN. Although political governments of internationally unrecognized or partially recognized republics are mentioned, this it is not intended to be a political statement. The historical maps used are intended only to give an indication of the location and size of the ancient states. Their borders are by no means exact, as these are often subject to intense debate – for example, some sources claim that the region of Nagorno Karabakh was included in Caucasian Albania in 387, while others claim this took place in 428.

1

GEOGRAPHY

Location, position and definition

The name Caucasus is the Latinized form of the Greek word Kaukasos, but its origin is highly debated. Still, there is no clear-cut definition for what constitutes the Caucasus. The notion or concept of the word is used ambiguously in geography, in politics, and even to a certain extent in culture. The Caucasus is customarily divided into a northern part and a southern part, and even here the geographical and political interpretations are different.

In the narrow physical-geographical sense the Caucasus denotes only the main Caucasian range. In a broader and more commonly used sense, it is the bridge between Europe and Asia and comprises an area of 440,194 km^2, i.e. almost the same size as Germany and Austria together, or a bit larger than California. The region occupies a strip of land of 700 to 900 km wide and stretches some 720 km north to south. Lying between the 39th and 47th parallels, it is located at the same latitude as southern France and northern Spain and the northern half of the US.

The borders of the Caucasus are the Kuma–Manych depression to the north, the Caspian Sea to the east, the border of Georgia–Armenia–Azerbaijan with Turkey–Iran to the south, and the Black Sea and Sea of Azov to the west. The Kuma-Manych depression is a post-Pliocene relic that once connected the Sea of Azov with the Caspian Sea. The southern border is characterized only partially by a real geographical feature – the eastern portion runs along the Araks River – and received its current form in 1921 through the Treaty of Kars. Through this treaty, the Bolsheviks ceded the region of Kars to Turkey, but received the Batumi area in return. When comparing the geographical map with the political map, one can see that under the physical-geographical definition the Caucasus comprises the three newly independent republics of Armenia, Azerbaijan and Georgia, but also part of the Russian Federation (the autonomous republics Adygea, Karachay–Cherkessia, Kabardino–Balkaria, North Ossetia–Alania, Ingushetia, Chechnya and Dagestan, the Krasnodar and Stavropol Krays and, in addition, a small piece of the Rostov Oblast and the autonomous Republic of Kalmykia). As previously mentioned, the Caucasus is subdivided into a northern and a southern part, the border between which is defined by the watershed and highest peaks of the main mountain range. The northern part is known as the North Caucasus, but

3

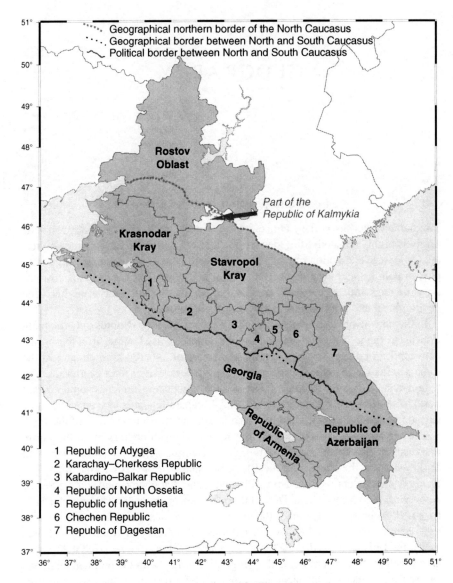

Map 1.1 Location of the Caucasus and its territorial entities

is often called Ciscaucasia in Russian literature. It comprises the Russian part of the Caucasus, except for the Black Sea coastline, but also includes some regions in northern Georgia and northeastern Azerbaijan. The South Caucasus, also known as Transcaucasus, encompasses the territory of Armenia, almost all of Georgia and Azerbaijan, and the Black Sea coastline of the Russian Federation.

The name Transcaucasus was used mainly until the break-up of the Soviet Union because seen from Moscow's perspective, this region is located behind the main Caucasian range. After gaining independence, the newly independent republics desired to be referred to as 'South Caucasus' so that they would not be associated with the Russian and Soviet past. Still, the word Transcaucasus remains in frequent use in Russian publications.

Some literature draws the southern border of the Caucasus eco-region even lower and includes the entire Chorokhi and Aras basins (in Turkey) and part of the Turkish Black Sea coast, as well as the northernmost part of Iran and part of its Caspian coast.

In terms of politics, the Caucasus is slightly bigger (i.e. 541,200 km^2). The South Caucasus groups the three newly independent republics Armenia, Azerbaijan and Georgia. The North Caucasus comprises what is known in Russia as the 'South of Russia', or '*Yug Rossii*': seven autonomous republics (Adygea, Karachay–Cherkessia, Kabardino–Balkaria, North Ossetia–Alania, Ingushetia, Chechnya and Dagestan), the two krays (Krasnodar and Stavropol) and the oblast (Rostov).

When talking about culture, and especially about linguistics, 'Caucasian' is interpreted mainly as the adjective for what is related to the ethnolinguistic groups that belong to the Caucasian language family (i.e. excluding Azerbaijani, Armenian, Russian, etc).

The question of whether the Caucasus belongs to Europe or to Asia has been and still is the subject of many intense discussions. The main interpretations and viewpoints are the following:

> The Caucasus belongs entirely to Asia because the Europe–Asia border passes through the Kuma–Manych depression.
> The Caucasus belongs entirely to Europe because the Europe–Asia border passes along the border between the South Caucasian countries on the one side and Turkey–Iran on the other.
> The Northern Caucasus belongs to Europe and the Southern Caucasus to Asia, because the Europe–Asia border passes along the main Caucasian range.
> The part of the Caucasus north of the rivers Rioni and Kura belongs to Europe and the part to the south to Asia, because these rivers form the Europe–Asia border.
> The main western part of the Caucasus belongs to Europe and a smaller part in the east (basically most of Azerbaijan and small parts of Georgia, Armenia and the Caspian Sea coast of the Russian Federation) to Asia, because the Europe–Asia border passes along the landscape borders. This last version is the most widely accepted one.

The South Caucasus falls within the UTC/GMT+4 time zone, with both Armenia and Azerbaijan observing Daylight Saving Time (i.e. advancing clocks in summer to have more daylight in the afternoon). The North Caucasus is part of the UTC/GMT+3 time zone, and also observes daylight saving time. So, consistently, during summer Azerbaijan and Armenia are one hour ahead of the rest of the Caucasus, and during winter the entire South Caucasus (with the exception of Abkhazia, which prefers to be closer to Moscow) is one hour ahead of the North Caucasus.

Main physical-geographical regions

The Pre-Caucasus or North Caucasus plain occupies the northern part of the Caucasus and is characterized by lowlands and lower elevations. It is a continuation of the great plains of Russia: the steppes of the rivers Don and Volga. The western part of the Pre-Caucasus contains the Kuban–Azov plain, at a level of 100 to 150 m (north of the River Kuban), the Pre-Kuban plain (south of the River Kuban) and the Taman peninsula, with its low wide ranges and mud hills. The Stavropol plateau in the centre of the Pre-Caucasus rises above these lowlands to a height of up to 831 m. To the south of the Stavropol plateau, in the region of Mineralnye Vody, are seventeen laccoliths, created by ancient volcano eruptions, of up to 1,400 m, such as Beshtau, Mashuk, etc. To the southeast of the Stavropol plateau lies the Terek–Sunzha plateau, which is composed of the Terek ridge (up to 664 m) and the Sunzha ridge (up to 926 m), separated from each other by the Alkhanchurt valley. The eastern part of the Pre-Caucasus consists of the Terek–Kuma plain, which in itself is the southwestern part of the Pre-Caspian lowlands. Its altitude varies from a maximum 100 m in the west to below sea level at the Caspian Sea coast.

The Greater Caucasus is situated around the main Caucasus range, stretching over a length of 1,500 km from northwest to southeast, and the lateral and rocky ranges, which run parallel. Although the main Caucasus range is difficult to cross, it does not preclude the many commonalities in the economic and socio-cultural aspects on either side. Nevertheless, throughout history the South Caucasus has experienced more and stronger foreign trade and influence from the Middle East and the Mediterranean area than from the North Caucasus. These mountains can be crossed by several passes, the most important ones being the Mamison Pass (Ossetian Military Road), the Roki Pass and the Daryal Pass (Georgian Military Road). For many Caucasian peoples, during times of war the mountains have been a refuge and shelter from which they employed guerrilla tactics and launched lightning attacks on the enemy. The main caucasus range can be split up into three major parts. The Western Caucasus starts as low hills close to the Taman peninsula at the estuary of the Kuban River, and extends over high hills with the elevation of the Alps to mount Elbrus. The highest peak in this Western Caucasus is Mount Dombay-Ulgen (4,046 m). The Central Caucasus stretches from Elbrus to Mount Kazbek. Mount Elbrus is the highest in the Caucasus (a western peak of 5,642 m and an eastern one of 5,621 m) and is situated on the border of the autonomous republics of Karachay–Cherkessia and Kabardino–Balkaria and only a few

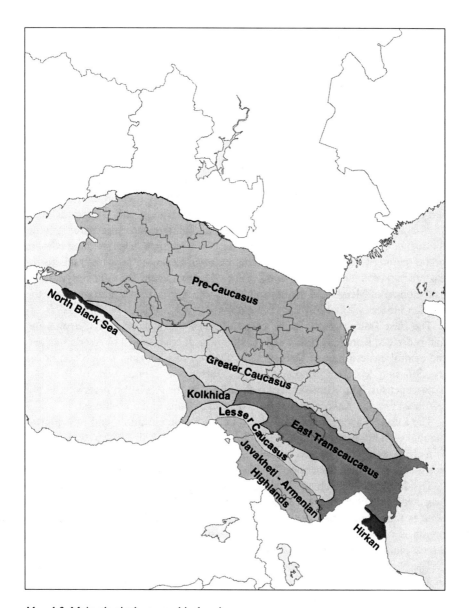

Map 1.2 Main physical-geographical regions

kilometers away from Georgia. Mount Kazbek (Mqinvartsveri in Georgian; 5,033 m), on the border between Georgia and North Ossetia, is famous in ancient legends, such as that of Prometheus.[1] According to this myth, Prometheus was chained to Mount Kazbek as a punishment for stealing the fire from the gods and giving it to humankind. Every day an eagle picked at his liver, which grew back

7

every night. Other peaks higher than 5,000 meters are Dykhtau (5,204 m), Shkhara (5,201 m), Koshtantau (5,152 m), Dzhangitau or Dzhanga (5,085 m) and Pushkin (5,033 m). The Eastern Caucasus runs from the top of Kazbek to the Absheron or Apsheron peninsula. It is not as high as the Central Caucasus, but still counts over thirty peaks of more than 4,000 meters, with Tebulosmta (4,493 m) and Bazardyuzyu (4,466 m) being the highest.

Kolkhida (Kolkheti in Georgian) constitutes the western part of the Transcaucasian depression (i.e. the lower elevations between the Greater Caucasus and the Lesser Caucasus). It is divided into three distinct units of relief: the Kolkheti lowlands, the foot-hills and the Imereti upland. The Kolkheti lowlands form the Georgian coastal region and contain wetlands located below sea level. These lowlands are ecologically important because they are both a shelter for many endemic species and a vital site for migrating and wintering birds. Drainage works have been conducted in the region, but were successful only on the higher elevations. Kolkhida has the form of a triangle, with its three corners in the region of Tuapse (northwest), the region of Zestafoni (east) and the northeastern part of Anatolia (southwest). It is well known in ancient Greek mythology as the home of Medea and the destination for the Argonauts on their quest for the Golden Fleece.

The East Transcaucasus is the eastern part of the Transcaucasian depression and is divided from Kolkhida by the Likhi range. It covers most of Azerbaijan and the central eastern part of Georgia. The Kura–Araks lowland, which comprises the Shirvan, Mil and Mughan steppes, forms the central part of the East Transcaucasus. The Kura–Araks lowland borders the Absheron peninsula in the northeast and the Kakhetian and Inner Kartlian plains in the northwest.

The Lesser Caucasus consists of a relief of alpine elevation, and runs almost parallel with but is not as high as the Greater Caucasus. This 200 km wide mountain chain, composed of several ranges, stretches over a distance of 530 km in a northwest–southeast direction. The highest mountain is Gyamysh (3,724 m).

The Javakheti–Armenian highlands, which are made up of lava ridges and a broad volcanic plateau, are located southwest of the Lesser Caucasus. The highest peak is the extinguished crater Aragats (4,090 m). The easternmost part of this region is considerably lower and is subdivided in the middle Araks basin, the Ararat plain and the Nakhchivan lowlands.

The North Black Sea is a narrow strip of land running from the city of Anapa to Tuapse, and lies between the Black Sea and the main Caucasus range. It is characterized by flat relief, rising into hills.

The Hirkan is an important ecological system because of its remnants of the Tertiary period, which ended 2 million years ago. It is composed of the Talysh Mountains and the Lenkoran lowlands. The Talysh Mountains are a continuation of the Lesser Caucasus, but are separated from it by a depression carved out by the Araks River. The highest mountain is Kyumyurkyoy (2,477 m). The Lenkoran lowlands are wedged between the Caspian Sea and the Talysh Mountains. This small strip is 5 km wide in the south and up to 30 km in the north.

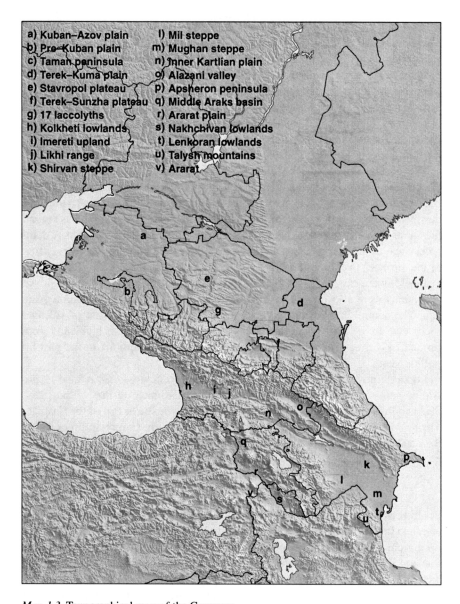

a) Kuban–Azov plain
b) Pre–Kuban plain
c) Taman peninsula
d) Terek–Kuma plain
e) Stavropol plateau
f) Terek–Sunzha plateau
g) 17 laccolyths
h) Kolkheti lowlands
i) Imereti upland
j) Likhi range
k) Shirvan steppe
l) Mil steppe
m) Mughan steppe
n) Inner Kartlian plain
o) Alazani valley
p) Apsheron peninsula
q) Middle Araks basin
r) Ararat plain
s) Nakhchivan lowlands
t) Lenkoran lowlands
u) Talysh mountains
v) Ararat

Map 1.3 Topographical map of the Caucasus

Although not directly on the territory of the Caucasus, it is important to mention Mount Ararat, where Noah's ark is controversially said to have been stranded. This mountain, with two peaks (one at 5,156 m and one at 4,030 m), is on Turkish soil but for many centuries was Armenian land and has been a symbol for Armenia.

Geology

The foundation of the platform of the Pre-Caucasus dates back to the early Carboniferous period of the Paleozoic era (345–290 million years ago). The sedimentary cover of the platform accumulated from the Middle Jurassic epoch of the Mesozoic era up to the Miocene epoch of the Cenozoic era (176–5.3 million years ago). In the middle of the Miocene epoch (23.8–5.3 million years ago), the Stavropol plateau was lifted up and divided the Azov–Kuban lowlands from the Terek–Kuma lowlands. The anticline zones of the Terek and Sunzha ranges appeared at the end of the Pliocene epoch of the Cenozoic era (5.3–1.8 million years ago).

The northern slope of the main Caucasus range is the edge of the Pre-Caucasian platform and was lifted up during the Late Oligocene epoch (33.7–23.7 million years ago) as part of the Alpine geosyncline (a vast structural downwarp of the Earth's crust) and then became subject to erosion. This is around the same time that the Alps were formed in Europe. In the western part, hard rocks such as schists, gneisses and granites (older than 206 million years) came to the surface. In the east, softer clay schist and sandstones (206–159 million years old) were exposed. The western part of the Lesser Caucasus and the Talysh Mountains were also formed by this Alpine geosyncline, some 50 million years ago. The central and eastern parts of the Lesser Caucasus consist of volcanic rocks that are at least twice that old. The Javakheti–Armenian highlands were formed by young volcanic debris during more recent eruptions in the past 50 million years.

Kolkhida and the Kura–Araks lowlands are both depressions, related to the Alpine geosynclines. The formation of Kolkhida is linked to that of the Black Sea, and the creation of the Kura–Araks lowlands is linked to that of the Caspian. Their surface consists of a metamorphic complex of Pre-Cambrian times (older than 543 million years), with younger sedimentary deposits.

Hydrology

Several scholars expect water to be *the* source of conflict for the twenty-first century, and in the Caucasus this is also likely to become a major issue. Water is used for agriculture, industry and domestic purposes, but also for hydropower generation and recreation. Many water reservoirs and canals have been built in order to increase the value even further. Whereas there is an abundance of water in the mountainous areas, the opposite is true for huge parts of the lowlands, both in the North and South Caucasus, where drinking water is often scarce. Azerbaijan suffers the most from such water shortages; Georgia has the fewest problems, and in fact draining water in the Kolkhida lowlands is a major issue. Another strategic importance of water is the access to the rest of the world created by seas. Both Russia and Georgia border the Black Sea, but Armenia is completely landlocked. Although Azerbaijan borders the Caspian Sea, the latter does not form an outlet to the world seas.

Seas

The Caspian Sea, at 28 m below sea level and with its 372,000 km^2, is the world's largest inland body of water. It was known in history as the Hyrcanian Ocean, the Khazar Sea and the Khvalissian Sea. It is surrounded by five countries – the Russian Federation, Kazakhstan, Turkmenistan, Iran and Azerbaijan – and is extremely important for the hydrocarbon resources that can be found beneath it. The sea is geographically divided into three parts: the North, Middle and South Caspian. The northern portion has a low shoreline and is very shallow, the middle portion is somewhat deeper, and the South Caspian contains the greatest depths as well as the largest oil and gas deposits. The Caspian is not really a sea in the physical-geographical sense, since it is not connected to the wider world oceans through natural waterways. It receives more than 80 per cent of its water from the Volga, with the remainder coming mainly from other rivers, rain and groundwater. The most significant problems relating to the Caspian are the status of legal ownership, the changing water levels and the high level of pollution, which seems to have improved in recent years.

The Black Sea is surrounded by the Russian Federation, Georgia, Turkey, Bulgaria, Romania and Ukraine, and measures some 423,000 km^2. It plays a strategic role for the Caucasus, as it forms an outlet to the world seas through the Bosporus. The Phoenicians sailed this sea as early as the second millennium BC. The Greeks first called it Pontos Axeinos (Hostile Sea), but after colonizing the area renamed it Pontos Euxeinos (Hospitable Sea). During the time of the Kievan Rus (ninth to twelfth century) it was called the Pontic Sea. Since 1821, all states have the right to navigate commercial fleets over the Black Sea, and it now has huge importance for transport, which in turn poses a considerable ecological threat. It is also highly significant for tourism. The Caucasian Riviera, with its warm climate, sandy beaches and picturesque scenery, was one of the most popular tourist regions during Soviet times and still attracts hundreds of thousands of visitors every summer.

The Sea of Azov is a shallow sea of 37,555 km^2 which is connected to the Black Sea by the Kerch Strait. It is situated in the border region between Ukraine and Russia and receives a huge inflow of fresh water – although this is heavily polluted by industrial waste – from the rivers Don and Kuban. Several parts of the sea are frozen during winter, but icebreakers keep the ports open. The Azov Sea is important for fishing, tourism, and oil and gas extraction, with its commercial importance increasing after the completion of the Volga–Don Canal in 1952. The Greeks, who called the sea Maiotis, founded their first colonies on its shores in the sixth century BC.

Rivers

On account of high levels of precipitation and the melting of snow, many rivers are found in the Caucasus. Most of them rise in the mountains, where they flow rapidly, but are calmer by the time they reach the lowlands. The flow of almost all rivers is very dependent on seasons. Most – especially the ones facing south – flood during the spring period, as the snowmelt and rainfall reach their peak. Summer floods are very common among rivers facing north and those on higher elevations. During other periods of the year, many rivers tend to dry up. In the Terek–Kuma lowlands, most rivers, except for the Terek, actually freeze during winter and do not even reach the Caspian Sea.

The main rivers flowing into the Sea of Azov are the Don, Yeya and Kuban. Most Caucasian rivers flowing into the Black Sea are relatively short but are extremely numerous where the mountainous region almost touches the coastline. The main ones are the Bzyp, Kodori, Inguri, Rioni (known as Phasis in antiquity) and Chorokhi.

In contrast, the rivers of the Caspian basin are in general much longer. These are the Kuma, Terek, Sulak, Ulluchay, Samur, Kura and Araks. The Kura (Kür in Azerbaijani and Mtkvari in Georgian) is the longest river in the Caucasus and was called Kuros or Cyrus in ancient times. The Kura basin encompasses the territory of five countries: Turkey, Iran, Armenia, Georgia and Azerbaijan. The romantic beauty of Dzhvari and Mtskheta at the confluence of the Mtkvari and Aragvi has been immortalized by the Russian poet Lermontov in his poem *Mtsyri*. The Araks (Aras in Turkish and Persian), the main tributary of the Kura, was known in antiquity as Araxes, a river often appearing in ancient mythology.

Lakes, wetlands, dams and reservoirs

The Caucasus does not have many large lakes. The largest one is Lake Sevan (1,256 km^2) in the eastern part of Armenia. It lies at 1,925 m above sea level and receives its water from the rivers originating in the surrounding mountains, but more water flows out for the lake through the Hrazdan River because of the high need for irrigation, human consumption and hydroelectricity. As a result, the water level has dropped almost 20 m since the 1930s and drinking water supplies are threatened. The second largest lake, the Manych–Gudilo Lake (800 km^2), is located right on the Kuma–Manych depression, the natural border of the Caucasus, and is also used as a reservoir (known as the Proletarskoye Reservoir). All other lakes, especially in the South Caucasus, are very small: the largest one in Azerbaijan, Sarysu Lake, is 67 km^2; the largest one in Georgia, Paravani Lake, is 37.5 km^2; the second largest in Armenia, Akna Lake, is only 0.5 km^2. The same is true of the North Caucasus, where most lakes are not bigger than 10 km^2. Still, several lakes can be found in the Kuma–Manych depression. Lake Paleostomi, Georgia's second biggest lake, is considered to be part of the Kolkheti wetlands. Many other wetlands and swamps can be found along the lower Terek, Sulak, Kuban, Kura and Rioni rivers, and the coastal zones of the Black, Azov and Caspian seas. There have been several attempts to drain wetlands, this being successful mainly on the higher elevations. In the coastal region of Abkhazia, imported Eucalyptus trees have helped to dry up the swampy territory.

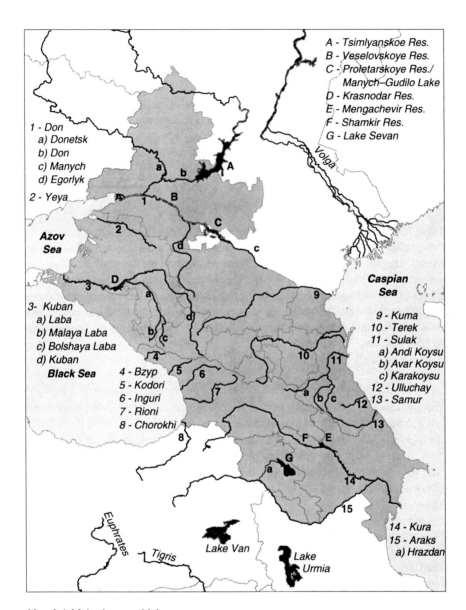

Map 1.4 Main rivers and lakes

During the second half of the twentieth century, many dams and artificial reservoirs were built on the tributaries of the rivers of the Caucasus, and they can be found on almost all the important rivers. Reservoirs and mountain rivers are used for hydropower and water from reservoirs and rivers in the plains is used for irrigation. Thanks to the creation of reservoirs, irrigation is available throughout the entire year and inhibits the spring floods in the lowlands; several reservoirs are important for drinking water.

The Mengachevir Reservoir (605 km²), constructed in 1953, is the biggest artificially created water storage basin in the Caucasus. It is located on the Kura in Azerbaijan, close to the Shamkir Reservoir, which is the second largest reservoir of the South Caucasus. The main water basins in the North Caucasus are the Veselovskoye, Proletarskoye and Krasnodar reservoirs and others on the Kuma–Manych depression. The Tsimlyanskoye Reservoir is partially in the Caucasus when the region is considered in political terms, but not in physical-geographical terms.

Glaciers

There are over 2,000 glaciers,[2] covering some 1,600 km², on the upper slopes of the Greater Caucasus – mainly in the western and central portions – and on Mount Aragats. Some 70 per cent of them are located on the northern side, primarily on the higher central slopes. The largest glacial systems are those of Elbrus (140 km²) and Kazbek (80 km²); five more glaciers have a surface of more than 40 km². Global climate change is severely affecting these glaciers. Their area, volume and length are reducing and they are breaking up into several smaller glaciers.

Groundwater and springs

The Caucasus is rich in underground waters and contains thousands of mineral and thermal springs. Hundreds of different mineral waters are sold throughout the region, and several of these are known all over the former Soviet Union and even beyond (e.g. Jermuk from Armenia, Borjomi and Nabeghlavi from Georgia, Yessentuki from the Stavropol Kray, and Arkhyz from Karachay–Cherkessia). Many tourists bathe in the famous Narzan springs in the Elbrus region.

Climate

The Caucasus, where humid Mediterranean and dry continental air masses meet, experiences almost all possible climate zones, several of them being micro-climates – i.e. extending over an area of only a few square kilometres. It is, however, generally accepted that the North Caucasus belongs to the continental belt and the South Caucasus to the subtropical one. The geographical location, topography and seas play an important role in this complexity.

Temperatures depend largely on elevation (i.e. a lower temperature at a higher elevation) and on the distance from the sea. The Black Sea, but to a lesser extent also the Caspian, has a moderating effect on the climate and the wide seasonal variations. This means that such seasonal variations are the greatest in the central and eastern part of the Caucasus: summers are hotter and winters colder. For example, winters are on average 5 degrees colder in Tbilisi than in Batumi, whereas summers are 2 degrees warmer. The mountain formations and highlands have a blocking effect. The main Caucasus range protects the south from cold air masses from the Russian mainland and thus raises the temperatures in the South Caucasus in winter, leading to an average January temperature 4 degrees colder in Mineralnye Vody than in Tbilisi. During summer, on the other hand, contrasts between north and south are not so visible. In general, weather conditions are more stable on the southern side of the Caucasus. Also the Likhi range, which separates Western Georgia from Eastern Georgia, tends to block streams of warm moist air from the west and dry continental air from the east.

Precipitation depends on both elevation and proximity to the sea. The areas with the highest precipitation are at the Black Sea coast and in the high mountains; the east of the Caucasus is more arid. The average yearly precipitation is 2,704 mm in Batumi, 497 mm in Tbilisi, and only 240 mm in Baku.

Almost the entire area of the North Caucasus has a continental climate. The Black Sea coast north of Sukhumi is rather moderate or subcontinental, but is still slightly colder and has less precipitation than the Georgian Black Sea coast.

The Greater Caucasus is alpine and has relatively cold winters and moderately warm summers. Permanent snow starts at 2,700 to 2,900 m in the west and at 3,000 to 3,500 m in the east. The climate is much drier in the eastern portion than in the western and central parts because of so-called condensers, which are obstacles to the moister air streams from the Black Sea. These condensers are the high mountain peaks, such as Elbrus and Kazbek. Their effect can be often seen when one flies over the region: whereas the lower lying areas may have a clear sky, the mountains are surrounded by clouds.

The Black Sea coast from Sukhumi to Batumi and the Kolkhida lowlands are subtropical and humid. This subtropical climate can be found to elevations of 650 m and freezing occurs very rarely. Palm trees grow in the coastal area, and cultivation of citrus and tea plants takes place in the lowlands. The southwestern part of Georgia, the region of Adjara, is even more humid. Precipitation, which is the highest of the entire former Soviet Union, can reach 4,000 mm per year, similar to that of a tropical rainforest.

The East Transcaucasus is subtropical but arid. Rainfall decreases towards the east, and thus irrigation is required for agriculture in the dry lowland regions. The Likhi range causes the contrast of climatic zones of Western and Eastern Georgia, i.e. precipitation in Eastern Georgia is only a third of that of Western Georgia, but temperature fluctuations are much larger. The region has good growing conditions for cotton – provided that fields are irrigated – and drought-resistant species. The southeast of Azerbaijan, the Talysh Mountains and Lenkoran lowlands, is also subtropical but much more humid (1,200 to 1,400 mm per year) than the rest of the country, with moderate winters, and bring the earliest crops of the former Soviet Union. Therefore the Lenkoran lowlands are also known as the Kremlin Kitchen Garden.

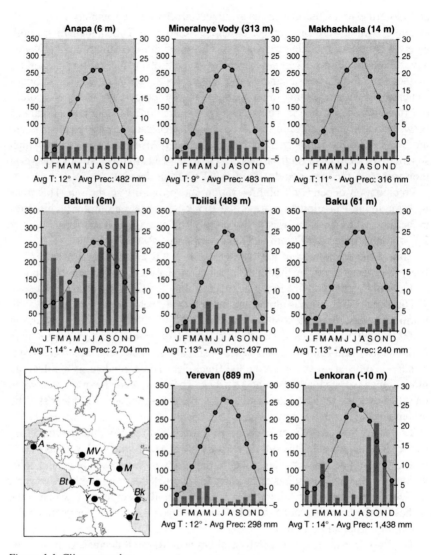

Figure 1.1 Climatographs

Sources: http://www.weatherbase.com/ and http://www.weatherpost.com

The Armenian highlands have a continental climate, with an average precipitation of 300 to 800 mm. The climate of the Lesser Caucasus is milder than that of the Armenian highlands, especially on its northern slopes. Winters are cool, summers are warm and humidity is relatively high.

The arid Middle Araks basin and Ararat plain have the highest variation in temperature. During summer the temperature can reach 43 degrees Celsius and in winter fall to minus 30. The annual average precipitation amounts to only 200 to 250 mm, the lowest in the entire Caucasus.

Main landscape types and ecosystems

The Caucasus is characterized by an enormous variety of landscape and ecosystem because of its complex orography (different altitudes), geology (different soils) and climate (the east is more arid than the west). In total there are twenty different types of landscape,[3] several of them occurring in only a small locality. This is quite exceptional, particularly given the small area of the Caucasus. On account of the long history of human habitation, many of these natural ecosystems have been affected. Approximately one-quarter of the entire territory remains in a reasonable condition but only one-tenth can be considered pristine.[4] For example, in order to accommodate agriculture and pasturelands, steppe vegetation was eradicated, semi-deserts were irrigated and developed, and forests were cleared.

The western and central parts of the Pre-Caucasus are dominated by steppes. In the northwest and centre these are grass or meadow steppes; in the Pre-Kuban plain and on the higher elevations they are broad-leaved forest steppes. The fertile black soil is cultivated (wheat, barley, maize, sugar beet, sunflower), and the meadows are used mainly as winter pasture for sheep. The major part of the Terek–Kuma lowlands and the Caspian coastline are characterized by desert and semi-desert, whereas there are wetlands and swamp forests in the delta and on the floodplains of the Terek. The lower and middle mountain elevations that form the transition from the Pre-Caucasus to the Greater Caucasus are covered with shrub vegetation and broad-leaved forests.

The mountainous landscape of the Greater Caucasus consists of forests, meadows and glaciers. These forests are mainly broad-leaved, although on the northern slopes, mainly at higher elevations in the central and eastern part, there are pinewoods. On the lower southern slopes, there are subtropical forests. The meadows are often used as summer pasture or mowing fields.

On account of its subtropical and humid climate, in earlier times the central part of Kolkhida used to be covered with forests and swamps, but these have been partially logged or drained to allow the cultivation of maize and subtropical produce. The low and middle-mountain regions have broad-leaved forests.

Deserts and semi-deserts are located in the arid regions of the East Transcaucasus, such as the Kura–Araks lowlands and the Absheron peninsula. These areas are used for winter pasture and for irrigation cultures, such as cotton. In the semi-arid regions there are steppes and shrublands, on which vines and cereals are grown. This is especially the case in the southeastern part of Georgia, which is home to many famous wines and is even held to be the cradle of the vine. The low and middle-mountain landscapes are covered with broad-leaved forests.

The mountainous landscape of the Lesser Caucasus is similar to that of the Greater Caucasus. It has mountain forests and meadows, but no glaciers.

Most common in the area of the javakheti–Armenian highlands are volcanic mountain steppes, shrublands and meadows. The steppes are good for the cultivation of vegetables, frost-tolerant fruit trees (lower altitudes) and fodder plants (higher altitudes). In the western and southern part there are also stony deserts and semi-deserts which require intensive irrigation for agriculture, which is not very developed here. The landscape of the region around Mount Aragats and in the south of Armenia is similar to that of the Greater and Lesser Caucasus.

The North Black Sea region is covered with oak and pine forests, and in the lower zones there are also Mediterranean shrublands (maquis).

In the Hirkan, the landscape of the Lenkoran lowland is similar to that of Kolkhida and is used for subtropical agriculture, including rice and tea. The lower parts of the Talysh Mountains are covered with oak and beech. In the middle high mountains the landscape changes to steppe, and to meadows at the highest elevations.

Biodiversity: fauna, flora and their protection

The wide array of landscape types results in an extremely rich biodiversity. It is further influenced by neighboring regions (e.g. from Asia Minor on the Armenian highlands, or from Iran on the Talysh Mountains) and human interaction. The latter has meant that several species are in danger of extinction. Two refugia (shelters) came into existence and are now of high ecological importance: Kolkhida and the Hirkan.

The fauna of the Caucasus is connected to that of both Eastern Europe and Central Asia. It is extremely varied, with 152 species of mammal, 389 of bird, 76 of reptile and 15 of amphibian.[5] Fifty-nine out of the 632 species are endemic (i.e. exclusively native to the region), mainly in the Greater Caucasus and Talysh Mountains.

In terms of flora, the Caucasus is the richest among the regions with a temperate climate, but not as diverse as tropical zones. According to the latest research, over 6,300 different plant species are known in the region.[6] There are more than 1,600 endemic plant species and also a large number of surviving ancient species, all of which can be found mainly in the Kolkheti wetlands and the Hirkan.

In order to reverse the threats to the environment and endangered species, several policy measures, including legislation and the creation of protected areas, have been undertaken. The first protected area was established in 1912, and the number of nature reserves increased rapidly in the 1920s and 1930s. However, most were closed in 1951 for economic reasons. From 1957 onwards, there were attempts to re-establish previously existing protected areas and to create new ones. Especially during the 1970s and 1980s, when the biodiversity was suffering tremendously from environmental problems and several species had become endangered, there was an increased interest in environmental protection. In the 1990s, many reserves failed as a result of economic difficulties, and even today illegal activities such as woodcutting are very common. The number of protected areas and their total size is in line with many other countries: the 40 nature reserves and six national parks occupy some 3 per cent of the territory.

Land use

Roughly 54 per cent[7] of the total land area of the Caucasus is used for agriculture. Most of this is located in the plains of the North Caucasus, on the Caspian coast, the Kolkhida lowlands and the Kura–Araks lowlands. Much arable land is located on the Kuban–Azov plain, the Stavropol plateau and the Kura–Araks lowland, as well as in the Ararat valley, where cereals, fodder, fruit, tea and tobacco are cultivated. Orchards, groves and vineyards occupy Kolkhida, the region around Tbilisi, the Alazani valley, the Ararat valley and the Lenkoran lowlands. Cotton, rice and alfalfa are cultivated in the arid but warm regions of Azerbaijan. Citrus fruits and tea are grown in the humid subtropical lowlands and foothills, mainly in Kolkhida and the Lenkoran lowlands. Summer pastures are traditionally in the high mountains of the Greater and Lesser Caucasus, whereas winter pastures can be found in the Terek–Kuma plain and the Kura–Araks lowland. In general, the main agricultural activity at higher elevations is the raising of sheep and cattle.

Forests cover 17 per cent[8] of the Caucasus. They are mainly broad-leaved and are located primarily in the mid-mountain zones at altitudes between 500 and 2,000 m as well as in the Black Sea coastal region. There are coastal temperate rainforests in southwestern Georgia and southeastern Azerbaijan.

Little of the total area of the region is urban. The biggest concentrations are the Baku–Sumgait agglomeration and the Black Sea coastline between Sochi and Tuapse. Other major urban areas are the Tbilisi–Rustavi agglomeration, the Kutaisi–Zestafoni agglomeration, Yerevan, Ganja, the Black Sea coastline between Tuapse and Novorossiysk, and the big cities of the North Caucasus.

Natural resources

The Soviet Union had a very strong mineral industry, a major portion of which was based in the Caucasus. A huge quantity of non-ferrous metals is found in the volcanic rocks of the lateral ridge and Lesser Caucasus and the Jurassic shale diabase formation of the main Caucasus range. After the fall of the Soviet Union, most mining industries collapsed, but in recent years many have started up again. These resources play an important role in the region's economic development, but the wealth thus created is not always spread equally among the population. This is definitely the case with the revenues from oil and gas.

Armenia mined one-third of the molybdenum of the Soviet Union and also excavated deposits of copper, zinc and gold. It was the largest producer of perlite and tuff and produced a number of other industrial minerals. It was also known for its diamond-cutting industry, but has virtually no mineral fuel production.

Azerbaijan's main natural resources are its oil and gas reserves. At the beginning of the twentieth century, half of the world's oil was extracted in Absheron,

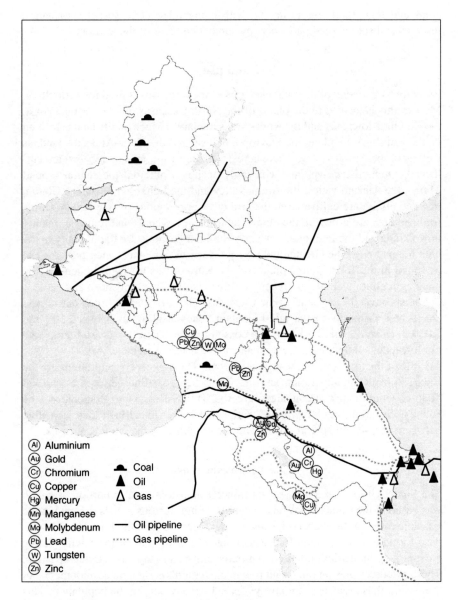

Map 1.5 Natural resources and oil and gas pipelines

and between 1897 and 1907 the Baku–Batumi oil pipeline was built, at 833 km the longest in the world at that time. Azerbaijan has also been a producer of aluminium, copper, molybdenum, iron, steel, lead and zinc, as well as many industrial minerals.

Georgia used to be a major producer of manganese from its deposits in Chiatura. The region of Marneuli still has deposits of copper, lead and zinc. Gold and silver can be found as a byproduct of other mineral excavation. Lead and zinc are abundant in Racha and arsenic was mined from the Lukhumi and Tsansa deposits in the north of the country. Many industrial minerals were produced, including several types of decorative stones. Coal and oil are also extracted in smaller quantities, and an oil refinery is located in Batumi.

Half of the minerals in the Russian Federation are found east of the Urals, but significant quantities are located in the North Caucasus. Many non-ferrous deposits are in North Ossetia (lead and zinc) and Kabardino–Balkaria (molybdenum, tungsten, copper). Large amounts of petroleum are present in most parts of the northern Caucasus, but primarily in Chechnya, Ingushetia, Dagestan, the Stavropol Kray and the Krasnodar Kray. In addition, these two krays possess large gas deposits.

Transport and communication infrastructure

During Soviet times, the Caucasus was just a peripheral region in a highly centralized system where very little external traffic took place. Now its location is strategic in terms of transport: it is the bridge between east and west and between north and south. Furthermore, it is located between the oil and gas extracting and consuming regions. Transporting goods through the Caucasus is quicker and cheaper than using alternative routes. As a result, the Caucasus has the potential to become a major transport hub, which would enable other economic sectors to revive. The Krasnodar Kray is already known as Russia's 'Southern Gateway' on account of its great economic significance to the country. Unfortunately, most of the transport and communication infrastructure is in poor condition, and at present the transport potential of the Caucasus cannot be capitalized upon as a result of the high level of corruption, slow border formalities, criminal activities, etc. Many governments, private consortia and multilateral development banks, notably the TRACECA initiative (Transport Corridor Europe–Caucasus–Asia) of the European Union, have already invested in the construction, rehabilitation and upgrading of the transport system, which should form the basis for economic development in the region.

Because of its flexibility, road transport has been gaining importance over rail. There is a dense network of paved roads and highways throughout the Caucasus, connecting cities and villages with each other and with the outside world. This network has existed since the times of the ancient Silk Road, but roads are generally in a bad state of repair, with their surfaces full of cracks and potholes. As a result, transport costs increase and the road capacity is not fully used. The most important roads are the east–west highways from Baku to Batumi and from Baku to Rostov-na-Donu. Several roads cross the main Caucasian range and link the North Caucasus with the South.

Since the end of the nineteenth century, a well-developed and comprehensive railway system has been established in the Caucasus, linking the northern part with the southern part and connecting them with the rest of the world. The Poti–Tbilisi railway was brought into use as early as 1872, the Rostov–Vladikavkaz railway three years later, and the main components of the railway infrastructure were built up during the following forty years. No single railway crosses the main Caucasian range, but two connect the North with the South and run close to the shores of the Black and Caspian seas. The one from Baku to Makhachkala and further north was closed for more the ten years, but is now functioning again, though the one on the Black Sea shore is still closed on account of unresolved conflicts and political tensions. The Black Sea and Caspian Sea are connected through the Transcaucasus Railway (Batumi–Tbilisi–Baku). A link between Georgia and Armenia (and further to the Persian Gulf in Iran) also exists. While there are railways from Armenia to Azerbaijan and to Turkey, they are not in use because of the blockade against Armenia. Branches from these main lines run through many valleys or to industrial centres. Most lines are 1.520 meter broad gauge, and the principal routes have been electrified.

Freight increased steadily during Soviet times, and rail was the main transport system during this era. However, the fall of the Soviet Union, the economic decline and many conflicts have had a huge impact on rail transport. There has been not only a decrease of some 80 per cent in railway freight turnover,[9] but also a lack of essential maintenance, resulting in a need for reconstruction. Some improvements and investments have been made to the network in the past few years, but the poor conditions of the rails mean there are speed restrictions on a considerable part of the network. Despite this there are regular trains travelling between the North Caucasus and other parts of Russia, including to Moscow and St Petersburg.

The Caucasus has a number of international airports and many smaller ones. Several major international airlines fly directly to the capitals of the three South Caucasian republics and to Krasnodar, Stavropol, Mineralnye Vody, Vladikavkaz, Anapa and Sochi. There are daily flights from Moscow to most major airports in the Caucasus. Several regional airlines fly to international destinations, whereas many more, mainly smaller, companies facilitate plane and helicopter flights to destinations within the Caucasus region.

There are some ten significant commercial seaports located along the Caucasian Black Sea and Azov Sea coast, the main ones being Poti and Batumi in Georgia and Novorossiysk, Sochi and Tuapse in Russia. The Krasnodar Kray offers the prime sea gateway to the Russian Federation and provides approximately 40 per cent of Russian port cargo handling capacity, mainly through the port in Novorossiysk. All the ports are connected to the railway system, and some (i.e. Novorossiysk, Tuapse, Poti, and Batumi) have links to pipelines from the Caspian and other Russian oil and gas fields. Most of the transported cargo consists of oil and oil-based products, but many terminals also handle general cargo, building materials, metals, coal, etc. There are passenger terminals in most of these seaports, but none are of major economic importance.

The key seaports on the Caspian are Baku, Dyubendi (Azerbaijan) and Makhachkala (Dagestan), but they are not large because they are only trans-shipment

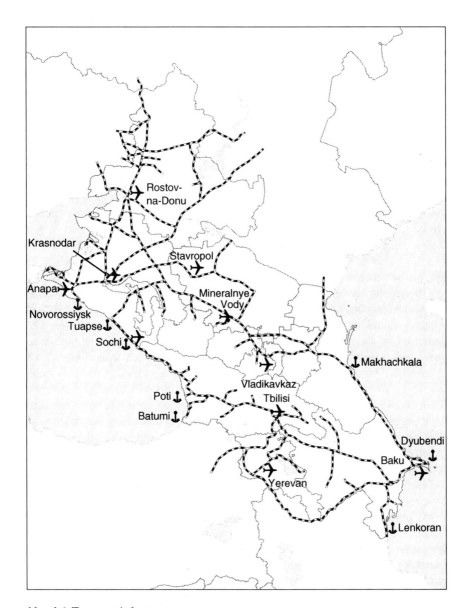

Map 1.6 Transport infrastructure

points for goods that are destined for the west or for passengers who travel to Turkmenistan or Iran. Most rivers in the Caucasus, apart from the lower reaches of the Kura, Kuban and Rioni, are not deep and hence not suitable for navigation. Water transport is very uncommon in Armenia as a result of the nature of the rivers and the landlocked position of the country.

The Caucasus is important not only for the extraction of oil and gas, but also for their transportation to the consuming countries. The first oil pipelines in the region were laid as early as the nineteenth century, but their significance increased mainly in the 1980s. Although the transport sector crumbled with the collapse of the Soviet Union, it has been regaining importance. The centre for gas and oil transport is at Baku and Sumgait, from where one high-capacity oil pipeline connects with Supsa and Batumi (Georgia) and one with Novorossiysk (Krasnodar Kray) on the Black Sea coast. A third pipeline, the so-called Main Export Pipeline, was opened in July 2006 and runs over a distance of 1,760 km from Baku over Georgian territory to the Turkish Mediterranean seaport of Ceyhan, while yet another takes oil from Tengiz in Kazakhstan to the Black Sea port of Novorossiysk and runs in part through the Caucasus. Two main natural gas pipelines run from the North Caucasus to Azerbaijan, Georgia and Armenia. Since February 2003, gas has been transported from Russia to Turkey through the Blue Stream pipeline, which runs along the bed of the Black Sea. These large new projects, which depend on geopolitical and geo-economical considerations, are projected to export huge quantities each day, but have met some degree of resistance because they harm the environment and pose a considerable ecological threat.

The system of public transport was well developed in Soviet times, and remains so. Bus and minibus (*marshrutka*) services operate not only countrywide but also on international routes to Russia, Turkey and Iran, and even to Greece. Trains are seldom used for short distances, but are convenient and inexpensive for long-distance travel. However, because of various conflicts, many of these train connections are not in use (i.e. Tbilisi–Moscow, Baku–Yerevan, etc.) Buses, trams, trolley-buses and *marshrutki* form part of the extensive and inexpensive city public transport systems. Subways run only in the capitals of the three South Caucasian republics, but there are plans for the construction of a similar rapid transit system in Rostov-na-Donu as well. The world's most serious subway accident occurred in 1995 in Baku: over 300 people died of carbon monoxide poisoning after fire broke out. Many people also use taxis, which are not always official vehicles, but often are regular private cars.

Telecommunications and the internet are of ever increasing importance and have received growing attention from regional political players. Telephone networks are present in the entire region, but are old and of low quality. They have been partially upgraded in the main urban areas in the past decade, but this is not the case in rural regions. Mobile phone networks have been set up throughout the Caucasus and competition has risen in this field. The internet emerged at the end of the 1990s and has since grown exponentially, first in companies and organizations but later also in private homes. The quality of these connections is not up to that in developed countries but is gradually improving.

Environmental problems and natural hazards

The Caucasus experiences many environmental problems and natural hazards. Recently, the number of natural disasters has been increasing, with wide-ranging results, from changes in the landscape, damage to the cultural heritage and economic difficulties to death and destruction. The main problems induced by human activity are caused primarily by a lack of state control; a poor economy leading to illegal activities; agriculture, with its unsustainable land practices; deforestation; overfishing; (irresponsible) tourism and recreation activities; the inefficient storage of agrochemicals and the high use of fertilizers; bad town planning; and industrialization, including the construction and operation of gas and oil pipelines. However, several natural disasters – excessive wind and rain, earthquakes, etc. – can affect the Caucasus.

Water pollution and overexploitation are among the major environmental concerns. In the past, losses were high in irrigation and water supply systems, and recycling was uncommon. The lack of metering has made problems of overconsumption even worse, and as a result certain parts of the Caucasus now face problems concerning the supply of potable water. Water use diminished during the 1990s, basically because of general economic decline. There is also a high level of pollution, mainly from industrial and household waste-water discharges which contain traces of heavy metals, oil products, phenols and other toxic substances. All main rivers in the Caucasus are polluted, with the part of the Terek between Vladikavkaz and Mozdok being the most affected. Other rivers with a high level of pollution are the Kura, Araks, Rioni and Kuban. This also disturbs the ecosystems of the Black Sea and Caspian Sea, and has contributed to the extinction of several species.

Soil pollution, soil erosion and land degradation are especially serious for Georgia and Armenia, which are both short of arable land. The causes can be both natural (e.g. flooding) and anthropogenic (e.g. bad agricultural practices or deforestation). Soil pollution is mainly the result of the ecologically irresponsible Soviet industry and agriculture policies, though it was aggravated by the sudden fall of the system. Heavy metals and oil products in urban and industrial centres, as well as road traffic, contribute to soil pollution.

Air pollution is caused mainly by transport and industry. The emissions reached their peak in the late 1980s and early 1990s, before the general economic decline. Nowadays, domestic heaters are also a source of pollution and create a problem of indoor air quality.

The rising level of the Caspian Sea poses a huge problem for and threat to the population living on its banks. Until 1978, the water level was becoming steadily lower; over a period of 100 years it had gone down by more than 2.5 meters.[10] The highest deficits of water inflow were experienced between 1930 and 1941, when the reduction averaged 16 cm per year. This was caused largely by the extensive irrigation activities and the filling of reservoirs with water from the Volga River. There were several Soviet plans to bring water from the rivers Pechora and Dvina to the Caspian through canals, but because of financial restraints these plans were never realized. This lowering of level led to a desertification of new lands, an increase in the amount of salt in the water, navigational problems and lower incomes in the fishery sector. Since 1978, the sea level has been rising again, with equally disastrous consequences: negative ecological effects, environmental contamination because of inundation of oil industry infrastructure, economic problems, and social catastrophes such as the need for the resettlement of several thousand people. The causes for these changes have not been fully studied, which makes it difficult to take adequate counter-measures. Several hypotheses point to long-term cyclical changes, tectonic movements, climatological factors and anthropogenic influences.

A contrasting problem is the water level of Lake Sevan, which since the 1930s has dropped by almost 20 m and severely threatens drinking water supplies. This is the result of the use of the late as a source for hydropower.

Earthquakes are the consequence of geodynamic processes, and seismic activity in the region has caused the deaths of many people. Several powerful earthquakes have taken place in the Greater Caucasus and the Javakheti–Armenian highlands. The devastating earthquake of 7 December 1988 in Spitak (Armenia), with a magnitude of 6.9 on the Richter scale, was one of the most catastrophic of the twentieth century. It took the lives of at least 25,000 people and the consequences are still visible.

Landslides are widespread in the southeastern part of the Caucasus, in the foothills of the western and central part of the main Caucasus range, and in the Meskheti and Trialeti ranges in Georgia. They have been occurring more frequently and devastatingly on account of excessive humidity, earthquakes and certain economic activities, destroying topsoil, vegetation and, often, settlements.

Mudflows are prevalent in the mountainous regions and often wash away entire communities. They are caused mostly by intensive woodcutting, overgrazing and unsustainable land use practices. Examples of such catastrophes were seen in 2000 in Tyrnyauz (Kabardino–Balkaria) and a year later in Karmadon (North Ossetia).

Flooding occurs after peak discharges of water into the rivers when snow melts in spring and after downpours in autumn. The rivers Kuban, Terek, Kura, Araks and Rioni have the largest flood areas; dykes have been erected along their shores and many reservoirs have been built to regulate the water flow.

Avalanches are frequent during winter in regions which are not forested. They impose a danger to populated areas, industry and communication, and frequently block traffic between the North and South Caucasus or on mountain roads, often at the cost of human lives.

Droughts occur frequently, because only a small part of the Caucasus has an annual precipitation of more than 1,000 mm. This problem goes hand in hand with the process of global warming and desertification, which is acute in the lowlands in the east.

Some geopolitical and geo-economical considerations

On first sight, the Caucasus might seem to be a remote part of the world, but this is definitely not the case. On the contrary, it is impossible to disconnect geography from politics and economy in the region, although it seems as if the newly independent states have not been able to make fully positive use of their geopolitical potential. Geo-economically there are even greater prospects, but this potential is heavily disrupted because of ongoing political instability and insecurity. In brief, the strategic location of the Caucasus and its energy resources are leading not only to international attention but also to a sharpened polarization in regional politics.[11]

The Caucasus lies on the border of Europe and Asia and its population is neither fully Asian nor fully European, but rather a mix of both. It is the type of cultural area that might be described by Samuel Huntington's controversial theory of the 'clash of civilizations'.[12] This theory claims that, in the post-Cold War period, cultural divisions rather than ideological or economic reasons will be the fundamental source of conflict and would be particularly prevalent between Islamic and non-Islamic civilizations. The Caucasus lies at the fault line of two major civilizations that could enter into such a conflict. At the same time is an important link in the Silk Road, the trade route between Europe and Asia. Through the expansion of the EU and NATO, the entire European security architecture is moving eastward, and the Caucasus is already at its new border. Even if the South Caucasian republics are not members of these organizations, the border makes the region crucial for European security, which means that the resolution of conflicts on Caucasian territory is of concern to Europe.

Throughout its long history, the South Caucasus has been a buffer or zone of influence for surrounding empires. On land, it is locked between three large countries – Russia, Turkey and Iran – each of which has a considerable interest in the region. Even though the status of these former empires has been reduced to one of 'regional superpower', the weak and small states of the South Caucasus are at their intersection and have to take them into account as a result. The key players in determining the future of the region are not the Caucasian states themselves but these three regional powers. Unfortunately, their presence and policies are often more of an impediment than a support. By their control or influence on the Caucasus, they could increase their regional and even global power significantly. Nowadays, the existence of the United Nations and other factors, such as public opinion and financial means, makes it less easy to invade the region and abuse it. The best alternative is cooperation. In order to have this positive and prosperous cooperation, stability is a prerequisite but difficult to accomplish.

Armenia's landlocked location does not only lead to its geographical isolation but hinders the development of its international relations. The eastern and western borders of Armenia are closed because of the blockade of Azerbaijan and Iran. Christian Armenia is therefore a close friend of the Islamic Republic of Iran and, in order to have a friend in the north, does not support pan-Armenian movements in the south of Georgia.

The 13-km common border of Azerbaijan and Turkey is extremely important, as these countries are allies and both have an anti-Armenian policy. This border is located at Nakhchivan, which implies that there is no direct land route between

Baku and Ankara. One of the proposals for the solution of the Nagorno Karabakh conflict was a territorial swap: Nagorno Karabakh would be exchanged for the Zangezur region in the south of Armenia. Armenia declined, as this solution could have had fatal consequences. First of all, there would have been a direct land route between its two main adversaries, which could imply more Turkish support for Azerbaijan against Armenia. Second, Armenia would have isolated itself even more by losing its common border with Iran.

2

TERRITORIAL DIVISION, GOVERNMENT AND ADMINISTRATION

For most of the twentieth century, the Caucasus was part of the Soviet Union. The USSR formed one single country, with no demarcated internal borders, and was subject to a single administrative and judicial system. During perestroika, national movements had freedom of operation, which resulted in the three South Caucasian republics declaring independence. However, the Armenian, Azerbaijani and Georgian authorities do not see this independence as a new phenomenon, but rather as the restoration of the republics that existed from 1918 until 1921. Indeed, there are several visible parallels between the new and those earlier republics: similar flags, national anthems, national holidays, etc. The North Caucasus also witnessed a number of national and liberation movements. This often led to conflict, but in the end none of them were able to obtain more than a limited degree of autonomy within the Russian Federation.

Soon after independence, the three South Caucasian republics reinstated their constitutions from pre-Soviet times (1918–21) but all adopted a new one in 1995. The constitution of the Russian Federation dates from 1993, and the different entities of this federation have their own constitution or charter, depending on their level of autonomy. The content of these documents is very similar to that of the constitutions of Western democracies, and follows the division into a legislative, executive and judicial power. Each charter ensures many rights to the population, but in reality not all of them are fully applied. This is especially the case with human rights and the freedom of expression. Both public administration and the political system suffer from problems, mainly from bad governance: there is a high level of corruption and little observance of the law. Strong pressure groups or clans hold too much influence, while many civil servants have a limited degree of knowledge and competence. These issues have not only led to the people losing their trust in the system, but have also greatly damaged individual economies and foreign investment.

The governments of both sovereign states and autonomies are headed by a president, the only exceptions being the two krays and the Rostov Oblast, where a governor is the head of state. In general, the president is vested with considerable power and a wide range of responsibilities. Several of the presidents held senior positions in the Communist Party during the Soviet era, though in recent years there has been a trend towards the election of younger people without this experience. Many leaders in the North Caucasus are former high-ranking military officials (e.g. Dudayev, Aushev and Semenov). Since they were among the very few members of the small ethnic groups of the North Caucasus who had reached high-level positions in the Soviet leadership, they were well respected by the populations who voted them into office.

Legislative power is exercised by parliaments, which in many cases do not have much power, but governments also have a partially legislative function.

The courts are nominally independent of the legislature and the executive. However, because of the high level of corruption people often do not use or trust the legal system. In some areas customary law and even Islamic law is applied. Historically, the state's rule of law was very weak and often did not extend to the mountainous regions. Despite this, there was no chaos in the relations between people. An unwritten code of standards and rules was observed and was supervised by the clans and the community in general. This combination of customary law, local norms and traditions is also known as *adat* in Muslim regions. One example of this customary law is the blood feud, which prevented society from descending into anarchy and which is still practised in remote areas or in regions where the rule of law cannot be fully imposed by the central authorities, for example in Ingushetia and Chechnya. Islamic law, the Sharia, is the collection of juridical norms, regulations and principles that every Muslim has to respect. This divine law originates from the Koran, hadiths and revelations of religious authorities. Many Muslims in the northeastern part of the Caucasus try to follow this law – which often contradicts the customary law – but there are no real Islamic courts. Although the creation of such extraordinary courts is not officially sanctioned, there have been several cases where an Islamic court, based on the Sharia, has ruled over specific cases. This fact should not be seen as especially unusual, as similar cases have occurred in Western countries with minority Muslim populations.

The political systems are based on the principles of pluralism. As a result, there are a huge number of small political parties which receive very few votes: most parties are built around the personality of their leader rather than on a particular ideology.

The conduct of elections remains a major issue, and most elections in the region have been classified as neither free nor fair by international organizations such as the OSCE and the Council of Europe. While there have been certain improvements, there are still many cases of ballot-stuffing, intimidation of opposition party members, poor maintenance of electoral lists, flawed counting processes and manipulation of the turnout figures.

The army of the Soviet Union was one of the most powerful of its time, but most of its successors are in dire straits. The armed forces rely mostly on conscripts, mainly on young men from poor families who are unable to pay the necessary bribe to be exempted. The conditions in army barracks are similar throughout the Caucasus, and diseases such as tuberculosis, diphtheria and typhoid are often diagnosed. This is a direct result of the economic problems in

Map 2.1 The Republic of Armenia (Hayastani Hanrapetutyun)

the country and the lack of funding for the military. In addition, all armed forces in the region suffer from endemic corruption, the organized extortion of soldiers by their officers, and bullying. The leadership also continually ignores, and fails to deal with, the causes behind the many deaths unrelated to combat, including the fact that every year there are large numbers of suicides.

The Republic of Armenia (Hayastani Hanrapetutyun)

The Republic of Armenia became independent on 23 September 1991, but there had already been a short-lived independent Democratic Republic of Armenia in the early twentieth century (28 May 1918 to 2 December 1920). The national holiday is celebrated on 21 September and goes back to the same day in 1991 when the referendum on independence was held in the country. The capital is Yerevan, the official currency is the Armenian dram and the official language is Armenian.

Armenia is divided into ten administrative provinces (sg. *marz*; pl. *marzer*) plus the capital city region (*kaghak*).

The president, elected by direct popular vote for a period of five years, is the head of state; he can serve for a maximum of two consecutive terms and holds considerable power under the constitution. Levon Ter-Petrossian was first elected chairman of the Armenian Supreme Soviet in July 1990, when the National Democratic Union Party defeated the Armenian Communist Party. He also became the first president of the new Armenia in October 1991, with 83 per cent of votes, and was re-elected in September 1996, but resigned in February 1998 after public protests against irregularities in the 1996 elections and disapproval of his policy towards the problem of Nagorno Karabakh. Ter-Petrossian was succeeded by Robert Kocharyan,[1] former president of Nagorno Karabakh and prime minister of Armenia. While Kocharyan was re-elected in March 2003, these elections were followed by allegations of election fraud, and one year later demonstrators asked for his resignation. In February 2008, a former prime minister, Serge Sargsian, another native from Nagorno Karabakh, won the election during the first round of a vote in which also Ter-Petrossian also participated. The former president contested the election results and demonstrations took place in Yerevan. Several people were killed during violent confrontations between the demonstrators and law enforcement agencies.

The Azgayin Zhoghov, or the National Assembly, is the single-chamber parliament of Armenia and consists of 131 seats. The deputies are elected by popular vote for a period of four years: 56 members in single-seat constituencies and 75 members by proportional representation, based on a list among those parties that receive at least 5 per cent of votes. The parties that obtained seats in the May 2007 elections are the Republican Party of Armenia (HHK, the party of President Sargsian; 64 seats), Prosperous Armenia (18 seats), the Armenian Revolutionary Federation – Dashnaktsutiun (HHD; 16 seats), Rule of Law (Orinats Yerkir; 9 seats) and Heritage (Zharangutiun; 7 seats). Dashnaktsutiun, the main opposition party, which was founded as early as 1890, was banned by Ter-Petrossian in 1994, but was legalized again when he stepped down in 1998.

In order to ensure administrative stability, the provinces are ruled by governors appointed by the president. However, these provinces have no budgets of their own. Local government is exercised by a council of elders and a city or village mayor, each elected for a period of three years.

A tragic event took place in Yerevan on 27 October 1999. Armed gunmen entered the parliament and opened fire, killing eight people, including the speaker of the parliament, Karen Demirchian, and Prime Minister Vazgen Sargsyan. These two strong personalities had formed the Unity Block, a coalition of the Republican Party and the Armenian People's Party, which had won the May 1999 parliamentary elections. As a result of the assassinations, the Unity Block fell apart, and there were fears of political and public turmoil. The opposition tried in vain to force President Kocharyan to resign.

In 2007, Armenia's active armed forces[2] numbered some 42,080 men, composed of an army (38,945) and air and defence aviation forces (3,135). Since the country is landlocked there is no navy. Some 60 per cent of the forces are conscripts, and the law requires 24 months of service from adult males. Armenia has a peacekeeping battalion which has served in both Kosovo and Iraq. Apart from the regular armed forces, there are paramilitary forces (numbering about 4,748), consisting of the troops of the Ministry of Internal Affairs and the Border Guard (Ministry of National Security). Armenia has supposedly received significant military support from Russia and also a limited amount from NATO member states, such as Greece.

Armenia has a good relationship with Moscow and agreed to accept a Russian military presence. In 2007 there were some 3,170 Russian troops in the country, mainly as part of the 102nd Russian military base in Gyumri.[3] The latter is important as it is close to the border with Turkey. In addition, a MIG-29 squadron and an S-300 Zenith anti-missile complex are situated in Armenia.

The Republic of Azerbaijan (Azarbaycan Respublikasi)

The Republic of Azerbaijan gained independence on 30 August 1991 and had previously been independent for almost two years (28 May 1918 to 28 April 1920). The capital is Baku, the official currency is the Azerbaijani manat and the official language is Azerbaijani. The national holiday is celebrated on 28 May, referring to the independence day of the first republic in 1918.

Azerbaijan is divided administratively into 66 districts (sg. *rayon*; pl. *rayonlar*) and 12 cities (sg. *sahar*; pl. *saharlar*). The Nakhchivan Autonomous Republic (Naxcivan Muxtar Respublika) is an integral part of the Republic of Azerbaijan, whereas the previously existing Nagorno Karabakh autonomy was abolished in November 1991 by a decision of the Azerbaijani Supreme Soviet and is not mentioned in the constitution. It is important to note that Azerbaijan is not in control of some 20 per cent of its territory – not only Nagorno Karabakh, but also some of the strategic surrounding territories.

The executive branch is headed by the president, who is elected directly for a five-year term and cannot serve more than two consecutive terms. Ayaz Mutalibov, the former first secretary of the Azerbaijani Communist Party, became the first president of Azerbaijan through his election by the Supreme Council in October 1991. He resigned after the March 1992 massacre of Azerbaijanis in Khojaly, but was restored to power in May. Opposition mounted, forcing Mutalibov out again one week later. In June the pan-Turkic leader of the Popular Front, Abulfaz Elchibey, won the first democratic elections, but his government was unable to deal with either the war in Nagorno Karabakh or the economy. As a result, an armed uprising started in Ganja and moved towards Baku in June 1993, forcing Elchibey to flee to his native Nakhchivan. Heydar Aliyev – at that time speaker of the National Council, but also first secretary of the Azerbaijani Communist Party from 1969 to 1981, former member of the Soviet Politbureau and former deputy prime minister of the USSR – was appointed head of state by the National Council and elected president in October 1993. Aliyev was re-elected in October 1998 and died in December 2003, two months after stepping down.

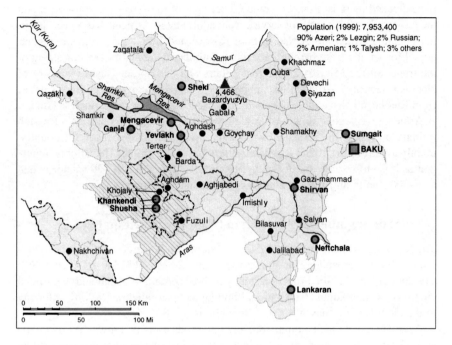

Map 2.2 The Republic of Azerbaijan (Azarbaycan Respublikasi)

His son Ilham Aliyev was elected president in October 2003 and re-elected five years later with almost 90 per cent of votes cast. The president appoints all ministers and other heads of central executive bodies.

The legislative body was the Supreme Soviet until May 1992 and the National Council from May 1992 until November 1995. Thereafter the Milli Majlis, or National Assembly, became the unicameral parliament, which is made up of 125 deputies, directly elected for a period of five years in single-seat constituencies. During the November 2005 elections, ten parties obtained seats in the parliament: the New Azerbaijan Party (YAP – Yeni Azarbaycan, headed by Ilham Aliyev) won 56 seats, the Freedom coalition (Azadliq) won six seats, and eight smaller parties obtained either one or two seats; the remainder of elected parliamentarians were not affiliated to any party.

Local power is very weak, and the first local elections were held only in 1999. The president still appoints the heads of the executive branch in the cities and districts.

In 2007, the total armed forces of Azerbaijan numbered some 66,740, composed of an army (56,840), a navy (2,000) and the Air Force and Air Defense (7,900).[4] This large number can be explained by the unsolved conflict over Nagorno Karabakh as well as the instability at its northern border (Dagestan, Chechnya). The armed forces rely mostly on conscripts, who serve for at least 12 months. Azerbaijan has been participating in peacekeeping operations in Kosovo, Afghanistan and Iraq. Apart from the regular armed forces, there are paramilitary forces estimated to number at least 15,000, consisting of the Militia (10,000 or more, under the Ministry of Internal Affairs) and the Border Guards (*c.* 5,000). There is a large military opposition (est. 18,000) in Nagorno Karabakh, made up largely of Karabakh Armenians. Whereas Armenia received support from Russia (which was not always so covert), Azerbaijan sought assistance from Turkey and other Muslim countries.

Azerbaijan was the first former Soviet republic to see the withdrawal of Russian troops, with the result that there is now only a very small Russian military presence, in the form of a radar station in Gabala, with some 800 Russian technical personnel. Although the Azerbaijani government previously demanded that the Russians leave altogether, in recent years they seem to have reached an informal agreement. However, this station may in future become a political card. Azerbaijan has furthermore refused a Russian peacekeeping role in Karabakh and strongly disapproves of the large Russian military involvement in Armenia.

The Autonomous Republic of Nakhchivan
(Naxcivan Muxtar Respublikasi)

Nakhchivan is an Azerbaijani exclave which is bordered by Armenia, Iran and Turkey. Its isolation from the main part of Azerbaijan dates from 1924, when Stalin transferred the province of Zangezur to Armenian control. Although it suffered severely from the war between Armenia and Azerbaijan and was bombed several times, it was never invaded. The autonomy of Nakhchivan originates in the treaties of Moscow and Kars of 1921 and has held its current form since 17 November 1990. The administration of the Autonomous Republic of Nakhchivan is stipulated in the Azerbaijani constitution of 1995, and as a result is very similar to that of Azerbaijan. Nevertheless, Nakhchivan has its own constitution, which was adopted by referendum in November 1995. The capital is the city of Nakhchivan, which according to Armenian tradition was founded by the biblical Noah.

Legislative power rests with the Ali Majlis (parliament), consisting of 45 members elected for a period of five years. Its chairman is the highest official of the republic. Heydar Aliyev was chairman from 1991 until 1993, when he became president of Azerbaijan, and was replaced by Vasib Talibov. The heads of the local administrations are appointed by the president of the Republic of Azerbaijan on recommendation of the chairman of the Ali Majlis. The official symbols (i.e. flag, coat of arms and hymn) are the same as those of the Republic of Azerbaijan.

Republic of Nagorno Karabakh (Artsakh)

The independent Republic of Nagorno Karabakh (Lernayin Gharabaghi Hanrapetutyn, or Artsakh) was declared on 2 September 1991 but is not recognized by any UN member state, not even Armenia. 'Nagorno' (translates as 'mountainous'). The region suffered from a devastating war from February 1988 to May 1994, and its status remains disputed. The city of Stepanakert, known as

Khankendi by Azerbaijanis, is its capital. Although President Bako Sahakyan, who came to power in autumn 2007, welcomed the Russian recognition of Abkhazia and South Ossetia, Russia has made it clear that a similar recognition of Nagorno Karabakh is out of question.

Nagorno Karabakh's head of state is the president, who is elected by popular vote for a period of five years and cannot serve more than two terms. Robert Kocharyan was elected president in 1994 by the parliament of Nagorno Karabakh and re-elected by popular vote two years later. He left office in March 1997 after accepting the post of prime minister of Armenia. Arkadi Ghukasyan won the second democratic presidential elections in September 1997, was re-elected five years later, and was succeeded by Sahakyan.

The National Assembly is the highest legislative organ, composed of 33 members all elected for a period of five years. The parties that obtained seats in the 2005 elections are the Democratic Party for Artsakh (12 seats), Free Motherland (ten seats) and the coalition of Movement 88 with the Armenian Revolutionary Federation – Dashnaktsutiun (three seats). The other seats were taken by independents.

Georgia (Sakartvelo)

On 9 April 1991, Georgia (Sakartvelos Respublikis; renamed Sakartvelo in 1995), with its capital in Tbilisi, became the first Caucasian republic to declare independence. It saw itself as a continuation of the republic that had existed some 70 years before (26 May 1918 to 25 February 1921), and the national holiday is celebrated on 26 May in commemoration of the original independence day. The official language is Georgian, but Abkhaz can also be used as an official language in Abkhazia. The lari is the official currency, but in reality the Russian rouble is in use in south Ossetia and Abkhazia (except for the Gali district) and the Armenian dram is commonly used in Javakheti as well.

The 1995 constitution changed the territorial administration and led to unrest among certain minority groups. This was the case, for example, with the Megrelians and the Javakheti Armenians, who were both merged with ethnic Georgians. The main administrative areas consist of nine provinces, or *mkharebi*, one autonomous republic (Adjara), one region without specified political status (Abkhazia) and the capital, Tbilisi. The previously existing Autonomous Region of South Ossetia was abolished in 1990 and now belongs to the province of Shida Kartli, but is now sometimes referred to as the Tskhinvali region. As a result, the regional level consists of 12 entities, but the legal status of only three of them (Abkhazia, Adjara and Tbilisi) is defined. The status of the *mkharebi* remains uncertain. At a lower level, there are 67 administrative districts (sg. *raioni*; pl. *raionebi*) and six independent cities (sg. *kalaki*; pl. *kalakebi*).

The president is the head of state and possesses wide-ranging responsibilities, which were extended through a reform to the constitution after Mikheil Saakashvili took office. The president is elected for a period of five years and cannot serve more than two consecutive terms. Zviad Gamsakhurdia was elected

Population (2002-3): 4,645,551
80% Georgian; 6% Armenian; 6% Azeri;
2% Abkhaz; 2% Russian; 2% Ossetian;
2% others

Ab:	Abkhazia
Adj:	Adjara
Gu:	Guria
Im:	Imereti
Ka:	Kakheti
KvK:	Kvemo Kartli
Mt:	Mtkheta
Ra:	Racha-Lechkhumi
S-J:	Samtskhe-Javakheti
Sa:	Samegrelo-Zemo Svaneti
ShK:	Shida Kartli
T:	Tbilisi

Map 2.3 Georgia (Sakartvelo)

chairman of the Supreme Council of the Republic of Georgia in November 1990
and elected the first president of the independent Georgia six months later, but
was ousted after another six months. Following a short period of leadership by a
military council, the former minister of foreign affairs of the USSR, Eduard
Shevardnadze, returned to his native country to be its new leader. However, he
was forced to step down after massive street protests in 2003 led by Mikheil
Saakashvili, who was elected president in 2004 and re-elected four years later.

According to the 1995 constitution, there should be a two-chamber parliament
(Sakartvelos Parlamenti; also known as Umaghlesi Sabcho, or Supreme Council),
consisting of a Republican Council, with members elected according to proportional representation, and a Senate, with members elected from all territorial units
plus five deputies appointed by the president. In reality and based on constitutional amendments, the parliament consists of only 150 deputies elected by proportional representation. Five parties obtained seats in the 2008 elections: the
United National Movement (led by President Saakashvili; 119 seats), the electoral bloc Joint Opposition (17 seats), the Christian-Democrat Movement (six
seats), the Labour Party (six seats) and the Republic Party of Georgia (two seats).

Local government exists, but only where it does not contradict Georgian interests or the constitution, thus severely limiting its powers. Councils, or *sakrebulebi*
(sg. *sakrebulo*), are at the level of regions, districts and villages/communities, and
governors are appointed by the president in each of the nine regions.

The main political event in recent years was the Rose Revolution, the peaceful uprising of November 2003 which led to the resignation of President Shevardnadze. Shevardnadze had been ruling Georgia for 11 years, and he and his family had become increasingly associated with corruption. The country had not developed economically, huge socio-economic problems persisted, Adjara was ruled by a local leader who did not submit to the central authorities, and there was no change in the status of the conflicts in Abkhazia and South Ossetia. The parliamentary elections on 2 November 2003 were marked by major fraud perpetrated by Shevardnadze's Citizen's Union of Georgia party and as a result Mikheil Saakashvili, the main opposition candidate, called on the Georgian people to demonstrate and engage in civil disobedience. This culminated on 22 November, when Saakashvili, with hundreds of supporters, most of them holding a rose in their hand, stormed the parliament building during the opening session of the new parliament. President Shevardnadze fled and resigned the next day. Saakashvili was subsequently elected president and new parliamentary elections were held. A second Rose Revolution took place in May 2004 in Batumi and led to the ousting of Aslan Abashidze, the authoritarian leader of Adjara.

Street protests broke out on 28 September 2007, one day after the former defence minister, Irakli Okruashvili,[5] was arrested on charges of corruption, money laundering and abuse of office. Protests grew bigger in the first days of November, calling for the resignation of Saakashvili and early elections. Tens of thousands of people rallied in the centre of Tbilisi, but the largely peaceful crowd was dispersed by police. The situation deteriorated so much that on 7 November President Saakashvili declared a state of emergency. He refused to resign, but the following day he announced early elections, thereby cutting his term in office by one year. Saakashvili won those 2008 presidential elections again, but gained only 52.5 per cent of votes compared with the 96 per cent he had obtained four years earlier.

There has also been some debate, albeit low key, about the restoration of the monarchy in the country, and the Georgian Orthodox Church in particular has argued for the return of the royal Bagrationi family. Nevertheless, this is an unlikely future scenario.

In 2007, Georgia's active armed forces[6] numbered some 21,150 individuals, made up of an army (17,767), a navy (495), an air force (1,310) and the National Guard (1,578). During recent years there have been several reforms made to the armed forces, and the number of conscripts (only 3,767 in 2007), who usually serve for a period of 18 months, is being gradually reduced. Georgia has been participating in peacekeeping operations in Kosovo and Iraq, and there have been talks about taking part in Afghanistan as well. Paramilitary forces number 11,700 persons and are made up of Ministry of Interior troops (6,300) and Border Guards (5,400). A large military opposition, however, consisting of the armed forces of the partially recognized republics of Abkhazia and South Ossetia, together with some Russian forces, exists in Georgia's conflict zones. Georgia has received large military support from NATO member states over the past years, especially from the US.

Until 2007 there was a large Russian military presence in Georgia, though this has been reduced. The CIS peacekeeping force in Abkhazia is composed exclusively of Russian military (c. 2,500)[7] and the joint peacekeeping force in South Ossetia has a Russian component (530). After obtaining independence, Georgia had to accept the stationing of four bases of 'Groups of Russian Forces in Transcaucasia', which housed approximately 9,200 troops. At the 1999 OSCE summit Russia agreed on the withdrawal of those troops, but they did not leave Vaziani (near Tbilisi) and Gudauta (in Abkhazia) until January 2004. The bases in Akhalkalaki (in the Armenian populated Javakheti region) and Batumi (in Adjara) were abandoned in May and September 2007 respectively. UNOMIG (the United Nations Observer Mission in Georgia) also has more than 130 observers originating from over 30 different countries.

The Republic of Abkhazia (Apsny)

The political status of Abkhazia, which declared independence on 23 July 1992, is not yet clear. It is not under the control of the Georgian central authorities but has a de facto government, president, parliament, laws, and a constitution which was adopted in November 1994. The Republic of Abkhazia and Apsny are equivalent names for the republic that is subdivided into seven districts.[8] Sukhum(i) (Aqua in Abkhaz) is the capital and the Russian rouble is the common currency. The official language is Abkhaz, but Russian is also used. Abkhazia is recognized only by Russia and Nicaragua.

Executive power is granted to the president, who is elected by direct vote for a period of five years and cannot be in office for more than two consecutive terms. The first president, Vladislav Ardzinba, sat for two terms (1994 to 2005), but serious illness meant that he did not appear in public after 2002. The lengthy and strongly contested presidential elections in the autumn of 2004 between Sergey Bagapsh and former prime minister Raul Khadzhimba (favoured by Ardzinba) resulted in an alliance of the two, with Bagapsh becoming the new president and Khadzhimba vice president.

Legislative power rests with the People's Assembly or Parliament of the Republic of Abkhazia, which consists of 35 members elected by direct vote for a period of five years. During the 2007 elections the three pro-Bagapsh parties, Revival (Aitara), Signal Lights (Amtsakhara) and United Abkhazia, obtained 28 seats, and three opposition parties took the remaining eight seats.

According to the most reliable estimates, the Abkhaz armed forces number between 5,000 and 10,000 persons.[9]

There is also a pro-Georgian Abkhaz government in exile. In September 1993 the Council of Ministers of Abkhazia left Sukhumi and relocated to Tbilisi, where it was led by Tamaz Nadareishvili. He resigned in January 2004 after internal controversy and was followed by Londer Tsaava, who in turn was replaced by Iralki Asatiani in September of the same year. Three months later, the official name of this government was changed from the Council of Ministers of the

Autonomous Republic of Abkhazia to the Government of Abkhazia (in exile). Malkhaz Akishbaia was elected its head in April 2006. After disarming the militia of local warlord Emzar Kvitsiani in July 2006 in the Kodori gorge, the Georgian leadership decided to install the Government of Abkhazia there, back on Abkhazian territory. But in August 2008 the Abkhaz took control over the Upper Kodori gorge and forced them out.

The Republic of South Ossetia (Respublika Hussar Iryston)

In 1990, South Ossetia lost the status it had held since 1922 as an autonomous region. As a reaction to this, it declared independence and adopted its own constitution. Tensions resulted in August 2008 in war, and South Ossetia is now de facto independent. Although the UN does not consider it to be a sovereign state, its independence has been recognized by Russia and Nicaragua. Certain Ossetian forces have called for a unification of South Ossetia with North Ossetia (i.e. inclusion in the Russian Federation),[10] but so far there have been no concrete attempts to bring this about. Tskhinval(i), known as Staliniri between 1934 and 1961, is the capital and the Russian rouble is used as currency. Ossetian is the official language, but Russian and Georgian can be used as state languages.

Until November 1996, the head of the South Ossetian state was the chairman of the parliament – successively Znaur Gassiyev (1991–2), Torez Kulumbegov (1992–3) and Lyudvig Chibirov (1992–6). The post of president was introduced in 1996, and the post has been occupied by Lyudvig Chibirov (1996–2001) and Eduard Kokoyty (from 2001; re-elected in 2006). Four out of the 34 seats of the South Ossetian parliament are allocated to ethnic Georgians, but they remain empty as the Georgians boycotted the elections.

In November 2006, an alternative election was organized in the ethnic Georgian villages of the breakaway region. Dmitriy Sanakoyev, a former prime minister of the South Ossetian de facto government under President Chibirov, became an alternative president and set up an alternative pro-Georgian government. In May 2007 President Saakashivili appointed Sanakoyev head of the South Ossetian Provisional Administrative Entity. This provisional administration had its seat in Kurta until it was forced to leave in the August 2008 war, uses the Georgian lari as official currency and has both Georgian and Ossetian as official languages. In meetings with Georgian officials, Sanakoyev actually often speaks in Ossetian.

The armed forces of South Ossetia number probably 3,000 troops.[11]

The Autonomous Republic of Adjara (Acharis Avtonomiuri Respublika)

On 16 July 1921, the Soviet leadership declared the Adjarian Autonomous Soviet Socialist Republic (Adjarian ASSR), largely for political reasons. First, Turkey had ceded the region to the Bolsheviks on the condition that it would grant autonomy to the Muslim Georgians of Adjara, and, second, it prevented the

Georgians from exercising full control over the port of Batumi. After the break-up of the Soviet Union, Adjara retained its status as an autonomous republic, but remained politically separate from the central authority until May 2004. The situation of Adjara cannot be compared to that of Abkhazia or South Ossetia, as the Adjarian leadership has never tried to secede from Georgia.

Adjara's government is headed by a chairman. Aslan Abashidze was nominated chairman in March 1991, and in 1998 he was elected to the newly introduced post of president, which was abolished after he was ousted. Abashidze's authoritarian style was not appreciated by the central authorities, and his refusal to provide Tbilisi with any tax revenue led to great tension. On 5 May 2004, after several days of street protests in the capital, Batumi, Abashidze resigned; the next day he left for Russia. Levan Varshalomidze was appointed as President Saakashvili's envoy to Adjara, and two months later he was nominated as the new chairman. Since 2004 the chairman has been appointed by the Georgian president.

The local legislative body is the Supreme Council of the Autonomous Republic of Adjara and consists of 30 members, each elected for a period of four years.

The Russian Federation

The Russian Federation or Russia – the constitution gives equal value to both names – is made up of 83 constituent entities[12] or territorial-administrative units of six different categories, all of whom signed the treaty of 21 March 1992 establishing the Russian Federation. These six categories are republics, krays, oblasts, autonomous okrugs, one autonomous oblast, and cities of federal significance. The 21 republics replace the Autonomous Socialist Soviet Republics and Autonomous Oblasts that existed during Soviet times.[13] The fundamental laws and principles of government of the republics are formulated in their own individual constitutions. These were changed during the 1990s in order for presidents to be elected by their populations, but this trend changed in 2005, and now candidates are proposed by the Russian president and approved by the legislative power of the respective republic. There are nine krays (territories), which have a charter that conforms to the constitution of the Russian Federation; their administration/government is led by a governor or head of administration. There are 46 oblasts (provinces), which also have a charter, an administration and a governor. In addition, there are four autonomous okrugs (autonomous districts), one autonomous oblast (autonomous province), and two federal cities (Moscow and St Petersburg). The North Caucasus has seven republics, two krays and one oblast. The two krays and the oblast are politically and economically the most stable in the North Caucasus, although skirmishes (e.g. with the Cossacks or anti-Russian rebels) do occur there too.

In May 2000, President Putin divided the Russian Federation into seven federal districts (okrugs) with the aim of strengthening the vertical governmental powers. The North Caucasus is part of the Southern Federal Okrug, which also includes the Republic of Kalmykia and the Astrakhan and Volgograd oblasts. While the latter have nothing in common in a physical-geographical or environmental sense with the North Caucasus, they do in an administrative sense. The city of Rostov-na-Donu is the administrative centre of the Southern Federal Okrug, which is seen as the most troublesome of the seven in political and socio-economical terms. The Russian president appoints special plenipotentiaries for these okrugs. Since May 2008 this position for the Southern Federal Okrug has been held by Vladimir Ustinov. He was preceded by Viktor Kazantsev (May 2000 – March 2004), Vladimir Yakovlev (March – September 2004), Dmitriy Kozak (September 2004 – September 2007) and Grigoriy Rapota (October 2007 – May 2008).

Russia is further split into 12 economic regions, which have nothing in common with the federal districts. The division into economic regions is only for economic and statistical purposes, and not for administrative use. The North Caucasus forms one single economic region.

The president is the head of state, elected for a period of four years,[14] and cannot serve more than two consecutive terms. The post, which was created when Russia was still an SSR, was initially held by Mikhail Gorbachev (April 1991 – July 1991), the first and only leader to be titled president of the Soviet Union. Boris Yeltsin came to power in July 1991 after having won the elections one month earlier. He was re-elected five years later, but resigned on 31 December 1999, resulting in the prime minister, Vladimir Putin, serving as acting president. Putin won the 2000 and 2004 elections and held the highest office for more than eight years (May 2000 – May 2008). Dmitriy Medvedev was inaugurated in May 2008, just three months before the war with Georgia broke out, and appointed Vladimir Putin as his prime minister.

The highest legislative body is the Federal Assembly. This bi-cameral parliament consists of the Council of the Federation and the State Duma. The Council of the Federation is composed of one representative of the legislative and one representative of the executive body of state authority for each of the 83 federal subjects. The State Duma has 450 deputies, elected for a term of four years through a party-list proportional representation system, and replaces the former Supreme Soviet. The four political parties that passed the 7 per cent threshold in the December 2007 Duma elections are United Russia (315 seats), the Communist Party of the Russian Federation (57 seats), the Liberal Democratic Party of Russia (40 seats), and Fair Russia (38 seats).

There is a high degree of local government, not only at the level of the 83 subjects, but also on the level of districts and municipalities, who have their own budget and property and can impose local taxes.

The Russian armed forces, subdivided into the Strategic Deterrent Forces and the Army, Navy and Military Air Forces, number over one million people[15] and the paramilitary forces number over 418,000. Service for conscripts is between 18 and 24 months. There are six military districts, and the deployment of troops in the Caucasus (90,000 in total) is arranged through the North Caucasus Military District –which also includes the South Caucasus group of forces – and has its headquarters in Rostov-na-Donu. Its largest component consists of ground troops, which are focused particularly on Chechnya and surrounding regions. The parts

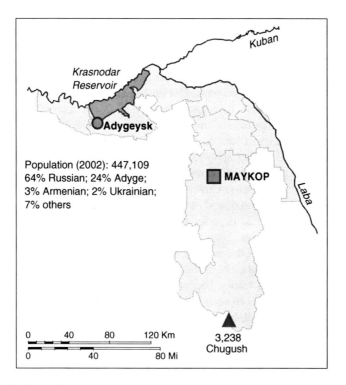

Population (2002): 447,109
64% Russian; 24% Adyge;
3% Armenian; 2% Ukrainian;
7% others

Map 2.4 The Republic of Adygea

of the navy which relate to the Caucasus are the Black Sea Fleet, with headquarters in Sevastopol (Ukraine) and two more bases, located in Novorossiysk and Temryuk, and the Caspian Sea Flotilla[16] with headquarters in Astrakhan.

Although the South Caucasian states are independent, Russia still has a considerable military influence, as has been explained above. Thus the Russian presence in the South Caucasus is an issue of much debate, and the withdrawal of Russian troops from Georgia has received much international attention. Whereas Armenia welcomes the Russian presence, Azerbaijan is gratified that it has almost no Russian forces on its territory. Foreign military bases can be seen as a threat not only to the sovereignty of the Caucasian republics but also to neighboring countries. Until September 2007 Russia controlled the entire former Soviet border with Turkey through its military presence on the Batumi–Akhalkalaki–Gyumri line.[17]

The Republic of Adygea

The Republic of Adygea is a curious case of both geography (it is a land-locked enclave inside the Krasnodar Kray) and history. It was an autonomous oblast during Soviet times, but became an independent entity and constituent republic within the Russian Federation in 1991. There are seven districts and two cities which have their own administration.

The head of state and executive is the president, who can serve two five-year terms. His candidature is proposed by the Russian president, but needs to be approved by the State Council (Khase) of the Republic of Adygea. In January 2007 Aslan Tkhakushinov was inaugurated as president. His predecessors, elected by direct suffrage, were Aslan Dzharimov (January 1992 – February 2002), who had previously been the chairman of the Supreme Soviet of the Adyghe SSR (March 1990 – January 1992), and Khazret Sovmen (February 2002 – January 2007).

The State Council of the Republic of Adygea is the highest legislative body and consists of two chambers: a Council of Representatives (upper chamber) and a Council of the Republic (lower chamber). The Council of Representatives consists of 27 deputies – three being directly elected by secret vote in each of the two cities and seven districts. The 27 deputies of the Council of the Republic are directly elected in 27 constituencies. Their mandate runs for a period of five years.

A major issue has been the possible unification of Adygea with the Krasnodar Kray, which was looked at early in 2006 by Dmitriy Kozak, special plenipotentiary for the Southern Federal Okrug. Factions within the republic warned of the possible negative consequences of such a move, and in April tensions rose so high that the then Adygean President, Hazret Sovmen, sent a letter of resignation to Vladimir Putin. The unification project was taken off the table and Sovmen stayed in office.

The Karachay–Cherkess Republic

The borders and status of the Karachay-Cherkess Republic changed several times in the 1920s. Because it was accused of collaboration with the Germans, Karachay–Cherkessia temporarily lost its local autonomy and between 1944 and 1957 came under direct rule from Moscow. It consists of eight districts and two cities which have their own administration.

In 1991, the Supreme Soviet of the Russian Federation appointed Vladimir Khubiyev – who had been holding the highest office in the Karachay–Cherkess Autonomous Oblast since 1979 – as head of the executive committee. This title became head of the republic in 1992 and president in 2000. In September 1999 Karachay–Cherkessia was the last republic to be 'liberalized' – in other words, to hold democratic elections for the head of the republic – and those who have served as president are Vladimir Semenov (Karachay; November 1999 – September 2003), Mustafa Batdyev (Karachay; September 2003 – September 2008) and Boris Ebzeyev (Karachay; September 2008–). The People's Assembly (parliament) has 73 members who are directly elected for a period of four years.

Ethnic tensions are quite high in the republic. The 1999 elections were won by Vladimir Semenov after allegations of fraud and protests by the supporters of his rival Stanislav Derev (Cherkess). Protests continued after a court ruling upholding the election results, and there were even demands for a partition of the republic. Viktor Kazantsev, the special plenipotentiary, brokered a solution in which the vice-president

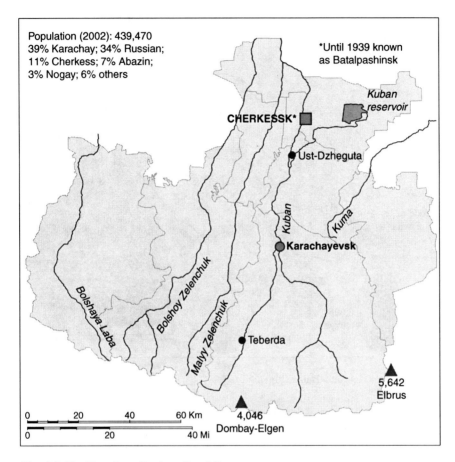

Population (2002): 439,470
39% Karachay; 34% Russian;
11% Cherkess; 7% Abazin;
3% Nogay; 6% others

*Until 1939 known
as Batalpashinsk

Kuban reservoir

CHERKESSK*

Ust-Dzheguta

Kuban

Kuma

Karachayevsk

Bolshaya Laba

Bolshoy Zelenchuk

Malyy Zelenchuk

Teberda

5,642
Elbrus

0   20   40   60 Km
0   20   40 Mi

4,046
Dombay-Elgen

Map 2.5 The Karachay–Cherkess Republic

must be a Russian and the prime minister a Cherkess. Although the situation later settled down, no comprehensive resolution to these ethnic tensions has yet been found.

The Kabardino–Balkar Republic

The Kabardino–Balkar Autonomous Oblast was created in 1922 and further upgraded to an ASSR in 1936. In December 1943, after being accused of collaboration with the Germans, the Balkars were deported and the Balkar part of the name was deleted. The Kabardino–Balkar autonomy was re-established in 1957, after which the Balkars were allowed to return. The Kabardino–Balkar Republic is subdivided into ten districts and three cities which have their own administration.

Arsen Kanokov became president in September 2005, following his nomination by the Russian president and the approval of the Kabardino–Balkar

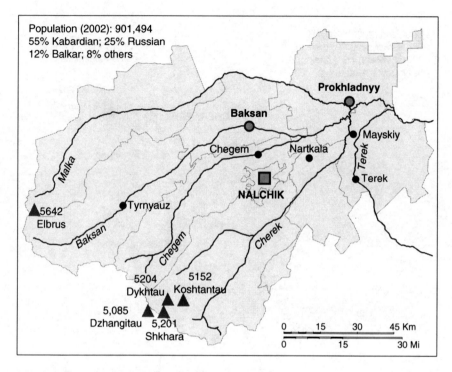

Population (2002): 901,494
55% Kabardian; 25% Russian
12% Balkar; 8% others

Map 2.6 The Kabardino–Balkar Republic

parliament. His predecessor, Valeriy Kokov, was elected in 1992 and served almost three full terms. Kokov submitted his resignation due to health problems in September 2005 and died one month later. There are 110 members of parliament, who are directly elected for a period of five years.

The Republic of North Ossetia–Alania

North Ossetia's status changed several times in the first few years after the 1917 Civil War and became an ASSR in 1936. In 1944, following the deportation of the Ingush for alleged collaboration with the Germans, the Prigorodnyy Rayon and part of the Stavropol Territory were added to North Ossetia. The republic's name was changed to North Ossetia–Alania in November 1994 in order to reflect the ancient Alan heritage. There are eight districts and two cities which have their own administration.

Akhsarbek Galazov, who was the chairman of the Supreme Council from 1990 to 1994, became the first president after winning the elections in the latter year. He was followed in 1998 by Aleksandr Dzasokhov, who was re-elected in 2002 but resigned in May 2005 – according to one view as a consequence of the Beslan tragedy one year previously, but according to another linked to his attitude towards the settlement of the Ingush–Ossetian problem. One week later,

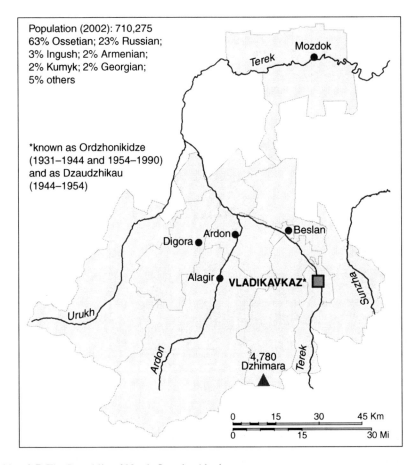

Population (2002): 710,275
63% Ossetian; 23% Russian;
3% Ingush; 2% Armenian;
2% Kumyk; 2% Georgian;
5% others

*known as Ordzhonikidze
(1931–1944 and 1954–1990)
and as Dzaudzhikau
(1944–1954)

Map 2.7 The Republic of North Ossetia–Alania

Taymuraz Mamsurov, who had been proposed by President Putin, was appointed president by the parliament. This parliament consists of 75 deputies elected for a four-year period.

Since 1 September 2004, North Ossetia, or rather its second biggest city, Beslan, has been known to the whole world as a group of armed rebels took hostage more than 1,100 people, mainly children, in a school. On the third day of the crisis, Russian forces stormed the building and a chaotic battle started. Hundreds of people died[18] and the full story of what happened remains unclear.[19] The conflict over the region of South Ossetia has led to calls from both sides to unify North and South Ossetia. The war of August 2008 further strengthened these calls and seems to receive support from Moscow. Naturally, such a move would not be simple as the international community would consider it to be an annexation of Georgian territory by the Russian Federation.

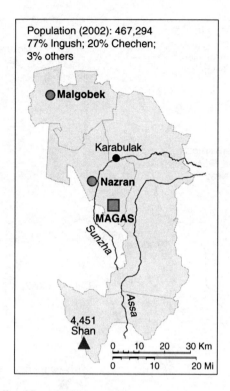

Population (2002): 467,294
77% Ingush; 20% Chechen;
3% others

Malgobek

Karabulak

Nazran

MAGAS

Sunzha

Assa

4,451
Shan

0   10   20   30 Km

0   10   20 Mi

Map 2.8 The Republic of Ingushetia

The Republic of Ingushetia

Ingushetia was part of the Mountain People's Autonomous Socialist Soviet Republic until 1924, the year in which the Ingush Autonomous Oblast was created. From 1934 until 1992 it was part of the Chechen–Ingush ASSR, although during the period 1944 to 1957 both Ingush and Chechens lived in exile in Central Asia and the territory was divided among its neighbors. In 1991 the Chechen-dominated parliament of the Chechen–Ingush Republic declared independence, but the Ingush did not wish to separate from Russia. They split away from the Chechens in November of that year to become a de facto separate republic, choosing to remain part of the Russian Federation. This status was formalized in June 1992. The Republic of Ingushetia, which is the smallest constituent republic of the Russian Federation, has four districts and three cities which have their own administration. Although Nazran is the largest city, and served as the temporary capital, the recently built city of Magas became the capital in December 2002. Magas was the name of the capital of Alania, the state that ruled most of the North Caucasus in the tenth to twelfth centuries.

In November 1992 Ruslan Aushev was appointed to lead the provisional administration of Ingushetia; he was elected president in March 1993 and re-elected four years later. After a short interim period under the leadership of Akhmed Malsagov (December 2001 – May 2002), FSB Major-General Murat Zyazikov was elected the new president; he was also re-elected four years later. Zyazikov survived an attempt on his life, but in general instability in the republic increased. When Magomed Evloyev, a key member of the opposition, was killed by law enforcement agencies in bizarre circumstances, civil unrest increased further and the close entourage of the president and the minister of interior were under constant attack. Zyazikov finally resigned in October 2008 and Yunus-Bek Yevkurov was appointed acting president.

The People's Assembly is the legislative body of Ingushetia. It has 27 deputies, elected for a period of four years.

The Chechen Republic

The history of Chechnya after 1917 was tied to that of Ingushetia until the Chechen declaration of independence and sovereignty in 1991. The current constitution, which was accepted by a controversial referendum in March 2003, replaces the previous constitution of 1992. It does not mention the word 'sovereignty', which appears in the constitutions of other ethnic republics, such as Tatarstan and Bashkortostan. The Chechen Republic is administratively divided into eighteen districts and three cities which have their own administration.

From March 1990 to September 1991, Doku Zavgayev was the chairman of the Supreme Soviet of the Chechen–Ingush ASSR. Dzhokhar Dudayev was the Chechen Republic's first president, elected in November 1991, and he remained in power until April 1996. He was replaced by Zelimkhan Yandarbiyev, who lost the February 1997 elections and was followed by Aslan Maskhadov. Maskhadov abandoned Groznyy in February 2000 and was killed in March 2005. In June 2000, the Russian authorities, who had taken control of most of Chechnya, appointed Akhmad Kadyrov as the head of administration. The post of president was introduced again through the new constitution in March 2003, and Kadyrov remained in power until he was assassinated in May 2004. Sergey Abramov served as acting president and Alu Alkhanov became the new president in October 2004. According to the new constitution, the Chechen president can be removed by the Russian president at any time. Ramzan Kadyrov, the son of Ahmad Kadyrov, became prime minister in 2004 and, following criticism of Alkhanov, was appointed president by Vladimir Putin.

The Chechen Parliament consists of two chambers: a Council of the Republic (21 members) and a People's Assembly (40 members), each elected for a four-year period. However, in June 2008 a new law was enacted whereby the new parliament – elections are scheduled for October 2009 – will be unicameral, with 61 seats.

The Republic of Dagestan

Dagestan, on the western shore of the Caspian Sea, is the largest republic of the North Caucasus. It is also the republic with the largest number of different

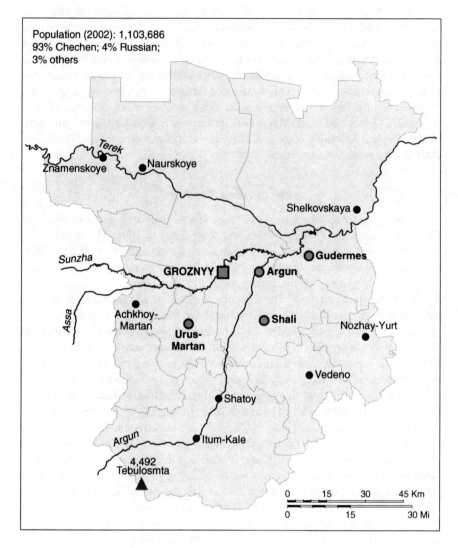

Population (2002): 1,103,686
93% Chechen; 4% Russian;
3% others

Map 2.9 The Chechen Republic

indigenous nationalities, many of them numbering only a few hundred people. Dagestan has 41 districts and ten cities which have their own administration.

The government of the Republic of Dagestan was formerly known as the State Council and the Supreme Council. The People's Assembly is a one-chamber parliament, and has 72 deputies directly elected for a period of four years. The president is nominated by the Russian president and approved by the People's Assembly. Since its creation in February 2006 this post has been held by Mukhu

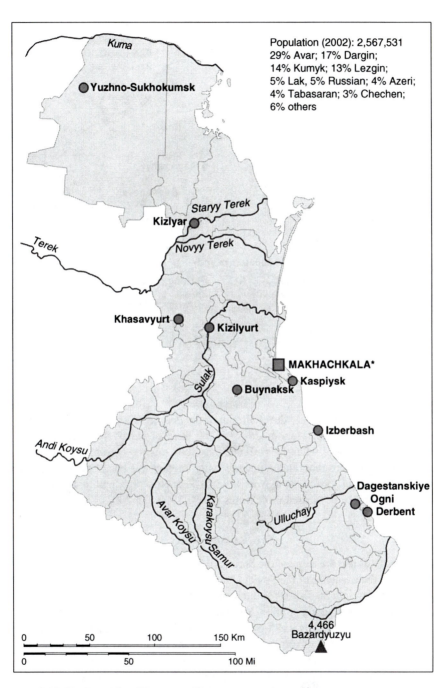

Population (2002): 2,567,531
29% Avar; 17% Dargin;
14% Kumyk; 13% Lezgin;
5% Lak, 5% Russian; 4% Azeri;
4% Tabasaran; 3% Chechen;
6% others

Kuma

Yuzhno-Sukhokumsk

Staryy Terek

Kizlyar

Terek

Novyy Terek

Khasavyurt

Kizilyurt

MAKHACHKALA*

Kaspiysk

Buynaksk

Sulak

Izberbash

Andi Koysu

Dagestanskiye
Ogni
Derbent

Avar Koysu

Karakoysu

Samur

Ulluchay

4,466
Bazardyuzyu

0   50   100   150 Km

0   50   100 Mi

Map 2.10 The Republic of Dagestan

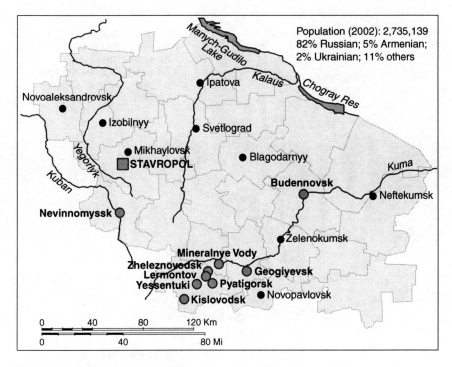

Map 2.11 The Stavropol Kray

Aliyev, who was previously the chairman of the People's Assembly for more than a decade. Magomedali Magomedov was the head of state[20] from August 1987 until February 2006, when he resigned just four months before the end of his mandate for reasons that remain unclear. Magomedov was one of the few leaders under the Soviet system who was able to keep his post within the Russian Federation and to be elected three times (1994, 1998 and 2002).

The Stavropol Kray

Both the status and the name of the Stavropol Kray changed several times in the first decades of the existence of the Soviet Union, and its present name dates from 1943. It is subdivided into 26 districts and ten cities which have their own administration.

The first head of administration, Yevgeniy Kuznetsov, was appointed in October 1991 and replaced in July 1995 by Petr Marchenko. In November 1996 the post was replaced by that of governor, to be elected for a period of five years. Aleksandr Chernogorov was elected in November 1996 and re-elected in 2000. From 2005 the governor has been presented by the Russian president and endowed with plenary powers by the Stavropol State Duma; Chernogorov remains in power. The State Duma has 50 members, each elected for a period of five years.

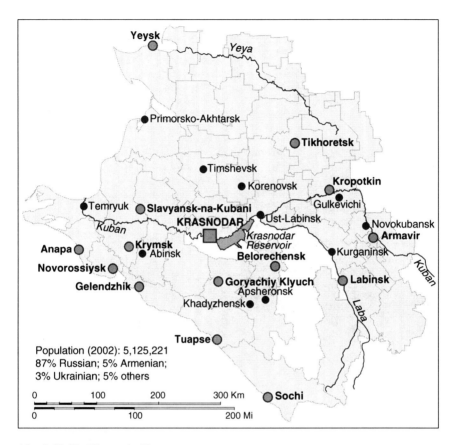

Map 2.12 The Krasnodar Kray

The Krasnodar Kray

The Krasnodar Kray – still often referred to as Kuban – was until 1937 part of the Azov–Black Sea Kray, and is the southernmost kray of the Russian Federation. The Republic of Adygea, which became a separate subject of the Russian Federation in 1991, forms an enclave in its centre. The Krasnodar Kray has 38 districts and 15 cities which have their own administration.

The head of administration also has the title of governor and is nominated by the Russian president and appointed by the Legislative Assembly for a period of five years. Aleksandr Tkachev was elected governor in December 2000. Previous governors were Nikolay Yegorov (December 1992 – August 1994; July 1996 – January 1997), Yevgeniy Kharitonov (August 1994 – July 1996) and Nikolay Kondratenko (January 1997 – January 2000). The Legislative Assembly is composed of 70 deputies, elected for a period of five years.

53

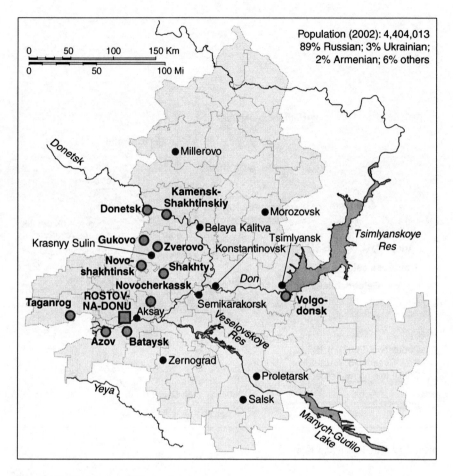

Population (2002): 4,404,013
89% Russian; 3% Ukrainian;
2% Armenian; 6% others

Map 2.13 The Rostov Oblast

The Rostov Oblast

The Rostov Oblast was created on 13 September 1937, when the Azov–Black Sea Oblast of 1924 was divided into the Rostov Oblast and the Krasnodar Kray. The Rostov Oblast contains 43 districts and 12 cities which have their own administration.

The executive is overseen by the head of administration, or governor. Vladimir Chub was appointed to this post on 8 October 1991 by a decree of the Russian president, and he was elected by popular vote for a period of five years in September 1996; he was re-elected in September 2001. Chub was proposed again by president Putin and endowed with plenary powers by the Legislative Assembly in June 2005. The Legislative Assembly has 45 members, elected for a period of five years.

3

POPULATION AND SOCIETY

The Caucasus is renowned for its large number of different ethnic groups, languages and religions. This is not only an object of study for academics; it also forms one of the cornerstones for understanding the dynamics of the region.

Demographic data

There is an acute lack of accurate information and statistics concerning the population of the Caucasus. While censuses were taken frequently in the nineteenth century, when the entire Caucasus was part of the Russian Empire, and during the existence of the Soviet Union, the latest censuses were in 1999 in Azerbaijan, in 2001 in Armenia, in 2002 in Georgia and in the Russian Federation, in 2003 in Abkhazia, and in 2005 in Nagorno Karabakh. No census has been organized in South Ossetia since the fall of the Soviet Union, and it did not participate in the 2002 Georgian census. Although Nagorno Karabakh did not take part in the 1999 Azerbaijan census, it is included in the official data: the number of Armenians in the region was simply copied from the 1989 census, and thus is probably not very accurate. The official data are also not fully reliable in the case of Chechnya and Ingushetia: the status of the many internally displaced people (IDPs) and refugees is not clear, and the 2002 census looked at where people were officially registered and not where they actually lived. Most of the data in this book are taken from these censuses, which are unlikely to be fully accurate. For example, the total population of Azerbaijan in early 2008 was estimated at 8.6 million[1] rather than the 8 million at the time of the 1999 census. For reasons discussed below, data on certain minorities often come from unofficial estimates from academic publications.

The total population of the Caucasus amounts to almost 35 million people. At the beginning of the 1970s it was 22.7 million and in 1985 it was 25 million. Population growth in the 1970s and 1980s was the result mainly of births in the static population, with, in general, the fertility rate among Muslims being higher than that among other ethnic groups. During the post-Soviet years, migration and the movement of refugees have been the main determining factors in changes in the population. There has been an inflow in the North Caucasus and an outflow

Table 3.1 Population statistics

Region	Population (in 1,000)	Area (in 1,000 km²)	Pop 1,000 density
Republic of Amenia	3,213	29.8	108
Republic of Azerbaijan	7,953	86.6	92
Georgia	4,646	69.7	67
Republic of Adygea	447	7.6	59
Karachay–Cherkess Republic	439	14.1	31
Kabardino–Balkar Republic	901	12.5	72
Republic of North Ossetia–Alania	710	8.0	89
Republic of Ingushetia	467	4.2	111
Republic of Chechnya	1,104	14.8	75
Republic of Dagestan	2,577	50.3	51
Stavropol Kray	2,735	66.5	41
Krasnodar Kray	5,125	76.0	67
Rostov Oblast	4,404	100.8	44

Sources: National Statistical Service of the Republic of Armenia, State Statistical Committee of the Republic of Abkhazia, Department for Statistics of Georgia, Department of State Statistics of the Republic of Abkhazia, Federal State Statistics Service of the Russian Federation.

in the South Caucasus. This has been the result of armed conflict, the poor economic situation, and the outmigration of native Russians and Ukrainians from the South Caucasus and the North Caucasian autonomies. For example, between 1989 and 2002, 65 per cent of Russians, 83 per cent of Ukrainians and 85 per cent of Greeks left Georgia. There are two types of migrants. Poverty, low salaries, high unemployment, the absence of legal protection, political instability, and the lack of opportunities are the main reasons why some look for a better life elsewhere. Highly qualified people move to Russia, Europe and the US in search of better prospects. This brain drain leads, in turn, to a decrease in the quality of the labour force and a decline in purchasing power in the Caucasus, thereby creating a vicious circle. Other migrants are refugees, IDPs or just people not feeling at ease in a minority group. The emigration from Chechnya is clearly linked to the two consecutive wars and the absence of a solution. Whereas Groznyy was once a multi-ethnic and multicultural centre, most non-Chechens have now left.

The population of the Caucasus is not evenly distributed. The most densely populated areas are along the Black Sea coast, in the Rioni River valley, and in several other valleys in the South Caucasus. The mountain areas and the arid steppes along the Caspian coast, on the other hand, are sparsely populated. There are only four cities with a population of more than a million: Tbilisi, Baku, Yerevan and Rostov-na-Donu.

Ethnic composition

The Caucasus is an ethnolinguistic mosaic, since more than a hundred different ethnic groups, each with completely different languages and customs, populate this small area. The ancient Greek geographer Timosthenes (third century BC) claimed that there were 300 languages spoken in the markets of Kolkhis, although this figure is probably exaggerated. Strabo (64 BC – AD 24) was probably more accurate when he declared that there were 70 different peoples in the Caucasus. Medieval Arab geographers called the Caucasus *jabal al-alsun*, or the Mountain of Tongues. Since those times several nations have died out or have been assimilated, and some new ones have arrived in the region.

It is difficult to estimate the size of every ethnic group as official data are often hard to find, are outdated or else are manipulated by either not including or underestimating the numbers of certain ethnic groups. A very clear example is that several minor Dagestani nations, such as the Andi and Dido, are counted as Avars. Another is that of the Budukhs, who appear in statistics as Azerbaijanis. On the other hand, the Azerbaijani government claims that there are only some 77,000 Talysh in Azerbaijan, but Talysh nationalists talk about a figure of more than a million.

The question of ethnic groupings is not always entirely clear. First of all, in order to avoid discrimination, some people prefer to see themselves as belonging to the majority population. There are also many cases where mountain people have moved to the plains and 'adopted' a new nationality – for example many ethnic Rutuls call themselves Lezgins. Second, it is unclear whether or not certain groups belong to a larger group: some claim, for instance, that the Tabasarans, Aguls, Rutuls and Tsakhurs are all Lezgins. And, as a result of assimilation and intermarriage between different ethnic groups, it is difficult for certain people to determine their nationality. In general, most people will identify with the ethnic origin of their father. While Russians are especially exogamous, Armenia is almost a mono-ethnic state since the war in Nagorno Karabakh, with an impressive 98 per cent of its population ethnic Armenian; 91 per cent of the population of Azerbaijan is Azerbaijani and 80 per cent of that of Georgia is Georgian.

The preservation of one's ethnic and national identity is a very important issue in the Caucasus and is especially acute for the younger generations of smaller ethnic groups such as the Andi and Dido. Territorial isolation kept foreign influence away and helped to preserve languages and customs, although several elements of Soviet urban culture have influenced clothing, household equipment, furniture, food and architecture. The construction of roads and urbanization made these regions more vulnerable to Russification, anti-Islamism, forced collectivization and general oppression. The growing number of mixed marriages and the rise of education standards further contributed to this problem. However, Soviet policies also had a reverse effect, as they actually strengthened hatred of the Russians and heightened the feelings of national identity among many of the minorities.

This chapter gives an overview of the main ethnic groups in the Caucasus. It discusses their territory, language, religion and roots, as well as some main historic events. The numbers given in parentheses refers to the population in the Caucasus only. The genesis of each particular ethnic group is the most widely accepted account, though many of these are contested, especially if one ethnic group is in conflict with another. It is very important to consider to what extent the indigenous ethnic groups of the region remain linked to their ancestors. Armenians, Georgians and others have often been intermingled with Persians, Arabs, Mongols and other conquerors.

The Russians (11.8 million) constitute the largest ethnic group in the Caucasus and form the majority population in the Krasnodar Kray, Stavropol Kray and Rostov Oblast; they are also found in large numbers in the other Caucasian territorial-administrative entities. While their number used to be greater, many Russians moved away after the collapse of the Soviet Union, mainly for economic reasons. Most Russians are Orthodox Christians, but there are several other Christian sects, such as Molokanism or Catholicism. Only a limited number of Russians also speak the language of the titular nation of the region in which they live. They call themselves *russkie*, which is not the same as *rossijanin*, the latter referring to any citizen of the Russian Federation regardless of his or her ethnic background. The Russians are the descendants of Eastern Slavic nomadic tribes who were residing in the north but who expanded from the Baltic to the Black Sea and had Kiev and Novgorod as their main centres. The first Russian dynasty originated in 862, when the Russians invited the Viking Rurik to become their ruler. They multiplied to the northeast and northwest, and Kiev became the centre of imperial power, known as the Kievan Rus, which reached its zenith in the eleventh century. In 1223, the Mongols invaded the Kievan Rus, and gradually the centre moved to Moscow. When the power of the Mongols began to diminish at the end of the fourteenth century, the Russians started to reconquer all the territory that had previously been ethnically Russian. They went even further in the sixteenth century by annexing the Tatar khanates of Kazan and Astrakhan. During the Middle Ages there were several Russian–Cherkess treaties, and active trade contacts existed between Russia and the Caucasus. One of the seven wives of the Russian Tsar Ivan the Terrible actually came from Kabarda. The official inclusion of the Caucasus in the Russian Empire at the end of the eighteenth century resulted in several wars with the Persian and Ottoman empires. Many Russian resettlers, such as the Cossacks and sectarians, arrived in the region to control the newly gained territories, and by 1864 the entire Caucasus was recognized as Russian territory.

Most of the Azeris (7.7 million) in the Caucasus live in Azerbaijan, though there are a large number in the eastern part of Georgia. Smaller groups can be found in all other regions with the exception of Armenia, whence Azeris fled during the war over Nagorno Karabakh. The largest number of Azeris, however (estimated between 20 and 25 million), live in Iran, in so-called South Azerbaijan. Russia conquered the region of Azerbaijan in the early 1820s, and with the treaties of Gulistan (1813) and Turkmenchay (1828) divided the land into two parts: the north allotted to Russia, the south remaining part of Persia. In addition there is a large Azeri diaspora in Central Asia, Iraq and Turkey. Most Azeris are Shiite Muslims of the Ja'fari doctrine. Until the early 1900s they were called Azerbaijan Tatars – although they are not closely linked ethnogenetically to the Tatars – or sometimes even more falsely Azerbaijan Tartars. The word Azerbaijan most likely comes from Atropates, one of the satraps (rulers representing the king) during the Seleucid times, though another possibility is a derivation from the Persian *azer-bhaygan*, meaning protector of fire. The first Turkic tribes probably settled in the Caucasus in the second millennium BC, but the largest influx took place around the fifth century AD.

The Armenians (4.1 million) are primarily in Armenia, in Georgia (Samtskhe–Javakheti, Tbilisi and Abkhazia, although many left during the conflict) and in Nagorno Karabakh. More than half a million other Armenians live in different parts of the Russian Federation, and there is a huge diaspora (estimated at 2.5 million) in the US, Canada, France and the Middle East. These people are in general well educated, and several of them hold high positions which enable them to influence the foreign policy of their adopted country towards the Caucasus. This is particularly the case with the Armenian diaspora in the US and France. The Armenians are mainly Orthodox Christians, but there are also a few Catholics and Protestants. They claim to be the first in the world to have adopted Christianity as a state religion, in the early fourth century, and call themselves Hay, after the legend of Hayk Nahapet, who, according to tradition, was the first to unite the Armenians and crush the Assyrians, in 2492 BC. The word Armenian is probably derived from Aram, who united the Armenians into one state in 1824 BC (also according to tradition). The biggest tragedy for the Armenian nation was the genocide of 1915, which resulted in the death of hundreds of thousands of Armenians living in Turkey and forced many others to emigrate. Since then, many Armenians in Turkey have assimilated into Turkish society.

The Georgians (3.7 million) reside mainly in Georgia, but some 50,000 are spread over the rest of the Caucasus. Since the collapse of the Soviet Union many Georgians have emigrated for economic reasons, and as a result there is a large diaspora in both Russia and the rest of the world. There are four main groups of Georgians: the Georgians proper (living throughout Georgia), the Megrelians (in central West Georgia), the Svanetians (in the mountains in the central northern region) and the Laz (in the southwestern mountains, but mainly in Turkey). In total there are 17 sub-ethnic groups: 15 of them live in Georgia, but the Ingiloi and Fereidans are in Azerbaijan and Iran respectively. The Georgians, who trace their ancestry back to Japhet, son of Noah, call themselves *kartvelebi*, derived from the pagan god Kartlos, said to be the father of the nation. The internationally used name Georgian is mistakenly believed to derive from the country's patron, St George, though in reality it comes from the names Kurj or Gurj, by which the Georgians are known to the Arabs and Persians. Another theory is that it originates from the Greek word for earth: *ge*. When the Greeks arrived, they saw the Georgians working the land. Historically, the Georgians were known as Iberians, thus becoming confused with the inhabitants of the Iberian peninsula (modern Spain and Portugal). Christianity came to the region around the year 330, and now most Georgians are Orthodox Christians. They were forced to convert to Islam during the rule of the Mongols, Turks and Persians, but only the Adjars and the Ingiloi were genuine converts. Although their ethnic formation took place some 2,500 to 3,000 years ago, the Georgians were united for the first time into one kingdom in 1008.

The Abkhaz (100,000) live in Abkhazia and in the Krasnodar Kray, but there is a much larger community (approximately 500,000) in the Near East, predominantly in Turkey. This is the result of the mass emigration and deportation of the late 1860s. Interestingly, several families migrated from Turkey to Abkhazia during and after the Georgian–Abkhaz war of 1992–3. They call themselves *apsua*, and the word Abkhaz comes from the Georgian and Russian ethnonyms, which in turn come from Greek. Most of the Abkhaz in Abkhazia are Orthodox Christians, while the others and the majority of the Abkhaz diaspora follow Sunni Islam, which was brought to the region when it was under Ottoman influence in the sixteenth century. It was mainly the Muslim believers who left their native lands in the 1860s.

Most Abazins (40,000) are found in Karachay–Cherkessia, and there is a smaller community in the Stavropol Kray. A large number are in Turkey, and smaller groups in Syria, Jordan and Lebanon. They call themselves *abaza* and are divided into two main tribes: the Tapantas and the Ashkaras. It is generally accepted that the Abazins were a common ethnic group with the Abkhaz until, between the eighth and twelfth centuries, they gradually split. Up to the fourteenth century the Abazins lived north of the Abkhaz on the Black Sea coast, in the area between the rivers Tuapse and Bzyb. From the fourteenth to the seventeenth century they migrated eastwards to the rivers Laba, Urup, Zelenchuk, Kuban and Teberda, in present-day Karachay–Cherkessia, in the neighbourhood of the Adyghe tribes. This territory was contested between the Russians and the Ottomans in the eighteenth and nineteenth centuries, and in 1862 the Russians triumphed and demanded the Abazins who had fought against them leave the area between the Laba and Belyy rivers and move either to the Kuban plain or away altogether.[2] Some 40,000 people left – most of them migrating to Turkey – and fewer than 10,000 people remained in the Kuban lands allotted by the tsarist government. These areas were soon filled with immigrants from Russia, mostly Cossacks, and the Abazins became a minority group in their native land.

The Ubykhs lived on the Black Sea coast in the region of Sochi until 1864, when they emigrated en masse to the Ottoman Empire while the Russians took their lands. The Ubykh nation, which was ethnogenetically closely related to the Abkhaz and Abazins, no longer exists, and all those of Ubykh ancestry have completely assimilated into Turkish culture.

The Adyghe[3] (129,000) reside mainly in the regions of the Laba and Kuban rivers in Adygea, with a smaller community in the Krasnodar Kray; the Cherkess (58,000) are mostly in Karachay–Cherkessia; and the majority of Kabards or Kabardians (511,000) are to be found in Kabardino–Balkaria. There is a diaspora of these three ethnic groups throughout the Middle East and in smaller groups in Europe and North America. The Adyghe, Cherkess and Karbards are very closely related ethnically, and all call themselves Adyghe, but since the thirteenth century they have been known in Europe and the East as Circassians or Cherkess. The word Cherkess might derive from *ker-ket*, the name classical Greek authors gave to one of the several Adyghe tribes. Before the Bolshevik Revolution these three ethnic groups were indeed regarded as one people, but in the 1920s they were defined in two groups: the Cherkess and the Kabards. In the 1930s they were further subdivided into Adyghe, Cherkess and Kabards. In order to separate one from another, administrative borders between them were created and the status of their lands changed frequently. The hierarchical structure of their society (with aristocracy, free farmers and slaves) was destroyed when they came under Russian rule. The Adyghe originate from the Black Sea coastal region, and their ancestors, the Zikhi, moved to the Kuban region between the fifth and seventh centuries. As a result of pressure from the Mongol invaders in the thirteenth century, some of the Adyghe moved to the Terek River and created Greater Kabarda on the left bank and the Minor Kabarda on the right bank. These Adyghe intermixed with the native people of the Central Caucasus and became known as the Kabards, while those that stayed in the Kuban region are now known as the Cherkess. The Kabards were among the first Caucasian people to have close contacts with the Russians, and their territory became a Muscovite protectorate in as early as 1557. Even though the Adyghe, Cherkess and Kabards remained neutral during the revolt against Russia in the nineteenth century, many were forced to move to Turkey and the Middle East. Those who remained, however, were not deported by Stalin – unlike their neighbors the Karachay and the Balkars.

The Balkars (107,000) inhabit the northern slopes of the Greater Caucasus and constitute a minority in Kabardino–Balkaria. A few thousand are still left in Kazakhstan and Kyrgyzstan as a result of the deportation during the Great Patriotic War. They call themselves Taulula, which means mountain dwellers. The Karachay (187,000), who have much in common with the Balkars (ethnogenesis, language, religion, history), live in Karachay–Cherkessia and the neighbouring regions. They call themselves *k'rchaylylar*. The Balkars and Karachays are the result of a mixture of North Caucasian, Iranian and Turkic tribes. The Balkars and Karachays were deported to Central Asia in 1943, but were permitted to return to their lands in 1957, when autonomy was restored.

The Ossetians or Ossetes (557,000) live mostly in North Ossetia and Georgia, and in smaller numbers in the neighbouring regions. There are two sub-ethnic groups, the Iron and the Digoron. Most Ossetians (mainly the Iron, in the northeast) are Christian, and a minority (predominantly the Digoron, in the west) follow Sunni Islam. The Ossetians claim to be the descendants of the Alans, a Sarmatian tribe that used to inhabit the plains of the Northern Caucasus but which was pushed into the foothills in the fourth century and even further into the mountains by the Tatar and Mongol invaders. The enemies of the Ossetians (i.e. the Ingush and Georgians) claim this is Ossetian propaganda and that in reality the Ossetians are a comparatively new nation in the region.

The Ingush (391,000) are mainly in Ingushetia and in the Prigorodnyy Rayon of North Ossetia. There are also some Ingush in Kazakhstan, a remnant of the 1944 deportation. They call themselves *galgay*, which means builder or inhabitant of a tower. The name Ingush derives from the name of the old Ingush village

Angusht. The Ingush used to live on the northern slopes of the Greater Caucasus, and only in the sixteenth and seventeenth centuries did they descend to the plains.

The biggest groups of Chechens (1.3 million) live in Chechnya, Ingushetia and the Khasavyurt district of Dagestan. The rest are spread throughout the Caucasus. Many Chechens live in other parts of Russia but also in Central Asia following the deportation of 1944. They call themselves *nokhcho*. The name Chechen was given by the Russians after the name of one village, Chechen-aul. Chechnya is often referred to as Ichkeria, which comes from the Turkish word *ichker* (inner, land) and has its origin in the military history of the Chechens, who would retreat to the mountains and would launch guerrilla attacks against foreign invaders.

The Bats (est. 2,500) now inhabit the Akhmeta district of Georgia, but until the middle of the nineteenth century lived in Tushetia, a mountainous region in north-eastern Georgia. They call themselves *batsba nah* (Bats people) but are known by Georgians as the Tsova-Tushs. One theory is that the Bats are a Chechen tribe that moved across the high Caucasian mountains, but Georgians claim they are Chechenized Georgians.

A number of scholars consider the Ingush, Chechens and Bats to be one nation. Together they are actually known as Vainakhs (or Dzurdzuks in medieval Georgian literature). However, many Ingush and Chechens do not agree with this theory and foster unfriendly relations with each other.

The Avars (830,000) constitute the largest ethnic group in Dagestan and inhabit what is often referred to as Avaria (the basins of three rivers: the Avar Koysu, the Andi Koysu and the Karakoysu) in the western mountains. A large number reside in the north of Azerbaijan, near the border with Dagestan, where they arrived during their search for new pastures. Smaller groups can be found throughout other parts of the Caucasus and the former Soviet Union. The current Avars (Avartsy in Russian) should not be confused with the powerful Turkic-speaking Avars (Avary in Russian) of the sixth and seventh centuries. According to the nineteenth-century scholar Peter von Uslar, the word *avar* has been in use since the twelfth century and means unquiet or quarrelsome. The Avars call themselves *ma'arulal*, which means mountaineers. In official censuses, smaller ethnic groups such as the Andis and Didos are also classified as Avars.

The Lezgins or Lezgians (531,000), who refer to themselves as Lezgiar, live mainly in the border region of Dagestan and Azerbaijan.

The Laks (147,000) originate from the region of the Lak and Kulin districts in Dagestan, but were in part forcibly moved to the neighboring Aukhov district (renamed into Novolak district) in 1944 after the Chechens had been deported to Central Asia.

The Dargins (475,000) reside predominantly in the mountains of central Dagestan, but there are considerable communities in the Stavropol Kray as well. They call themselves Darganti or Dargwa. Because of their strong fundamentalist Muslim faith and anti-Russian feelings, they refused to resettle from the mountains to the plains, and many Dargins kept to their traditional lifestyle. Some scholars claim that the Kaitags and Kubachi are distinct ethnic groups, whereas others argue that they are Dargins.

The Tabasarans (120,000) inhabit southeast Dagestan. They are among the first Dagestani people mentioned in historical sources. Before the Russian Revolution they were classified as Lezgins, together with the Aguls, Rutuls and Lezgins proper. The name Tabasaran is a self-designation and comes from *tab* (top) and *seran* (district). In the past, Lezgi and Azerbaijani were the lingua francas, but they have been replaced by Russian. The Tabasarans refused to participate in the relocations from the mountains to the plains, which explains the retention of their traditional lifestyle.

The Aguls (26,000) populate the high mountains in southern Dagestan and, since the 1960s, in the plains of southeastern Dagestan. They call themselves *agular* (inhabitants of Agul). They speak Agul, which is not a literary language, but they write in Lezgi.

The Rutuls (27,000) live along the Dagestani–Azerbaijani border. Before the Russian Revolution they were classified as Lezgins, as was the case with the Tabasarans and Aguls. The internationally recognized name for the Rutul people comes from the Lezgin and Azerbaijani name for their main village, Rutul, though they call themselves *mjukhadar*, meaning inhabitant of the village Mjukhad. They use the Rutul language at home and at work, but Russian is the official language. In the late 1920s the Soviet government decided to assimilate the Rutuls and Tsakhurs with the Azerbaijanis. As a consequence, Azerbaijani became the official language, but gradually Russian was imposed for administrative purposes and in schools. Soviet collectivization proceeded a lot faster among the Rutuls in comparison with other Lezgin people.[4]

The Tsakhurs (25,000) may be found in the region of Kas and Zaqatala in the north of Azerbaijan and in the mountains of the upper reaches of the Samur River in the Rutul district of southwestern Dagestan. They originally lived in Dagestan, but during the thirteenth century many moved to Azerbaijan. Their self-designation is *iyhjby*, but they are better known as Tsakhurs, after the name of their central settlement. In ancient records they are mentioned as Tsakhaiks. One theory holds that they originated in Artsakh.[5] In the Zangezur region of Armenia there are two villages in which a language closely related to Tsakhur and Rutul is spoken.

The Budukhs (est. 1,000) live in a few auls (villages) in the Konakhkent district in northern Azerbaijan. They were counted as an independent nation only in the 1926 census, and since then have been considered as Azerbaijanis. They probably descend from a proto-Lezgin tribe, but almost all Lezgin cultural elements have been subsumed under Azerbaijani influence. The name Budukh derives from the name of their main settlement.

The Kryz (est. 6,000) dwell in the remote and least accessible regions of Azerbaijan, surrounded by mountain ranges separating them from their neighbours. Their self-designation is *kjrtuar*, and the internationally used name Kryz originates from the village of the same name.

The Khinalugs (est. 2,000) dwell in the high mountain village of Khinalug in the Konakhkent district of Azerbaijan and are separated from their neighbours by mountain ranges. The name Khinalug comes from the Azerbaijani name for the village, but the people call themselves *ketch halh* (people of the village Ketch) or *kayttiodur* (the inhabitants of one village).

The Udis or Udins (7,000) live in two villages in Azerbaijan and in one village in Georgia, but more recently also in the Rostov Oblast, Krasnodar Kray and Stavropol Kray. They call themselves *udi* or *uti*, and are believed to be descendants of Caucasian Albanians who lived in the area of the eastern Caucasus along the coast of the Caspian Sea. After the Albanian state came to an end the Caucasian Albanians were ruled by the Arabs, Turks and Persians, and before their incorporation into Russia were part of the Quba khanate.

The Archis (est. 1,200) inhabit the village of Archi in the Charodi district of southern Dagestan. Since the 1959 census they have been counted as Avars. They call themselves *arshishtib*.

There are eight Andi and five Dido (also known as Tsezic) ethnic groups, all of which have their own culture and language and descend from proto-Avar tribes that settled at latest in the fourth or fifth century. Most of them live in the mountainous Botlikh, Tsumada, Akhvakh and Tsunta districts in the western part of Dagestan and in some villages across the border in Azerbaijan and Georgia. Furthermore, a large number moved to the plains and lowlands of the Khasavyurt, Kizlyar, Kizilyurt and Nogay districts between the 1950s and the 1970s. The eight Andi ethnic groups are the Andis (est. 21,300), the Akhvakhs (est. 8,400), the Chamalals (est. 7,300), the Karatas (est. 6,400), the Bagulals (est. 5,000), the Tindis (est. 5,000), the Botlikhs (est. 3,000) and the Godoberis (est. 2,500), and the five Dido or Tsezic ethnic groups are the Didos (est. 16,200), the Bezhtas (est. 6,000), the Khvarshis (est. 1,800), the Hunzibs (est. 1,700) and the Hinukhs (est. 600). Many of these nations have been assimilated, especially after the introduction of Soviet nationality policies. All these distinct ethnic groups were counted separately in the Soviet census of 1926, but thereafter they were classified by the Soviet government as Avars. Although they do not want to be called Avars, they have a lot in common with that group when it comes to history, economy, religion and culture. Because of the absence of official population statistics, academic researchers can only approximate their number, and during the 1960s and 1970s there were attempts to explain the considerable ethnic variety by the theory of traditional territorial isolation.[6] However, this theory has now been abandoned, since there is no isolation between neighbouring ethnic groups in the Andi Koysu river basin and it is proven that there have been centuries-long economic and cultural ties. In the 1980s theories of both endogamy (L. Lavrov) and a polystructural political system (M. Aglarov) were proposed,[7] the latter suggesting that the stable society and fixed borders of small independent political units (free communities) favoured linguistic factionalizing.

The Kumyks (396,000) reside predominantly in the Terek–Sulak plains and foothills along the northeastern coastline of the Caspian Sea in Dagestan, but also in North Ossetia, Chechnya, the Stavropol Kray and the Rostov Oblast. Others live in different parts of Russia, the CIS and the Near East. The Dagestani capital Makhachkala is located within the Kumyk region, but only 15 per cent of its inhabitants are Kumyks. The Kumyks were mentioned by Pliny the Elder and Ptolemy in the first and second centuries AD. In the fifteenth and sixteenth centuries, they had their own state, the Shamkhalat of Tarki, and 100 years later they controlled many Avars and Dargins. They maintained good commercial and diplomatic contacts with Russia, but after the occupation of Derbent by Peter the Great in 1722 and the defeat of the Shamil rebellion, the Kumyks lost their autonomy and the Kumyk Shamkhalat was ended in 1867. Only the northern Kumyks supported the Shamil rebellion, whereas the central Kumyks sided with the Russians and the southern Kumyks remained neutral.

The Nogays (78,000) are descendants of Turkic and Mongolian nomad tribes and inhabit mainly the Nogay Steppe, without having a real homeland. More precisely, they live in northern Dagestan, the Stavropol Kray, Karachay–Cherkessia and Chechnya, but also in Turkey, Ukraine and Romania. In 1957 the region of the Nogay Steppe was divided between three administrative units (Dagestan ASSR, Chechen–Ingush ASSR and Stavropol district), and so the Nogays cannot easily form a political unit. Still, the organization Birlik (Unity), founded in the late 1980s, calls for a restitution of autonomy within the pre-1957 boundaries. This ethnic group received its name from Nogay, the grandson of Genghis Khan and ruler of the Nogay Horde between the Dnepr and Danube rivers. In older Russian texts, the people are misleadingly referred to as the North Caucasian Tatars. Historically they lived in the steppes between the Danube and the Caspian. After Tsar Ivan IV conquered Astrakhan and Kazan in the sixteenth century, the Nogay Horde split into a Great Horde (living in the Lower Volga region) and a Little Horde (occupying the lands further to the southwest). In 1634 the hordes reunited under Crimean Tatar rule, when the Great Horde was driven southward by the Kalmyks. Several of the Nogay tribes were forced to leave their steppe homes and move to the foothills of the North Caucasus, which explains the presence of Nogays in Karachay–Cherkessia. In the second half of the eighteenth century they lost their independence and many emigrated on account of the struggle between Russia and Turkey. A second main wave of emigration to Turkey, the Crimea and Romania took place between 1858 and 1866, when there was significant Russian expansion in Nogay territory.

The Talysh (77,000) live south of the Vilyazh-Chay River in the southeastern part of Azerbaijan and along a long strip of the Caspian coast, from Astara to Rasht in the Gilan province in Iran. Certain pro-Talysh sources talk about a million Talysh in each of these two countries. A Talysh khanate was founded in the seventeenth century, but through the Gulistan (1813) and Turkmenchay (1828) treaties the Talysh nation was split into two parts – a northern territory that was annexed to Russia and a southern part that remained with Persia. During Soviet times there were several attempts to assimilate the Talysh. In 1993 Talysh independence was declared in seven districts of Azerbaijan, but this Talysh–Mughan Autonomous Republic lasted for only a few months.

The Tats (12,000) reside in dense communities on the Absheron peninsula, in Baku, in the northeastern part of Azerbaijan and in Dagestan, and some

300,000 live in Iran. The Tats probably descend from Iranian tribes who moved into the Caucasus Mountains in the fourth and fifth centuries AD, although another theory claims that they are Israelites who arrived in the Caucasus during Achaemenid rule (550–330 BC). The word Tat is Turkish in origin and was used to denote the non-Turkish population. There are three religious groups among the Tats. One group embraces Judaism and is known as the Mountain Jews or Judeo Tats. Huge speculation exists about its origins: some claim its members are Jews who took the Tat language, while others say they are Tats who adopted Judaism. During the twentieth century the majority of the Mountain Jews moved to Israel, an emigration that is still ongoing. A second group of Tats has been Muslim (mainly Shia) since the seventh and eighth centuries, and a smaller third group has been Christian (Armenian Gregorian) since the eighth and ninth centuries.

The Georgian Jews (est. 30,000) are considered to be ancient inhabitants of Georgia. They live mainly in the western part of the country, in Tbilisi, and in other surrounding towns and small country villages. One of the most plausible theses is that these Jews arrived in the first century AD, though others claim that they arrived after fleeing from exile in Babylon in the sixth century BC. They speak Georgian but some also know Hebrew.

The Ashkenazi Jews or European Jews (27,000) now live in Azerbaijan, Georgia, the Rostov Oblast, the Krasnodar Kray, the Stavropol Kray, Dagestan and Kabardino–Balkaria. They arrived in the Caucasus after the region became part of the Russian Empire, but most of them were attracted by the oil boom in Baku in the nineteenth century.

There are Tatars (104,000) in Azerbaijan and throughout the entire North Caucasus. The main Tatar population is centred around the Volga region, though, outside the Caucasus, and the total number of Tatars in Russia is over 5.5 million. They have their own language, Kazan Tatar, but most Tatars now have Russian as their mother tongue. The word Tatar has for many centuries often been incorrectly used by the Russians to denote anybody from Asian, Muslim or Turkish descent (e.g. Azerbaijan Tatars and North Caucasus Tatars).

The Trukhmens, the Turkmens (14,000) of the Caucasus, inhabit mainly the Nogay Steppe on the territory of the Stavropol Kray. They call themselves *T'rpen* and are descended from Oghuz Turkmen tribes who migrated to the region in search of fresh pasturage in the eighteenth century.

Ukrainians (365,000) can be found in large numbers in the entire Caucasus. However, many left the non-Russian ethnic regions after the fall of the Soviet Union. The first Ukrainians, who live mainly in Western Ukraine, came to the South Caucasus at the end of the nineteenth century, having encountering economic problems in their own country. Other major waves of migration followed after the situation became even worse in the 1920s and 1930s.

The Meskhetian Turks (est. 45,000) resided in the Akhaltsikhe region (Meskhetia) in Georgia until they were deported in 1944. They are now in Azerbaijan, but a few have returned to Georgia. Many more live in Kazakhstan,

Kyrgyzstan, Uzbekistan and Ukraine. They call themselves Ahiska Türkleri (Akhaltsikhe Turks), but rather than create yet another nationalist problem many Georgians prefer to call them Georgians from the Meskhi tribe. Their ethnic origin is not fully clear. Some say they are Georgianized Turks, others that they are Turkified Georgians of the Meskhi tribe or Georgian Sunni Muslims. One thing is certain: they lived in southern Georgia and were under Ottoman rule for three centuries. The first Meskhetians arrived in Azerbaijan at the end of the nineteenth century, and more followed in 1918–20. Those who had remained in Georgia were deported under Stalin in November 1944, together with the Kurds and the Hemshins. In 1956, when all the other ethnic groups were permitted to return to their homelands, the Meskhetians were forced to stay in Central Asia, though thousands of Meskhetian families resettled in Azerbaijan in the period 1958–62. Some 90,000 of the 107,000 Meskhetians in Uzbekistan left the country after the pogroms in the Fergana valley in June 1989. While Georgia agreed in 1999 to the return of the Meskhetian Turks as a condition of entry into the Council of Europe, it is worried that their repatriation will lead to further problems in a region of the country that is already volatile.

The Greeks (88,000) of the Caucasus live mainly in the Stavropol Kray, the Krasnodar Kray, Georgia, the Rostov Oblast, North Ossetia, Adygea, Karachay–Cherkessia and Armenia. While most speak the local language and Russian, some also speak Pontic Greek and yet others Urum, a language very close to Crimean Tatar. The Greeks came to the Caucasus from the Balkan peninsula in two waves. They already had trade relations with the Scythians between 750 and 500 BC. The Greek city states established colonies leading to a first wave of migration, after which most of the Greeks were assimilated. The second wave was the result of the Russo–Turkish War of 1768–74. Many Greeks who collaborated with the Russians moved to tsarist Russia, mostly to the Crimea and the Caucasus. In addition, Greek miners were invited to Armenia in the late eighteenth century and were partially relocated to central Georgia in the 1820s. During the Civil War the Greeks fought against the Bolsheviks, and many were forced to return to Greece. However, in 1928 the Greek government refused to accept any more returnees, and in the following years the remaining Greeks were the subject of Soviet persecution, torture and mass deportation.

The Kurds (28,000) of the Caucasus are found in Azerbaijan, the Krasnodar Kray, Adygea, Georgia, Armenia and the Stavropol Kray. The total number of Kurds in the world, estimated at 17 to 20 million, live mainly in what they call Kurdistan, which is located across the territory of four countries – Turkey, Iran, Iraq and Syria. They call themselves Kurmanjand. While there are some indications that there were Kurdish villages in the region of Nakhchivan as early as the tenth century, most Kurds arrived in contemporary Armenia and Azerbaijan and in smaller numbers in Georgia after the peace treaties of Gulistan (1813) and Turkmenchay (1828). There was a further increase in migration after the Russo–Turkish wars. During the period 1923–9 there was a Kurdistan Autonomous Soviet Socialist Republic, known as Red Kurdistan, in the region of Lachin, but it was fully incorporated into Azerbaijan in 1930. Many Kurds in Georgia were deported, together with the Meskhetians, in 1944. On the introduction of perestroika there were some 6,000 Kurds in Armenia, mainly in Azerbaijani enclaves, but most moved out, together with the Azerbaijanis, as a result of the war in Karabakh. Many other Kurds from the South Caucasus moved to the Stavropol and Krasnodar krays.

The Yezidis or Yazidis (68,000) live in Armenia, Georgia, the Krasnodar Kray, the Stavropol Kray and the Rostov Oblast, but also in Syria, Western Europe and other parts of Russia. They call themselves *ezdi* and insist on their ethnic distinction from the Kurds, even though they speak the same language, Kurmanji; however, in order to stress their difference, they call their language Ezdiki. The Yezidis are not Muslims but have their own religion. They live in a caste society and are largely endogamous. The Yezidis arrived in Armenia mainly in 1877–8, during the last Russo–Turkish War. In the mid-nineteenth and early twentieth centuries some moved to Georgia, especially following repression during the First World War. Their fate was similar to that of the Armenians, and the two ethnic groups were strongly supportive of each other. After the Second World War a smaller number of Yezidis moved to Krasnodar, Stavropol and Rostov.

The Assyrians (14,000) constitute a small group in Armenia, Georgia, the Krasnodar Kray and the Rostov Oblast. Worldwide they number some 350,000 (mainly in Iran, Iraq, Syria and Turkey). They are among the first Christian nations in the world and now belong to the Nestorian Church (Assyrian Church of the East), the Jacobite Monophysite Church (Assyrian Church of the West) and the Assyro-Chaldaic Church. However, most Assyrians in the South Caucasus adopted Russian Orthodoxy because they could not find a Nestorian priest. The Assyrians claim to be descendants of the Assyrian Empire which existed from 2500 to 612 BC in what is now Iraq. Their nation was almost exterminated in the fourteenth century by Timur because of their refusal to adopt Islam. The first Assyrians appeared in Armenia in 1826–8 during the Russo-Persian War after leaving the region of Lake Urmia in Iran. They were loyal to the Armenians and consequently were also subjected to genocide: during and after the First World War about half a million Assyrians were killed by the Turks and Kurds, which led to a wave of emigration by the survivors. In 1923–4 some Assyrians from Yerevan founded a settlement by the name of Urmia in the Krasnodar Kray.

Romani, also known as Roma or (derogatory) Gypsies (est. 50,000), are spread throughout the Caucasus, but their real number is very hard to determine. They originated in South Asia and moved to the Caucasus and Europe no earlier than the eleventh century. In the Caucasus they are often falsely called Tajiks – with whom they do not share any direct genetic link – and are despised for their way of life.

Many other minorities can be found in the Caucasus, such as Belorussians (70,000), Germans (40,000), Koreans (30,000), Moldavians (18,000), Mordva (12,000), Chuvash (10,000), Udmurtians (9,000) and Poles (8,000). Several other groups number only a few hundred people, with most completely assimilated into the local population and not even knowing the language of their ancestors.

ა ბ გ დ ე ვ ზ თ ი კ ლ
მ ნ ო პ ჟ რ ს ტ უ ფ ქ
ღ ყ შ ჩ ც ძ წ ჭ ხ ჯ ჰ

Georgian alphabet

 Աա Բբ Գգ Դդ Եե Զզ
Էէ Ըը Թթ Ժժ Իի Լլ
Խխ Ծծ Կկ Հհ Ձձ Ղղ
Ճճ Մմ Յյ Նն Շշ Ոո Չչ
Պպ Ջջ Ռռ Սս Վվ Տտ
Րր Ցց Ււ Փփ Քք Օօ Ֆֆ

Armenian alphabet

Аа Бб Вв Гг Дд Ее
Ёё Жж Зз Ии Йй
Кк Лл Мм Нн Оо
Пп Рр Сс Тт Уу Фф
Хх Цц Чч Шш Щщ
Ъъ Ыы Ьь Ээ Юю Яя

Russian Cyrillic alphabet

Aa Bb Cc Çç Dd
Ee Ə Ff Gg Ğğ
Hh Xx Iı İi Jj Kk Qq
Ll Mm Nn Oo Öö
Pp Rr Ss Şş Tt Uu
Üü Vv Yy Zz

Azeri Latin alphabet

Figure 3.1 Major alphabets in use in the Caucasus

Languages

In general, people speak their titular and native language – i.e. Georgians speak Georgian, Armenians speak Armenian, etc. However, several minorities have partly taken up the language of the majority population in their region or speak that language at least as their second or third language. Most people in the Caucasus speak Russian as well, as it was imposed in schools and for administrative purposes.

Until the arrival of the Russians there was no single lingua franca in the Caucasus, and instead there was a considerable bilingualism and multilingualism between adjacent communities among the ethnic minorities. In most cases the highland population knew the language of the lowland population, since markets and winter pastures were to be found in the lowlands. Even now there is substantial multilingualism among small minorities in the Caucasus. Several Dagestani nations used and still use the Avar language to communicate. Many of the ethnic groups do not have their own literary or written tradition and use a more dominant language – for example the Tat use mostly Azerbaijani.

The expansion of the Russian Empire, and especially the creation of the Soviet Union, brought about the intense Russification of the Caucasus. Russian became the lingua franca and has been one of the major building elements among the many nations of the Caucasus, including between majority and minority populations. Based on nationalist and anti-Russian feelings, some Caucasian people now avoid learning Russian and study English instead. With this diminishing knowledge of Russian, mutual alienation is likely to increase in future, and could add fuel to potential new conflicts. Youth in Georgia in particular seems to be suffering from this hatred of the Russian language.

The languages indigenous to the Caucasus, and which do not show any affili-
ations with any other major language families, are grouped into the Caucasian
language family. The other languages spoken in the region belong to the Indo-
European, Altaic or Afro-Asiatic language families. Due to historic relations,
many Arabic, Persian and Russian influences can be found in the vocabularies of
most of these languages. The Russian influence is probably the strongest, as the
Russification process started at the time of the Russian Empire and in some
places is still ongoing. Many Russian loanwords were adopted and Russia
attempted to replace all Arabic and Persian words with Russian equivalents.

Most of the minority languages do not have a long written tradition, if any at
all. There are inscriptions and some documents in Arabic-based alphabets which
date from the Middle Ages, but there was no consistent history of writing. It was
only with the Russian conquest of the Caucasus that Russian linguists began
studying these languages and developed alphabets for them. In this context,
Baron Peter von Uslar is probably the most significant scholar and is seen as the
father of the study of the Northern Caucasian languages. There was a massive
move to create alphabets in the early years of the Soviet Union. In the 1920s most
of these were Latin-based, but between 1936 and 1938 they were replaced by a
Cyrillic alphabet, as the former had been an impediment to learning Russian. In
fact, this attempt at Russification had a reverse effect, as it actually served to
unify the smaller ethnic groups against the Russians. An exception was Abkhaz
and Ossetian in Georgia, which had been forced to adopt a Georgian-based
orthography; this was in use until the death of Stalin, after which it was changed
for a Cyrillic alphabet. Azerbaijan switched to a Latin alphabet in 1991, but the
Cyrillic alphabet is still in common use as well.

Caucasian languages

The indigenous languages of the Caucasus are known for their complexity (consonant systems, complex morphology and ergativity), but Georgian and Udi are
the only ones with an ancient literary tradition. The Caucasian languages are
divided into three main branches: the South Caucasian, the Northeast Caucasian,
and the Northwest Caucasian language groups. These languages are organized
more on a geographical than on a linguistic basis, as it is often very questionable
how much they are related to one another. To date there is no proven interrela-
tionship between the North and South Caucasian languages, and thus they should
actually be viewed as different language families. Similarities between the languages are probably only the result of centuries-long contact between the different families. Furthermore, attempts to find an ethnolinguistic relationship
between Caucasian languages and any other languages, such as Semitic and Indo-
European languages, have so far been unsuccessful.

The South Caucasian language group is also known as the Kartvelian or Ibero-
Caucasian language group and contains four languages. They all descend from a
proto-Georgian language that started to diverge some 5,000 to 6,000 years ago.

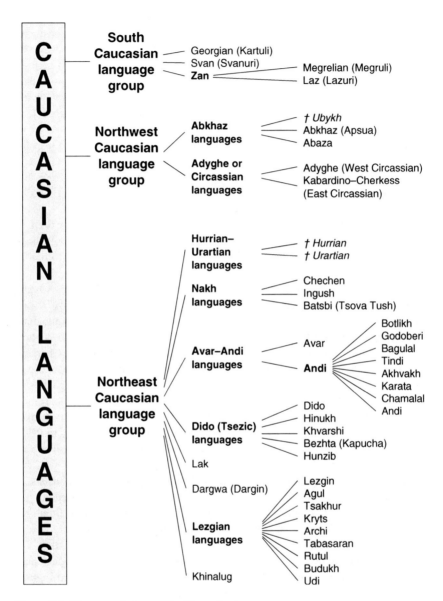

Figure 3.2 Ethnogenetic tree of the Caucasian languages

Georgian is spoken in the greater part of Georgia. It has its own alphabet and uses 33 letters that are unambiguous in pronunciation and make no distinction between upper and lower case. The old alphabet, Mtavruli (or Asomtavruli, meaning capital or capital letters), is thought to have been based on Aramaic script. Armenians claim that Mashtots, the creator of the Armenian alphabet, invented it

71

in the fifth century AD, whereas the Georgian tradition claims King Parnavaz of Iberia created it in the fourth century BC. It lost its role as the alphabet for manuscripts in the thirteenth century. Between the ninth and the eighteenth century a second alphabet, Nuskhuri (List), was used. Mkhedruli (Horsemen's), a third script, was developed in the eleventh century under the influence of Arabic style and forms the basis for current fonts. Georgian has a complex grammar with a difficult verbal system, seven cases and some long consonant clusters, such as seen in the word *mcvrt'neli* (trainer).

Svan is spoken in Svanetia in the central northern part of Georgia, and uses the Georgian alphabet.

Megrelian is spoken in Samegrelo in western Georgia. It existed sporadically in a written form and used both the Cyrillic (1860s) and Georgian (1920–33, 1990s) alphabets.

Laz is spoken by the Laz in northeastern Turkey and, to a very small extent, in southwestern Georgia. It has made use of the Roman alphabet sporadically since 1984 but remains largely unwritten. Laz is often seen together with Megrelian as Zan, but these languages are very different.

The Northwest Caucasian language group, also known as the Abkhaz–Adyghe or Akbhaz–Circassian language group, consists of four languages (five if one includes the extinct Ubykh) spoken in the Northwestern Caucasus and some diaspora communities in Turkey. During the second half of the nineteenth century there was a huge emigration of Abkhaz, Abazins, Ubykhs, Adyghe and Cherkess to Turkey. While many moved further, to Syria, Jordan and Iraq, most of those in the Middle East do not speak the language of their ancestors. The languages of the Northwest Caucasian group are Ubykh, Abkhaz (Apsua), Abaza, Kabardino–Cherkess (East Circassian) and Adyghe (West Circassian). The last native speaker of Ubykh, which had 82 consonants and only two vowels, died in Turkey in 1992. Abkhaz was the first Northwest Caucasian language to receive an alphabet,[8] created in 1862–3 by Peter von Uslar.

The Northeast Caucasian or Nakho-Dagestanian language group consists of some 30 languages spoken in the Central and Eastern Caucasus. The structure of this language group is based more on geographical proximity than on linguistic links, and as a result there are different branches. Figure 3.2 shows only one of the many different versions. Both Hurrian and Urartian have been extinct for about two millennia, but they are seen as predecessors of the Nakho-Dagestanian languages and shared many similarities with contemporary Chechen and Ingush. Sometimes the Nakh languages, comprising Chechen, Ingush and Batsbi (or Tsova Tush), the last having been influenced strongly by Georgian, are seen as an independent group. Both Chechen and Ingush have a written tradition, though Batsbi does not,[9] the Bats people using Georgian as their literary language. The 26 languages of the Dagestanian nations, each one spoken by perhaps only a few thousand people, are further subdivided into several groups, and here there are as many differing opinions as scholars on the subject. Most of these languages – some of which show only small differences from one another (e.g. Andi or

Dido) – have taken over many Avar loanwords, but were also influenced by Arab and Turkish. Some, especially the Dido languages, also borrowed many words from Georgian, which in turn had been heavily influenced by Persian. In the twentieth century Russian exerted the strongest influence, notably in terms of political and technical vocabulary. The Andi and Dido ethnic groups as well as the Archi employ their native language for domestic purposes, but most of them are bilingual in Avar, which serves as the lingua franca of the region, both for writing and for maintaining economic and cultural ties with other groups. The Tsakhur, Budukh, Kryz and Khinalug have Azerbaijani as their lingua franca. Most of the Dagestanian languages do not exist in a written form, but there have been some minor literary attempts. Avar, Lak, Dargwa, Lezgin and Tabasaran form the main exceptions and have their own literature.[10]

Indo-European languages

Russian, the only Slavic language widespread in the region, has an important function throughout the Caucasus. First of all, it is the native language of one-third of the population. Furthermore, it was the language of communication during Soviet times and remains to a certain extent the lingua franca. It is, however, gradually losing its importance, and the number of people with a good command of Russian is decreasing steadily in the South Caucasus.

While Armenian is a separate Indo-European language, with loanwords from the Iranian languages, most of its vocabulary has no connection with that of the other Indo-European languages. There are many grammatical and phonetic features from the Caucasian and Turkic languages, such as agglutination and the absence of gender. There are two main dialects – the eastern (Aravelian Hayeren: spoken in Armenia, the rest of the Caucasus and Iran) and the western dialect (Arevmdian Hayeren: spoken in Turkey and by most of the Armenian diaspora). At the end of the fourth century AD, King Vramshapuh saw the necessity to give his people their own alphabet, particularly for religious purposes, and the monk Mesrop Mashtots was ordered to create one. Mashtots, who developed his 36-character alphabet in 406 AD, had studied Syrian, Greek and Iranian and used this knowledge for his assignment. The creation of the alphabet was essential to the cultural development of the Armenians, the dissemination of Christianity, a strong position against Iranian Zoroastrianism, and independence from the Greeks, Syrians and Iranians. In the twelfth century, two further letters were added, bringing the total to 38. Old Armenian or Grabar, the classical Armenian, is used today only as a liturgical language in the Armenian Apostolic Church.

Ossetic (or Ossetian)[11] is a member of the northeastern branch of the Iranian subfamily of the Indo-European languages. The earliest known Ossetian inscription was written in Greek characters and dates from 941 AD, but the real written language has existed only since 1789, when Christian missionaries created an alphabet based on the Slavic Cyrillic. In 1844 the Russian linguist A. M. Shegren invented a new system using a Cyrillic script. A Latin alphabet was employed from 1923, when Ossetian became the official language of Ossetia, until it was replaced in 1938 with yet another Cyrillic script. On Georgian territory, the language was written in a Georgian alphabet from 1938 until the death of Stalin in 1954. Written Ossetian may be recognized immediately by its use of the æ, a character to be found in no other language using the Cyrillic alphabet. There are two main dialects in Ossetian: Iron, which covers South Ossetia and most of North Ossetia (four-fifths of the Ossetic-speaking population) and which forms the basis for the Ossetian literature, and Digor, spoken in the northwestern part of Ossetia (one-fifth of the Ossetic-speaking population).[12]

Tat, or Tati, seen as a dialect of New Persian, is a southwestern Iranian language and exists only in a spoken form. Some scholars see Judeo Tat (of the Mountain Jews) and Muslim Tat as two different languages. Most Tat speakers use Azerbaijani as their written and literary language.

Most of the Kurds of the South Caucasus speak (North) Kurmanji, a northwestern Iranian language. The Kurds of the former Soviet Union first began writing Kurmanji in the Armenian alphabet in the 1920s, followed by Latin in 1927, then Cyrillic in 1945; nowadays both Cyrillic and Latin alphabets are employed. In other countries, Kurds use modified Latin or modified Perso-Arabic alphabets. One of the main differences between Kurmanji and other Iranian languages is that it makes a distinction in gender.

Talysh, a northwestern Iranian language, has a Persian-based alphabet in Iran and both a Cyrillic and an Azeri Latin alphabet in Azerbaijan.

Turkic languages

There are four languages of the Oghuz group within the Turkic languages spoken in the Caucasus.

Northern Azerbaijani is spoken by the Azeris in the Caucasus and differs slightly from Southern Azerbaijani, which is used mainly in Iran. Azerbaijani is very close to Anatolian Turkish, and the differences between these two languages can be explained by Mongolian and Turkic influences. Due to Azerbaijan's close historic relationship with Persia, the Russian Empire and the Soviet Union, there are many loanwords from Persian and Russian. The Persian alphabet was used from the fourteenth century, and in 1924 Soviet officials forced the introduction of the modified Roman (Latin) alphabet for Northern Azerbaijani. In 1928 Turkey also switched to the modified Roman alphabet, which was one of the reasons for the imposition of the Cyrillic alphabet on the Azerbaijanis in 1939. Eight new letters were created to represent certain Azerbaijani sounds. Following the break-up of the Soviet Union the issue of the alphabet rose again. Iran tried to promote the Arabic alphabet, but at the end of 1991 the Azerbaijani Latin alphabet was reintroduced, which makes the link with Turkey obvious. Nevertheless, Azerbaijani Cyrillic writing is still widespread and publicly used. The Arabic alphabet is used for Southern Azerbaijani in Iran.

Turkish is known as a second or third language by some Azerbaijanis, but an East Anatolian dialect of Turkish is the native language for the Meskhetian Turks.

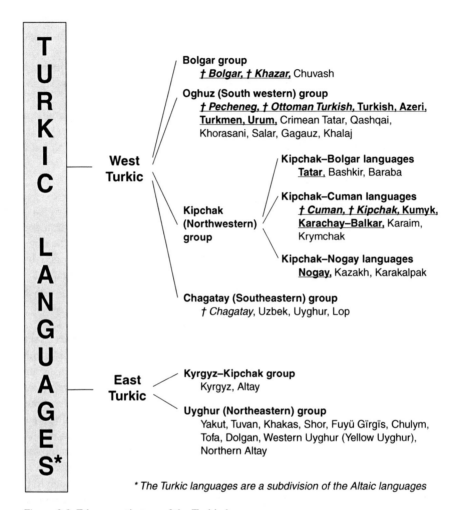

Figure 3.3 Ethnogenetic tree of the Turkic languages

Turkmen is spoken mainly in Turkmenistan, but the Trukhmen dialect is used by the Turkmens of the Stavropol Kray. The language comes from the Oghuz tribes and received a lot of Kipchak influences during its development. Although Turkmen has a literary tradition, the Trukhmens employ Russian for writing.

Urum (Greek Tatar) is used in the Caucasus by some Urum Greeks who moved from the Crimea to Georgia. However, in recent times most Urum Greeks emigrated to Greece and the Krasnodar Kray. The language is very similar to Crimean Tatar (Crimean Turkish) and has almost no links at all with Greek.

There are four languages of the Kipchak group within the Turkic languages spoken in the Caucasus.

Kumyk was subject to significant influence from the Scythians, Huns, Khazars and Oghuz. It was written first in an Arabic script, then from 1929 in Latin, and since 1938 has used Cyrillic.

Karachay–Balkar was known as Mountain Tatar, Tatar Chagatai and Mountain Turkish until the 1950s. It was sporadically written in Arabic until it was assigned a Latin alphabet in 1924. Since 1937 it has used a Cyrillic alphabet.

Tatar is used by some Tatars in the Caucasus, but it occurs as a native language only seldom.

Nogay was written originally in an Arabic script, but changed in 1928 to Latin and in 1938 to Cyrillic.

Afro-Asiatic (Hamito-Semitic) languages

Neo-Aramaic is a language spoken by Jews and Christians in Northern Iran and Iraq. The Assyrian community who moved to Georgia and Azerbaijan in the nineteenth century also speaks this language. It was initially called Aysorski by Russian linguists; however, since the 1930s it has been known as Assiriyskiy.

Religion

The profession of faith and its history in the Caucasus is almost as complex as the ethnolinguistic mosaic. A large number of different beliefs are followed, with many more having been practised in the past. Most people in the Caucasus are believers, but not all actively practise their religion. The history of state religions is related more to strategic and political considerations than to specific religious beliefs. For example, the Khazar leadership opted to accept Judaism as the state religion in order to avoid falling under the influence of Christian Byzantium or the Muslim Arab caliphate. The separation between state and religion was limited in the Caucasus until very recently.

Freedom of religion exists officially, and the Caucasus has not seen much religious intolerance or fanaticism. Jewish communities live throughout the region, Islam is freely practised by minorities in Georgia, Christian and Muslim Abkhaz live together in peace. Nevertheless, the last decade of the twentieth century brought some radical Wahhabism to the North Caucasus, and certain Georgian Orthodox priests have violently attacked people confessing other religions.[13]

Until the fourth century AD, the Caucasians worshipped pagan gods, Greek gods (in the west) and the sun or followed Anatolian (probably Hurrian) cults. Yet others were animists or Zoroastrians. Many influences of these ancient cults and beliefs are still apparent in modern-day religions, especially in the mountainous areas. Gradually Christianity spread over the region and lead to continual conflict with the Persian Zoroastrians. Still, the local population often accepted the new religions very slowly and kept many pagan aspects to their worship. The Arabs conquered large parts of the Caucasus in the seventh century and brought Islam with them. In the following centuries there was a constant struggle between

Muslim and Christian expansion, which reached its peak in the eleventh century. The attacks of the Mongols led to the collapse of the Georgian kingdom and to the prevalence of Islam in most of the Northern Caucasus. Then Russian conquests of the Caucasus in the eighteenth and nineteenth centuries and the Russo-Turkish War resulted in an enormous migration of Muslims – Abkhaz, Abazins, Ubykhs, Adyghe, Cherkess and Kabardians – from the northwestern part of the region. During Soviet times, especially throughout the Stalinist era, religion was suppressed and religious buildings were destroyed and converted into museums or concert halls. Many historically important buildings were torn down, such as the Bibi Eibar shrine in Azerbaijan. In addition, many Muslim nations were deported to Central Asia and Siberia during the Second World War.

A religious revival began in 1988, with Gorbachev's reforms, and many religious buildings were restored. This revival, especially of Islam, has been an important element in the building of national identity. Since the break-up of the Soviet Union there has also been a real expansion in the number of religious sects and their adherents.

Heathenism and animism

The first religious beliefs existed in the form of worship of nature and pagan gods. Even now, several centuries after the Christianization and Islamization of the region, almost all Caucasian people share certain traditional beliefs, and the Christian and Muslim ceremonies carry folk elements of faith, such as animism or fetishism. This is true mainly for the North Caucasians and particularly for those who live in the mountain areas. The most significant pagan heritage, however, is the Ossetian one, where Islam and Christianity are unique (i.e. they incorporate more pagan elements). Some examples are the beliefs and rituals related to agriculture; the reverence for gods of thunder and lightning; the honouring of nature – mountains, trees, stones, springs and wells; magical ceremonies; and the cult of family spirits. Many Turkic nations also share the cult of the deity Tengri,[14] the goddess Umay, and several 'master-spirits'. Several names of pagan deities have in fact become synonyms for Allah. These pagan customs and beliefs are still present because, when the monotheist religions spread across the region, many people adhered to the traditions of their ancestors and preserved the patriarchal customs, and also because their economic basis for survival and their dependence on nature remained.

Zoroastrianism

The prophet Zoroaster (Zarathustra) was probably born between the fifteenth and seventh century BC in the region which is now known as South Azerbaijan, i.e. Northern Iran. He founded one of the world's first monotheistic world religions, which is still practised by some 140,000 people. Its followers are often falsely termed fire worshippers: they do not worship fire, though fire – still one of the symbols of Azerbaijan – plays a central role in their rituals. The holy book is called the Avesta and is composed of Gathas, abstract sacred metrical poetry that explains the doctrine of the religion. There is only one god, Ahura Mazda, and all evil is caused by the fiendish spirit Angra Mainyu. Zoroastrianism spread under Persian rule in the Southeastern Caucasus (present Armenia, eastern Georgia, Dagestan and Azerbaijan) between the third century BC and the seventh century AD and was established as the state religion of the Sassanid Empire (AD 211–640; the empire included a large part of the South Caucasus). With the rise of Byzantine influence in Caucasian Albania, the Persian rulers tried to preserve their religion but had little success. Most Zoroastrian temples in the Caucasus were destroyed after Islam was introduced, but a few can still be found (e.g. in Surakhany, near Baku, and in Khinalug, near Quba). There are also remnants of the everyday culture, such as the Novruz celebration (21 March), which comes from the Zoroastrian New Year feast.

Judaism

Jews arrived in the Caucasus in several waves but many have emigrated again in the past few decades. According to archaeological findings and ancient Armenian and Georgian historiography, there must have been a considerable Jewish population in the South Caucasus for more than 2,000 years – some claiming they were present as early as 721 BC – but the precise date of their arrival is unknown. There was a steady influx of Jews to Greater Armenia from the first century BC until AD 360–70 and later in the fifth century. Georgian sources also mention the arrival of Jews from the Byzantine Empire to western Georgia in the sixth century and a further migration of 3,000 Jews to eastern Georgia. Western Georgia was under the strong influence of Byzantium, which suppressed the Jews in the sixth century, but eastern Georgia, ruled by the Persians, tolerated them.

The main political powers in the region in the eighth century were Christian and Muslim. The Khazar Empire, however, converted to Judaism in order to avoid dependence on either Byzantium or the Arab caliphate. Several Dagestani nations (e.g. the Aguls, Tabassarans and even some Kumyks) were partially Jewish for a period of time in their history but later converted to Islam. The Tiflis sect, a Jewish sect which denied certain Jewish laws and regulations, emerged in the ninth century in Tbilisi and existed for about 300 years. When the Mongols invaded the Caucasus, many Jews from eastern and southern Georgia moved to western Georgia, which remained independent. In the following five centuries most Jews in Georgia were serfs and some converted to Christianity in order to escape their serfdom. During this time many Jews migrated to the Crimea – some voluntarily (fifteenth to sixteenth centuries) and some forcibly (seventeenth to eighteenth centuries, under Persian pressure). Following the Russo-Persian War of 1826–8 a Jewish community (mainly Kurdish Jews) resettled from northern Iran to Armenia, but later most of them relocated to Israel and Georgia. As a consequence there are only a few hundred Jews remaining in Armenia. The Ashkenazi Jews arrived primarily in Azerbaijan in the nineteenth century, inspired by the oil boom. Zionist ideas spread at the end of that same century, especially among the Ashkenazi Jews, but only a few thousand Jews moved to the Holy Land. The real exodus to Israel started in the 1970s and reached its peak in the early 1990s. Twenty years later this trend of emigration to Israel (*aliyah*) persists, and the vast majority of Jews have already left the Caucasus.

The Georgian Jews, who see Georgian as their native language, claim that they are descendants of the Ten Lost Tribes of Israel, exiled by Shalmaneser in 721 BC, while other Jews claim they arrived in the Caucasus after Nebukhadnessar (Nabukodonosor) conquered Jerusalem and many Jews were sent into exile to Babylonia in 586 BC.

The Tat-speaking Mountain Jews live in the Quba and Baku regions in Azerbaijan and in Derbent and several villages in Dagestan. One theory postulates that they are descendants of the Khazars, another suggests that they are descendants of the Persian Jews or of one of the Ten Lost Ttribes of Israel, whereas yet another claims they came from Persia as late as the seventeenth century.[15]

Many Ashkenazi Jews migrated from European Russia to the Caucasus when the region became part of the Russian Empire. Many more European Jews relocated to the rapidly growing oil centre of Baku and actively participated in the development of the industry.

The Subbotniki (Sabbath keepers, Saturday People) are seen as a Jewish sect. Their ancestors were Russian peasants who relinquished the Russian Orthodox Church in the sixteenth century, just as the Molokans and Doukhobors did. The Subbotniki follow most Jewish laws and rules, including circumcision, prayers and, especially, the observance of the Sabbath. Under the rule of Russian Tsar Aleksandr I (1801–25) they enjoyed relative religious freedom as long as they did not engage Jewish preachers or proselytize among the Christians. Unrest started under the reign of Nikolay I (1825–55), as many of the Subbotniki desired to embrace real Judaism. In 1826 the Russian government decided to deport the Subbotniki to Siberia and the Caucasus, where they could also act as a buffer on the border of the empire. Currently, there are only a few thousand Subbotniki left in the region, and most now live in the US, Israel, France or Hungary.

Christianity

The Christianization of the Caucasus took place in several waves, spread across many centuries. This process did not always go very smoothly or quickly. The higher ranks of society often accepted the new religion easily, as this was based largely on political considerations. The broad masses of the people, however, especially in the mountains, initially reacted in quite a hostile manner. This early Christianity was fundamental in the development of the written language, and the fifth and sixth centuries witnessed the emergence of huge numbers of religious writings in Georgian, Armenian and Agvan (in Albania).

The first contact with Christianity occurred in the Caucasus through the apostles Andrew, Matthew and Simon the Canaanite, who all preached in western Georgia in the first century AD but were able to convert only a few people. Around the same time the apostles Thaddeus and Bartholomew preached in Armenia and Albania, and both suffered martyrdom there. St Elyseus, one of the five students of St Thaddeus, survived the violence and went to Caucasian Albania through Persia, thus bypassing Armenia, and started preaching in Derbent. In the following centuries Syrian missionaries came to the region, but although some of the population were converted Christianity was not adopted as the state religion immediately.

The Christian religion began spreading faster and more strongly in the fourth century, mainly through the cultural and political influence of Byzantium, which was very much linked to the fight against Zoroastrian Persia. St Gregory 'the Illuminator' converted King Tiridates III of Armenia, who had previously persecuted Christians and even tortured and imprisoned St Gregory for 13 years. Armenians claim that King Tiridates recognized Christianity as a state religion in 301, making Armenia the first Christian state in the world. However, there are several indicators that this did not happen until 314, one year after the Edict of Milan of Constantine the Great, which established religious freedom and the end of the persecution of Christians in the Roman Empire.[16]

Around 303, the Cappadocian slave Nino came to Iberia (eastern Georgia) to preach Christianity and convert the local population. She cured Queen Nana from a curious disease and was offered gold and silver by King Mirian III. Nino declined and pointed to the power she had received from her belief. Despite this, Mirian refused to accept the religion. However, following another miracle in 337 he proclaimed Christianity the state religion.[17] Western Georgia did not officially adopt Christianity until the fifth century, but its population had been largely Christian before that. Also in the middle of the fourth century, King Urnayr of Albania converted to Christianity under the influence of St Gregory and declared it the state religion. Initially the majority of the population remained Zoroastrian, but towards the fifth century Christianity became the main religion. At first the Zoroastrian Sassanid Empire did not oppose the spreading of Christianity, but in the fifth and sixth centuries its rulers feared the increase of Byzantine influence and the strengthening of power of the Albanian kings. It was in fact the spreading of Christianity and the end of polytheism that helped in the unification of Albania and its independence from Persia. In 451 AD the Christian allied forces (Armenian, Albanian and Iberian) lost the Battle of Avarayr against the Zoroastrian Sassanid army but remained loyal to their religion. In 484, however, the Persian king declared full tolerance of the Christian faith. Another important event in the history of Christianity took place in 451, when the Christian churches of the Caucasus refused to accept the decisions of the Council of Chalcedon and severed ties with the Byzantine and Roman Churches.[18] This resulted in the formation of autocephalous Armenian, Georgian and Albanian Churches.

Byzantine, Georgian, Abkhaz and Albanian missionaries crossed the main Caucasian range to continue their work of conversion. However, apart from a few small groups of people (e.g. Adyghe, Balkars, Ossetians, Avars, Kumyks, Andi and Dido), they were not very successful. With the arrival of the Arabs came new

competition in the religious life of the Caucasus. Between the ninth and the fourteenth century there was a constant struggle between the expansion of Islam
(coming from the south, from the Islamized part of the South Caucasus) and
Christianity (coming from Georgia in the west). The eleventh century in Georgia
was marked by prosperity, and the Georgian rulers tried to spread their religion to
the North Caucasus. The western part of the North Caucasus became almost
entirely Christian, whereas these attempts among the Ingush, Chechens and
Dagestanians were only partially successful. In many cases people took the religion nominally but did not profess it. In the fourteenth century, after the Mongol
invasions and the campaign of Timur, the Georgian state weakened, with the
result that the base for Christianity shrank and Islam prevailed.

From the seventeenth century onwards, the Russians also assisted in the
Christianization of the North Caucasus and were especially successful in Ossetia.
Other attempts, such as those with the Tatars, were not so fruitful.

The roots of the diophysite Russian Orthodox Church, the largest of the 15
autocephalous (independent) Orthodox churches, go back to the baptism of
Grand Prince Vladimir I of the Kievan Rus in 988. The Church was affiliated to
the patriarchate of Constantinople, and its centre moved to Moscow in the fourteenth century after the Mongols had destroyed Kiev. The Russian Church
became independent in 1589 with the patriarch of Moscow and All Rus at its
head. In 1653–7 Patriarch Nikon attempted to reorganize the Church and its rituals,[19] which led to a schism. Those who refused to accept these reforms became
known as Old Believers. In the following years the Russian Orthodox Church
experienced a tremendous growth, but Peter the Great abolished the patriarchate
in 1721. Instead, the Church was ruled by a Holy Synod under close state supervision. After the abdication of the tsar in 1917, a synod re-established the patriarchate and elected Tikhon as the new patriarch. Tikhon initially criticized
communism, but later he and his successor were able to normalize church–state
relations. The Church supported the government and in return was granted the
right to practise the liturgy in a limited way. The disintegration of the Soviet
Union also posed a threat to the unity of the Moscow patriarchate. In 1990 the
Russian Orthodox Council of Bishops decided to grant a degree of autonomy to
the Orthodox churches in Ukraine and Belarus. The same happened with Estonia,
Latvia and Moldova one year later. Patriarch Aleksey II, elected a year and a half
before the collapse of the Soviet Union, died in December 2008. His successor,
elected at the end of January 2009, is Kirill I.

The diophysite Georgian Orthodox Church forms the main religion in Georgia
and was initially under the heavy influence of the Byzantine Empire: it fell under
the jurisdiction of the Apostolic See of Antioch and its liturgy was in Greek. At
the Chalcedonian Council of 451 it separated from the teachings of other
Christian churches, in 466 it became an autocephalous catholicosate and in 1010
its status was elevated to a patriarchate, headed by the Catholicos-Patriarch of All
Georgia. Until the political unification of Georgia in 1008, the structure of the
Georgian Church had also been split (i.e. one catholicos in western Georgia and

another one in eastern Georgia). Between the fifteenth and eighteenth centuries, when Georgia was again divided, the Church broke up accordingly, and two catholicos-patriarchs ruled simultaneously. Georgia was annexed by Russia in 1801, and when the Georgian patriarch died in 1811 the Russians abolished the patriarchate, and Russian and Slavonic languages replaced Georgian in the liturgy. The Georgian bishops unilaterally restored the autocephaly of the Georgian Orthodox Church following the overthrow of the tsarist regime in March 1917 and elected a new catholicos-patriarch. However, this event was not officially recognized by the Russian Orthodox Church and the Soviet regime closed most churches or converted them into secular buildings. It was only in 1943 that the Russian Orthodox Church finally granted this independence, but it did not change the policy of the political authorities. Ilia II has became Catholicos-Patriarch of All Georgia in 1977, and in 1988 Moscow permitted him to reopen and restore churches.

The miaphysite (a form of monophysitism) Armenian Apostolic Church, or Armenian Gregorian Church as it is also known, embraces some 90 per cent of Armenians. Soon after the Christianization of Armenia, St Gregory the Illuminator built a cathedral in Vagharshapat (Echmiadzin), which is now the centre of the Armenian Church: the Holy See of Armenia. St Gregory became the first in an unbroken line of catholicoi: Karekin II was elected in 1999 as the 132nd catholicos. In 506 the Armenian Church rejected the doctrine of the Council of Chalcedon (451), and the Armenian Church became canonically independent. It has since been in communion with the other monophysite churches in Egypt, Syria and Ethiopia. The Armenian Apostolic Church is not related theologically to the Catholic or Orthodox Church, but its practices are similar. The Armenian liturgical tradition was formed between the fifth and the seventh centuries and reflects the strong influence of the Syrian, Jerusalem and Byzantine tradition. The structure of the Armenian Church is rather complex. There are four hierarchical sees: the catholicosate of All Armenians in Echmiadzin, the catholicosate of Sis, or the Great House of Cilicia (in Antelias, Lebanon), the patriarchate of Jerusalem and the patriarchate of Constantinople. The mother see of Holy Echmiadzin is recognized as the head of the whole church, whereas the other three have administrative autonomy and ecclesiastical jurisdiction but owe spiritual allegiance.

The autocephalous Albanian Apostolic Church was established in the fourth century after Christianity had become the official state religion. Initially the catholicos was ordained from Jerusalem. The Church became fully independent at the end of the fourth century, mainly because it was politically independent. This, however, did not mean it had no links with the Byzantine Church. During the first centuries of its existence its power was nominal, but it grew stronger in the seventh century. Around the same time, like the Georgian Church, the Albanian Church opted for the diophysite dogma. Because it preferred to see monophysitism in Albania as a counterweight to the diophysite Byzantine Empire, when the Arab caliphate crushed the Albanian state in 705 the Arabs

officially subordinated the Albanian Church to the Armenian one and simultaneously launched their own Islamization. In the following centuries only the Udins
refused to accept Islam and managed to survive in a few parts of the region. In
1836 the Albanian autocephalous patriarchal catholicosate was cancelled and
again subordinated to the Armenian Gregorian Church by a decision of the tsarist
government. The Udins tried unsuccessfully to avoid this Gregorianization and as
a result lost their religion altogether, though some became Georgian or Russian
Orthodox instead.

The Doukhobors (Spirit Wrestlers) form a spiritual Christian sect and have
completely broken away from Orthodoxy. The sect, currently numbering some
50,000 members across the world, originated in the late 1760s in the region of
Yekaterinoslav and Tambov in Russia. Their persecution began in 1793–4, and in
1801 they were resettled in the Crimea. In 1839 the Doukhobors were relocated to
Transcaucasia following a new wave of persecutions. In the period 1841–5 roughly
4,000 Doukhobors were exiled to the regions of Ninotsminda (formerly known as
Bogdanovka) and Dmanisi in present-day Georgia and Gadabey in present-day
Azerbaijan. Since then there have been three waves of emigration from the South
Caucasus. In 1899 the Doukhobors were persecuted again and 7,500 of them
moved to Canada, where the majority of Doukhobors live today. In 1921–3, 4,000
Doukhobors from the South Caucasus were permitted to resettle in the Rostov
Oblast, where they still live. Finally, a mass departure, mainly to the region of
Bryansk in Russia, took place in the early 1990s during the rule of Georgian
President Zviad Gamsakhurdia. Whereas in the early 1990s there were 7,000
Doukhobors left in the South Caucasus, at present there are only some 1,000.

The Molokans (Milk People) are Russian sectarians, many of whom moved to
the Caucasus in the nineteenth century, particularly to present-day Armenia. The
name of this Christian sect finds its origin in the Russian word *moloko* (milk)
because, contrary to the instructions of the Russian Orthodox Church, the
Molokans drink milk during the 200 fasting days each year. They evolved from
spiritual Christian Russian peasants who refused to join the Russian Orthodox
Church and rejected both its traditions and the divinity of the tsar. Molokan doctrine, which opposes the worship of material representations of God, spread in the
seventeenth century in the central provinces of Russia, but it was only with
Semeon Uklein, who broke away from the Doukhobors,[20] that the religious movement was officially formed. An 1805 manifesto of Aleksandr I allowed Molokans
and Doukhobors freely to profess their religion, but under Nikolay I their persecution started once again. In 1830 they were forbidden to live in certain parts of
Russia and as a result many accepted the voluntary resettlement to the
Transcaucasus. At the end of the nineteenth century, when they rejected military
service, a large number moved to the United States and, to a lesser extent,
Mexico. During the late 1980s and early 1990s there was a tremendous outflow
of the Russian population, including Molokans, from Armenia. There were
25,000 Molokans left in the nine Molokan communities of the Caucasus in the
early 1980s, but at present there are only 5,000. Today, Molokans are found

around the world, including several dozen communities in the US and a limited number in Australia.

Catholics can be found throughout the North Caucasus, in southern Georgia and in certain parts of Armenia (and its diaspora) but only in quite small numbers. From the twelfth century onwards Armenians in Cilicia came into contact with the Roman Catholic crusaders and were influenced by missionaries in the fourteenth century. Some Armenians became Catholics, but it was only in 1742 that the Armenian Catholic Church was created. It is headed by a patriarch who now resides in Beirut, and liturgy is celebrated in the classical Armenian language. Relations between the Russian Orthodox Church and the Catholic Church are very strained, and only limited contact exists between the two, especially after the Vatican established four dioceses in Russia in 2002.

From the second half of the nineteenth century and the beginning of the twentieth century other forms of Christianity emerged, such as Adventism, Baptism, Jehovah's Witnesses and Presbyterianism. These 'new' religions often experience administrative problems and are seen as inferior by a large part of the population. After the break-up of the Soviet Union and the loss of security and protection, several people looked at and adopted these new religions.

Islam

Islam is the second religion in Russia but also one of the leading religions in the Caucasus. The Islamization process, which was quite peaceful in general, took many centuries and started as early as the seventh century. Since the end of the nineteenth century Azerbaijan and the entire North Caucasus, with exception of most of the Ossetians, have followed Islam. There is also a Muslim minority on Georgian territory (Azeris, Adjars and some Abkhaz), but almost none are left in Armenia following the war in Nagorno Karabakh. As mentioned above, there are a lot of remnants of previous beliefs. Several nations still use the name of pagan deities to denote Allah: the Nogays talk about Tangir, the Karachays and Balkars about Teiri, the Chechen and Ingush about Djal. Religious Islamic literature used to be in Arabic and Persian, apart from Sufi poetry, which was often written in local Turkish dialects. However, since the late nineteenth century books on Islamic teachings have appeared in Caucasian languages. The spokesperson for the Muslims in the Caucasus is currently Sheikh Allakhshukyur Pashazade, the chairman of the Caucasus Muslim Board.

In 653 Arab invaders conquered Derbent and turned the city into a base for protection against the Khazars and to launch military campaigns against non-Muslims in the region. The Arab soldiers and merchants started spreading Islam among the local population in the eighth and ninth centuries in the lowlands of Dagestan and Azerbaijan, and thereby entered into a struggle with the attempts at Christianization emanating from Georgia. Islamization of the mountain communities was more difficult and was achieved much later in history. Derbent remained the basis for these efforts and gradually also turned into a centre for Sufi teachings. Islam spread slowly and peacefully, and became widespread among the Khazar population during the tenth century.

The next wave of Islamization in the Caucasus commenced in the fourteenth century through the influence of the Mongols. Uzbek Khan, great-grandson of Genghis Khan, adopted Islam in 1312 as the state religion of the Golden Horde. The successor states of the Golden Horde, especially the Crimean khanate supported by the Nogay Horde, played a crucial role in the slow Islamization process of the North Caucasus. Most of the western part had adopted Sunni Islam by the eighteenth century, and the final conversion took place at the time of the Caucasian War in the mid-nineteenth century. Islam started to spread from Dagestan to the Ingush and Chechens in the sixteenth century – first in the valleys and foothills, later in the mountainous regions – and in the nineteenth century it became the dominant religion. However, the influence of the Ottoman and Safavid Empire, especially in the southern part of the Caucasus, should not be underestimated.

Before the eighteenth century, Islam in the North Caucasus was a belief and a matter of identity, but not a real religion practised according to Koranic principles. The western part of the North Caucasus was also more Christian and pagan in its beliefs and had not been subdued by the Islamization efforts – though the advance and more aggressive attitude of the Russians would change this. The struggle against Russia resulted in an increase in religious enthusiasm, spiritual leaders became heroes and Islam, previously liberal in form, became more extreme. It was particularly the systematic activities of the Sufi brotherhoods in the eighteenth century that led to the Islamization of the mountain communities. With the Russian conquest of the Caucasus, resistance grew and Muridism developed. Because of their stubborn resistance, after their defeat in the 1860s many Muslim North Caucasian people were exiled to Turkey and the Middle East.

During the early Soviet times mosques were destroyed, representatives of the Muslim clergy were persecuted, religious holidays were banned, and the Arabic alphabets were replaced first by Latin and later by Cyrillic ones. During perestroika some 60 years later, when religion could be professed openly again, the role of Islam increased in social and political life. Mosques were constructed, Islamic schools were opened, and Muslims had an opportunity to make the *hajj*. It also led to a process of fundamentalization in the form of Wahhabism. Perestroika did not have the same effect on all ethnic groups in terms of religion. While for some it did not provoke a strong revival (e.g. Abazins), for others it meant a true revitalization (e.g. Adyghe, Balkars, Karachay); for those who had held their beliefs in secret (e.g. Avars, Andi, Dido), it meant that they were suddenly able to practise openly. In any event, the ethnic groups in the western part of the North Caucasus are not as religiously active as those in the east.

As is the case with most other religions, there are several movements within Islam. Muslim ideology was split into two main trends at the end of the seventh century: Sunni and Shia. In the early eighth century the Sunni trend was further subdivided into four *mazhabs*, or theological-legal schools: Hanafi, Maliki, Shafii and Hanbali. The western part of the North Caucasus (Adyghe, Abazins, Kabards,

Karachays, Balkars, Nogays and some of the Ossetians), having been influenced by the Golden Horde and later by Crimean Tatars, Turks and Nogays, is mainly Hanafi. The eastern part (Ingush, Chechen, most Dagestani, Kumyks and some Nogays) became mainly Shafii, under influence from Derbent, where the Shafii school of law and theology replaced the Hanafi in the twelfth century. Azeris and Talysh are mainly Shiite because the Safavid Shah Ismail I established Shia Islam as the state religion in the sixteenth century. Shia Islam in Azerbaijan is not as fundamentalist as in Iran. During the seventeenth century some Kumyks and Lezgins converted to Shia Islam after they had turned to the Persian Safavids for help in the struggle against Russian expansion.

Sufism (or *tasawwuf* in Arabic) is a mystical and psycho-spiritual dimension of Sunni Islam whose objective is turning away from everything but God; it is currently very widespread among the Ingush, Chechens, Avars and Laks. It developed in the middle of the eighth century and appeared in Derbent in the twelfth century, whence it spread to other areas of the Northeastern Caucasus. It was easily introduced in the region because it absorbed elements of the local beliefs and cults. Within Sufism there are several orders and mystical ways (*tariqats*) leading to God. The Yasaviyya and Kubrawiyya orders were the most popular with the Nogays and Kumyks until the nineteenth century, but from the fifteenth century onwards Naqshbandiyya and Qadiriyya enjoyed their greatest success. Naqshbandiyya and Qadiriyya were a source of inspiration and energy for the struggle against Russian oppression and thus laid the foundation for Muridism, a religious teaching that became the ideology of the Caucasian War in the nineteenth century and the establishment for the first theocratic state (imamate) in the North Caucasus. However, Muridism did not get much support from the Northwestern Caucasians. Sufism flourished during the Soviet era, when religious practices were officially forbidden, and especially when the Ingush and Chechens were deported to Central Asia. Today the brotherhoods also play an important factor in politics. Nevertheless, assessing the role of these *tariqats* is difficult because their practices are secret.

Wahhabism was founded by Muhammed Ibn Abd al-Wahhab in the eighteenth century in Arabia, where this fundamentalist Sunni movement is known as Tawhid (monotheism). In the Western world of today, fundamentalism has a very negative connotation, whereas in Islam, on the contrary, it is perceived positively by many because it goes back to the real roots of the religion. Wahhabists (*muwahhidun*) wish to purify their religion from innovation, superstition, deviance and idolatry. Wahhabism, and especially an aggressive Sudanese version, has been spreading in the eastern part of the North Caucasus, from Dagestan to Ingushetia, since the 1980s. It conflicts with Sufism, which is also prevalent in that part of the Caucasus, because the Wahhabist ideology does not permit the adoration of saints or the visiting of their graves. Wahhabists see it as their role to restore Islam but also to set up an Islamic state and Islamize the entire world population. The more moderate among them feel this should happen without violence, whereas the radicals do not want to wait and look for an open war with the non-Muslims. Since the early 1990s Wahhabism has become a politically loaded, one-size-fits-all description used arbitrarily for any form of Islamic worship outside the state-controlled religious structures. The first to use the term in this sense were the Russian security establishment and the official religious boards, the latter resenting the 'competition' by foreign religious groups even if those were not of Wahhabi inspiration or Saudi-funded. Arab and other foreign fighters who assisted some of the Chechen rebel factions are generally not adepts of Wahhabism but of Salafism, a more militant form of Islam whose puritanical teachings partly overlap those of the former.

Yezidism

Yezidism or Yazidism, into which one has to be born and to which nobody can convert, has existed in its current form since the reforms of Sheikh Adi, who died in 1155. However, this religion, which outsiders often falsely see as a form of Zoroastrianism, must have existed for even longer, and some think it goes as far back as 2000 BC. The religious centre is Lalish, northeast of Mosul, in Iraq. Yezidis live according to a rigid religious caste system. Although their traditions and faiths are passed on orally, there are two books with an important religious value: the *Kitêba Cilwe* (Book of Illumination) and the *Mishefa Reş* (Black Book). Yezidism is monotheistic and is a combination of Zoroastrian, Manichaean, Jewish, Nestorian Christian and Islamic elements. God created seven archangels out of his light, and the most important one, Melek Tawus, is symbolized by a peacock and takes the function of a form of substitute for God. The Yezidis maintain good relations with the Christians, because the groups have protected and helped each other on several occasions – for example during the times of the persecution of the Armenians by the Turks. However, they are not on such good terms with Muslims, who often falsely refer to them as devil worshippers, as the other name of Melek Taus is Shaytan, the name of the devil in the Koran.

Russian and Soviet nationality policies

After non-Russian regions and peoples had been absorbed into the structure of the Russian Empire, specific policies towards these ethnic groups were developed. This mainly meant Russianization (spreading the Russian language, culture and people into non-Russian cultures and regions) and Russification (the process of changing one's ethnic identity from non-Russian to Russian). These processes were relatively weak during the Russian Empire and Russification was largely a result of Russian chauvinism. However, these efforts were not particularly successful in the Caucasus.

During the 1920s and the early 1930s the Soviet nationalities policy was guided by the principle of indigenization (*korenizatsiya*), contradicting the Russification attempts of the Russian Empire: regional administrative units were created, non-Russians were recruited into leadership positions, and non-Russian languages were both promoted in government administration and public life and received a Latin-based alphabet.

The situation changed dramatically in the late 1930s as a result of the perceived threat of local nationalism. In 1938 Russian became a compulsory subject of study in all schools, and during the same period Cyrillic alphabets replaced the Latin ones. Russification and Russianization were reintroduced and ethnic Russians took on leading role in the Soviet family of nations. This included the recruitment of mainly ethnic Russians to the high administrative positions.

Starting in the late 1950s Russian became the main language of instruction in schools. In the 1960s the concepts of rapprochement (*sblizheniye*) and fusion of nationalities (*sliyaniye*) were launched, and in 1971 the idea of a 'Soviet people' with Russian as the common language was introduced.

Social structure

Although a discussion about the organization of society in the North Caucasus through history may not fully fit under this chapter, it deserves special consideration because in several ways it is closely related to current peculiarities in the region. The social order and self-government of the region attracted the attention of various Russian researchers in the eighteenth and nineteenth centuries. At that time there were, for example, both free communities (Dagestani nations), among them feudal societies headed by a shamkhal, maysum or bey (Dagestanians, Balkars and Karachays), and aristocratic societies (Adyghe). The most interesting case is that of the Chechens and Ingush, whose *teips* still form the cornerstone of society. There are approximately 150 *teips* – clan-like tribal communities which identify themselves by a common ancestor in the paternal line. These *teips* were grouped regionally into 13 *tukkhums* to solve common security and economic problems. The *teips* are subdivided into *gary* (branches) and further into *nek'i* (families), and their size varies from a few thousand to over 100,000. The largest are Benoy, Akkiy, Chinkho, Gendergenoy, Alleroy and Ersenoy. Over the years several *gary* and even *nek'i* have upgraded themselves to the status of a *teip*, and as a result the number of *teips* has increased fivefold over the past two centuries. The important decisions that have an effect on the *teip* are taken by a council of elders, composed of the oldest and most respected men. There is a strong competition among different *teips* trying to improve their status in society, which often leads to strong tensions. As a result, the *teip* forces its members to honour it and to live according to the *o'zdangala*, the ethical rules of modesty, education, orderliness, frankness and helpfulness. The status of a *teip* can be raised when its men are courageous at war and follow all ethical rules, or it can be downgraded in the opposite case. Every person is identified by his *teip*; thus the behaviour of a single person can ruin the image and honour of the entire *teip* and an insult to one person is an insult to all. Every *teip* has its own historical motherland, where most have some kind of symbol, such as a war-tower or mountain.

4

HISTORY

The history of the Caucasus is complex, and therefore is not always easy to comprehend. It is full of wars, changing coalitions, betrayals and a fair portion of ethnic cleansing. History is kept alive in the form of myths, stereotypes and prejudices, but not that much via objective historiography. Although it plays a major role in their minds, many Caucasians tend to have a very narrow and partisan knowledge of the history of their own nation and an even more limited understanding of that of their neighbors and enemies. This chapter aims to give a general overview of the overall trends without going into too much detail. More specifically, it deals with the history of the states and foreign rulers in the Caucasus, which should also make it clear how recent are the current geographical borders. A common mistake when studying history is to consider only what took place within the borders of the contemporary states rather than looking beyond them or taking into account the influence of neighbouring nations.

Historiography faces many difficulties, and this is certainly true as far as the historiography of the Caucasus is concerned. For the early history of the first states in the Caucasus and their relations with their neighbours, one often has to rely on Greek, Roman, Georgian, Armenian or Albanian authors who lived many centuries after the events actually took place and who had no first-hand knowledge of the region. These sources should therefore be treated with the utmost caution when considering their veracity. The biggest problem, however, is that, for many authors in the Caucasus, historiography is intended to give sense to nationalist propaganda. Such tendencies are common for all nations in search of their own identity, and historians and politicians involved in conflicts actively look for anything that could serve as proof that a certain region has 'always' been theirs. Making subtle alterations or absolute falsifications is therefore not uncommon. History is often romanticized or glorified, and celebrated kings were frequently responsible for genocides and massacres.

As an important aside, it should be mentioned that the Gregorian calendar – in use since the 1500s – and the Julian calendar – used in the Russian Empire until 1918 (i.e. after the revolution) – do not coincide. The difference between these two calendars is up to 13 days, which explains why the October Revolution actually took place in November according to the Gregorian calendar and why the Russian Orthodox Church celebrates Christmas on 7 January.

Human prehistory

The traditional three-age system of classifying human prehistory – Stone Age, Bronze Age and Iron Age, all named after the principal material for tools during those eras – applies to the Caucasus, although the indicative times are not the same in all parts of the world, and in fact many of these ages overlap one another.

Stone Age

The Caucasus, and the South Caucasus in particular, is one of the most ancient centres of human habitation, a fact that is confirmed by the large number of archaeological findings in the region. The Stone Age in the Caucasus is divided in several periods, but the exact dates of each are not very clear.

Throughout the Old Stone Age, or Paleolithic period (500,000–10,000 BC), people dwelt in small groups in the southern and western part of the Caucasus. At first they were in caves, but gradually they spread over the entire Northern Caucasus and started living in tents made from skins. Their life consisted mainly of hunting, fishing and gathering. People made their tools out of stone and volcanic material, but later bones and horn were also used. Gradually, the techniques for producing these tools improved and their variety increased.

There are few remnants of the Middle Stone Age, or Mesolithic period (10,000–8000 BC). During this period, significant changes took place in the lifestyle of people: hunting became more individual, bows and arrows came into use, and fishing gained in importance.

In the New Stone Age, or Neolithic period (8000–5000 BC) there was a change from hunting, fishing and gathering towards agriculture and cattle breeding. It is also the time when the first pottery was made, but tools were still produced mainly from stone or bones. These tools showed a greater level of workmanship and were often polished or ground.

During the Copper Stone Age, or Eneolithic/Chalcolithic period (5000–3000 BC), most artefacts were still made of stone, volcanic material or bones, but people became gradually familiar with bronze, gold, silver, tin and lead. During this period, the people of the Caucasus expanded their ties with the Near East, built the first fortified settlements, and made revolutionary inventions such as the wheel, canvas and the potter's wheel. The Shulaveri–Shomu Culture is the earliest culture known to the region of present-day Georgia and the Armenian highlands.

Bronze Age

There were tremendous changes in social and economic life, as well as culture, as a result of the improved manufacture of metal utensils and pottery and the appearance of weaving. Along with bows, arrows with bronze tips, swords, daggers and slings were produced. The main activities were cattle breeding and agriculture, but hunting and gathering retained their importance. While some cultures were still matriarchal, males generally became the dominant sex. Widespread archaeological evidence hints that people started settling in the third and second millennia BC. The Bronze Age in the Caucasus can further be subdivided into three distinct periods.

Two archaeological cultures are known from the Early Bronze Age, both of which were in close contact with the civilizations of the Russian mainland and Asia Minor. The tribes of the Maykop Culture, which takes its name from the place where the main archaeological finds were made, occupied the northwestern and central part of the North Caucasus. The tribes of the Kura–Araks Culture lived in the South Caucasus and in the eastern part of the North Caucasus.

Three cultures developed in the Middle Bronze Age. The Trialeti Culture developed from the Kura–Araks Culture, and artefacts have been found in Georgia and Armenia. They show many similarities to those of Iran and Iraq of that time. The North Caucasian Culture had its centre in the pre-Kuban area, and was influenced by both Maykop and Kura–Araks cultures. The Dolmen Culture originated in the Early Bronze Age but spread to the Caucasus and Black Sea region in the Middle Bronze Age. Dolmens are monumental constructions of huge stones that look like tables and were used as burial tombs.

More cultures emerged in the Late Bronze Age: the Koban Culture in the central mountainous part of the North Caucasus and the very similar Colchaian Culture in the Southwest Caucasus, the Kayakent–Kharachoy Culture in the Northeast Caucasus, and the Kobyakov Culture in the region of the Lower Don River. The first tribal unions (Diaukhi, Kolkha, Cimmerians, etc.) were formed during this time.

Early Iron Age

The extraction of iron was already known to the Koban Culture and others in the second half of the second millennium BC, and this metal was used to make expensive tools; however, it was only in the eighth and seventh centuries BC that its use became widespread and gradually replaced bronze and stone. By the fourth century AD, the use of iron was omnipresent in the Caucasus. It is during this time that cities, the first class societies, state formations (such as Caucasian Albania, Kolkhis and Iberia) and unions of warring tribes (Scythians, Sarmatians and Alans) were created.

The first tribal unions and states

Towards the end of the second millennium BC, the political map of the Near East changed completely, and around the same time the first tribal unions and states appeared in the greater Caucasian region. The Hittite Empire and Mitani disintegrated, Egypt and Babylon were weakened and new world powers such as Assyria and Urartu emerged.

From the fifteenth century BC, the tribes of the Armenian plateau came to fear Assyria, and two centuries later the Assyrian King Salmanasar I led campaigns to

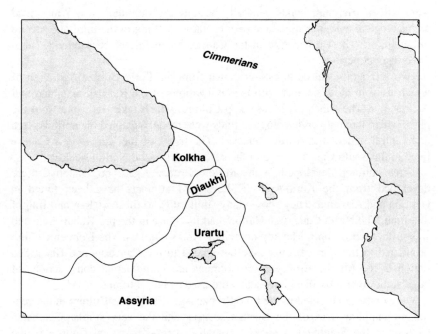

Map 4.1a Urartu and its neighbours around 800 BC

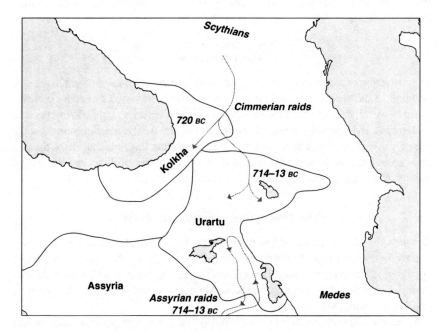

Map 4.1b Urartu and its neighbours around 720 BC

the heart of the region. As a result, the local tribes – not only Urartians, who were closely related to the Hurrians, but also Armenian groups – united, and they appear in Assyrian sources as Nairi and Uruatri. Around 860 BC the state of Biainili (Urartu in Assyrian) was created in the area around Lake Van. This state probably corresponds to the kingdom of Ararat in the Old Testament. It had a centralized government, led by a king, and Tushpa (present-day Van in Turkey) as capital. The people used mainly the Urartian language and the Assyrian cuneiform writing system.

The Cimmerians, a collection of nomad tribes whose origin is unclear,[1] occupied the steppes of southern Russia and the plains north of the Caucasus Mountains from about 1200 BC. They are also credited as the first people to domesticate and use the horse on the battlefield.

Around the twelfth century BC, the first Georgian tribal union arose, in the region around the sources of the Euphrates and Chorokhi rivers. It was known as Diaukhi (Diaeni, Diochi, Diaoki, Diaochi, Taochi or Tao), and during the first centuries of its existence it was able to resist the attacks of the Assyrians.

Kolkha (Kulkha, Kolkhis or Kolkheti), a second Georgian tribal union, emerged around the thirteenth century BC on the Black Sea coast of contemporary Georgia and was often at war with Diaukhi. This country is known as Aia (or Aea) in ancient Greek mythology. It was the home of King Aeetes and Medea, and the land where Jason and the Argonauts sought the Golden Fleece.

Urartu rose and expanded its territory during the rule of the kings Sardur I, Menuas and Argishti I (840–760 BC), and its borders were fortified. Several Assyrian provinces, including Babylon, were invaded and conquered. Urartu and Kolkha frequently clashed with Diaukhi and eventually destroyed the latter in the mid-eighth century BC. The territory was distributed among the two victors, who unleashed another war among themselves, resulting in the loss to Urartu of several provinces. Thus, under the rule of Sardur II, Urartu reached its greatest proportions and stretched from the South Caucasus (including present-day Armenia and parts of Georgia) to Lake Urmia (in Iran) and deep into present-day Turkey. As a result, the Urartians cut Assyria from the trade routes between Asia and the West and enjoyed a monopoly in the region.

From 735 BC onwards, Urartu was severely weakened owing to Assyrian attacks, the threat from the Cimmerians from the north, and internal struggles between the feudal states. The Urartians were able to recover their position and influence over trade routes, but suffered again in 714–13 BC from several raids by both the Assyrians and the Cimmerians. It was only in 585 BC that Urartu was finally annihilated. A large part of the territory was integrated into Media; another part went to the Armenians.

The Scythians were a group of nomadic tribes who initially lived in Central Asia. They were probably not a well-defined ethnic group, but rather a network of ethnically related peoples who migrated westward in the eighth century BC under pressure from Altaic tribes. They came into contact with the Cimmerians, who were probably ethnically related, and in a war which lasted for about 30 years pushed the Cimmerians away from their lands. As a result, the Scythians inhabited the steppes and lowlands north of the main Caucasus range and the lowlands of contemporary Azerbaijan. One branch of the Cimmerians moved west, invaded the Hungarian plain and survived there for a few centuries. Another group moved into the Crimea,[2] where they were known as Taurians. Most of the Cimmerians, however, were driven out of southern Russia, over the Caucasus Mountains and through Kolkha into Urartu. Around 720 BC they devastated Kolkha, whose tribes did not revive and regain their old glory for another century. In 714 BC the Cimmerians assaulted and looted Urartu, which had already been weakened by Assyria, then in 705 BC moved towards Anatolia, having noticed the strength of Assyria. Phrygia (present-day western Turkey) was conquered in 696–5 BC, and the Cimmerians returned to their nomadic existence, this time in western Anatolia. A second group, who had been operating to the west of Lake Van, moved to Anatolia and defeated Lydia (the region around present-day Izmir in Turkey) in 652 BC. From that point on the Cimmerians declined, and a few decades later they were completely defeated by the Assyrians.

Although Media did not include much of what is now defined as the Caucasus –its northern border was almost certainly the Araks River – it should be mentioned since it played an important role in relation to the Armenians and to what would later become Azerbaijan. Media was probably united around 715 BC by Deioces and was most likely more a confederation of various Persian and non-Persian people than a kingdom. At its height it took in parts of Iran, Azerbaijan, Armenia and Kurdistan. Media ruled its immediate neighbours and posed a serious military threat to Assyria. The Assyrians therefore formed an alliance with the Scythians and overwhelmed Media, which was ruled by the Scythians during the second half of the seventh century BC. The Median King Cyaraxes launched an attack on Assyria in 615–14 BC, but was not fully successful. Through the marriage of his granddaughter with the son of the Babylonian king (an enemy of Assyria) a new alliance was formed, and in 612 BC most of Assyria fell. Babylonia took the fertile lands, whereas the highlands, including parts of Armenia, came under Median rule. In the early sixth century BC the alliance with Babylon was weakened, but Media was not considered a threat as Cyrus, king of Anshan, formed a new coalition with other Persian tribes and revolted. Cyrus became king of Persia and Media, which formed the basis of the Achaemenid Empire and the end of Media as a state.

As already mentioned, the Scythians remained in the Caucasus but also moved into Asia Minor, where they allied themselves with the Assyrians to fight the Medes and Cimmerians. However, when Nineveh fell in 612 BC and the power of the Assyrians collapsed in 609 BC, the Scythians lost their allies and came under pressure from the Medes, who finally drove them out of Anatolia and pushed them back over the Caucasian Mountains around 600 BC. The Scythians founded a rich and strong empire between the Carpathians and the Don and exercised a strong influence on the Kuban lowlands and the North Caucasus, where they intermingled with the Meotian and Sindi tribes. Scythia was powerful enough to repel the invasion of the Persian king Darius I in 513 BC. Because of the growing wars with neighbouring tribes in the following decades, the Scythian king Atey

(Atheios) requested the help of Philip II of Macedonia. However, Atey was not willing to accept the condition that Philip would become the new ruler of Scythia. As a result relations worsened, and a war erupted between the two powers in 339 BC in which King Atey died and which initialled the decline of Scythia.

The early Caucasian kingdoms between independence and foreign occupation

The formation of new kingdoms in the South Caucasus

Throughout history, Armenia has been considered as two regions. Greater Armenia (Armenia Maior) was located to the east of the Euphrates and included northeastern Turkey, contemporary Armenia and parts of northern Persia (also called Iranian Azerbaijan). Lesser Armenia (Armenia Minor) was located to the west of the Euphrates. Many other Armenian kingdoms have existed, such as Sophene, Commagene and Cilicia. Although Armenians consider themselves to be direct descendants of the biblical Noah and claim that their first dynasty (Haykazuni) dated from as early as 2492 BC in the region of Lake Van, there is no historical evidence to support this. Modern scholars, on the other hand, think that the Armenians arrived in Asia Minor in the eighth century BC and intermarried with the indigenous peoples in Urartu to form a homogeneous nation two centuries later. After the fall of Urartu, the kingdom of Armenia was ruled by the Orontid (Yerevanduni) dynasty, which was at times independent and at times a Persian satrapy.

In the sixth century BC, the kingdom of Kolkhis/Kolkhida re-emerged in the valley of the Rioni River under the leadership of the Kolkh tribe. The ports of Kolkhis played an important role as they established the link between Europe and the inner region of the Caucasus, mainly for trade. However, Kolkhis had powerful neighbours, and so could not always act unilaterally. Around the same time the various factions of the Sasperi tribe, who lived to the south of Kolkhis, were in the process of unifying as well, but were unable to form their own state.

In the eastern part of Georgia between the sixth and the fourth century BC there was a struggle for leadership among the various confederations which was finally won by the Kartlian tribes from the region of Mtskheta. According to Georgian tradition, the kingdom of Kartli (known as Iberia in Greek and Roman literature) was founded around 300 BC by Parnavaz I. Mtskheta served as capital and Persian institutions were taken as models. The territory of Kartli expanded under Parnavaz I and his successor Saurmag to cover not only the eastern part of Georgia but also the southwestern region of historical Georgia (Tao-Klarjeti, Speri, etc.), which gave it access to the Black Sea. In addition it incorporated a part of western Georgia and had political influence over the rest of Kolkhis, which contributed to closer contacts among the Georgian population and assisted in their unification. Mtskheta was strategically located on international commercial routes to Caucasian Albania, Armenia and Asia Minor. The development of

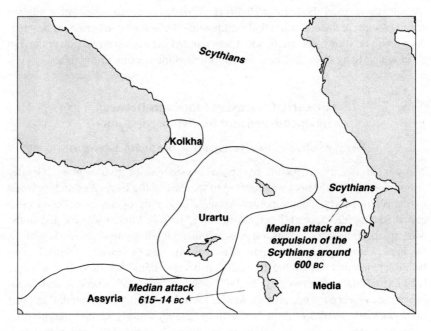

Map 4.2a Urartu and its neighbours around 610 BC, before the fall of Assyria

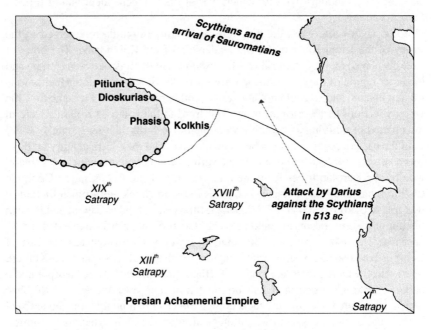

Map 4.2b The Caucasus as part of the Achaemenid Empire, around 500 BC

trade changed the ancient lifestyle of the region: roads, bridges and fortresses were built, and art flourished. However, just as was the case with Kolkhis, Kartli had to repel foreign invaders in order to preserve its independence.

Caucasian Albania was a military democracy and the first state on the territory of the modern-day Republic of Azerbaijan. The Albanian tribes started gathering as a tribal union in the fourth century BC and were headed by a king (military leader) from the second to the first century BC. The exact territory and borders of this state are heavily debated, because they are used as an argument in the conflict between Armenia and Azerbaijan. Its territory remained largely constant during Albania's 1,000 years of existence, and included Kakheti and probably also southern Dagestan. Parts were probably ruled by Armenia during the invasions and wars of the Artashesians. According to the Greek geographer and historian Strabo, Albania was populated by 26 tribes of Turkic, Persian and indigenous Caucasian descent. Among these were the Udins, now the only surviving tribe to have retained its language and religion; the Legi and Geli, the ancestors of some Dagestani nations; and some Turkic-Albanian tribes, such as the Chols and Gargars, who merged with the Azeris.

The leading tribes of the North Caucasus: the Sauromatians, Sarmatians and early Alans

According to Greek historiography, the Sauromatians were descendants of Scythian men and Amazon women. Although the existence of the Amazons, warrior women who removed their right breasts in order to be better fighters, is probably a myth, historic evidence suggests that Sauromatian women fought alongside men in battle. However, legends and theories that Sauromatian society was initially matriarchal have no archaeological support. In reality, the Sauromatians were most likely an amalgamation of Persian nomadic tribes who moved from Central Asia to the steppes on the east of the Don and the northwestern parts of the Caucasus around the sixth century BC. Their neighbours to the south were the Meotians and the Sindi. The Sauromatians lived in good relations with the Scythians, with whom they intermarried and jointly fought against the Persian Achaemenids. The Scythians and Sauromatians were both nomadic and pastoral, and probably ethnically related. Their society was hierarchical, with an aristocratic warrior elite and a large working class together with slaves. When the Scythians began to lose power around the fourth century BC, the Sauromatians gradually took over the leading role in the region and pushed the remaining Scythians westward.

Around the fourth to the third century BC the Sarmatians penetrated the areas previously dominated by the Sauromatians and became the new rulers. They moved further westward and at the beginning of the second century BC brought down Scythian rule. In fact, at its height, Sarmatia was a coalition of several tribes who formed the majority population in the region of the Don River and assimilated a large portion of the population in the plains of the north Caucasus. They were allies of King Mithradates of Pontus, one of the major enemies of the Roman Empire. After Mithradates' defeat by Pompey, the Sarmatians continued their anti-Roman fight in the lower Danube region and later formed an alliance with Germanic tribes.

In the second half of the first century AD, the Alans began to dominate the Sarmatian tribal union and built up a great kingdom between the Don, the Volga and the Caucasus Mountains. But the rule of the Alans would change dramatically in the third and fourth centuries with the arrival of the Goths and the Huns.

The rule of regional superpowers in the South Caucasus

Greek colonies on the Black Sea coast

In the sixth century BC many permanent settlements of Greek colonists – coming mainly from Milete – were established on the Black Sea coast. Examples are Phasis (Poti), Dioskurias (Sukhumi) and Pitiunt (Bichvinta or Pitsunda). These Greek settlers set up trade relations with the local population, but their culture influenced only the higher classes. A genuine Hellenization started in the fourth century BC, at the time of Alexander of Macedonia. It was also during that time that the commercial role of the Caucasus became much stronger. Gradually, the Greek cities became influenced culturally by the local ethnic groups, and as a result their character changed in the third and second centuries BC.

The Achaemenid Persian Empire (550–330 BC)

In 550 BC, Cyrus the Great became the ruler of the Persians and Medes. He is mentioned in the Old Testament, for he set the Jews free after the Babylonian exile and gave them back the ornaments that had been stolen from the Temple of Jerusalem. Cyrus aimed to set up a large empire and succeeded in a short period of time. He conquered huge parts of Central Asia, campaigned in India and, more importantly, in 539 BC captured Babylonia, the leading power of that time. Cyrus developed a system of satrapies, administrative provinces, which were ruled by a satrap appointed by the central government. After his death in 530 BC, his successors further expanded the empire and optimized the system of satrapies. Probably the best-known Achaemenid ruler was Darius, whose defeat by the Athenians at Marathon has become legendary. There were many rebellions (Egypt, but also the proto-Georgian tribes) during the reign of Darius II in the last quarter of the fifth century BC, and the situation was further aggravated in the fourth century BC when Egypt reclaimed independence and many other satraps, including Orontes of Armenia, tried to increase their own power and wealth.

The Achaemenids dominated most of the South Caucasus, but their grip remained strong only until the middle of the fifth century BC. The Armenian king Tigran I had allied himself with Cyrus the Great and helped him to conquer the Medes, but the alliance did not hold very long and soon the Armenians themselves were conquered and made up the thirteenth satrapy. The Sasperi (a Georgian tribe in the southwest of Kolkhis) were part of the eighteenth satrapy, and other proto-Georgian tribes, such as the Mushki, Tibal and Mares, formed the nineteenth satrapy. The kingdom of Kolkhis was an autonomous vassal state which for a few decades paid tribute to the Achaemenids but freed itself from Achaemenid control before the end of the fifth century BC. The Albanian tribes, which were in the process of forming a state, made only occasional contact with the Achaemenid Empire, and during the last decades of its existence they fought as mercenaries in the Persian army. The other Georgian tribes who would later make up the kingdom of Kartli had also freed themselves from Achaemenid rule by that time. The high mountains of the Caucasus formed a natural border, and so the North Caucasus never fell under Achaemenid control.

Macedonian and Seleucid rule

Alexander the Great of Macedonia started his first campaigns in Asia Minor in the 330s BC and was able to conquer the entire region in only a few years. In 330 BC he took over the entire Achaemenid Empire. The Armenian lands became independent, but its rulers formally recognized the power of Alexander, even though he never visited the region himself. The Persian commander Atropates was appointed satrap of the north of Persia (the region which now is often referred to as South Azerbaijan), where he would later found an independent kingdom: Media Atropatena.

After Alexander's death in 323 BC his empire was divided into three. The Asian portions of his realm became part of the Seleucid Empire, which was in fact a continuation of the Achaemenid Empire. In the following years semi-independent Armenian kingdoms arose, and in 332–1 BC Lesser Armenia became an independent Armenian kingdom. Armenia proper, and Sophene, which later split from Armenia, were special satraps in the Seleucid Empire but had their own hereditary dynasty. Initially only certain parts of Armenia came under Seleucid rule, but by the end of the third century BC almost all Armenian lands were under their authority. However, the Seleucid Empire did not exercise much authority over the rest of the Caucasus. The strength and unity of Kolkhis broke during the third century BC and leaders of the several regions ruled quite independently. Iberia, which had actually grown more powerful, added some of these Kolkhian territories but also exerted a strong influence over those territories it did not incorporate.

Artashes I the Great led the Armenian uprising against the Seleucids after the latter had been defeated by the Romans in 190 BC. He declared the independence of Great Armenia in 189 BC and founded the Artashesian (Artaxiad) dynasty, which would rule the state until 62 AD. King Zarekh of Sophene also saw the chance to declare himself an independent king. Both kingdoms, but especially Greater Armenia, enlarged their territory at the expense of neighbouring peoples, and Artashes moved the capital from Armavir to the newly built city of Artashat, located on a commercial route. Around 165 BC the Artaxiad ruler tried in vain to

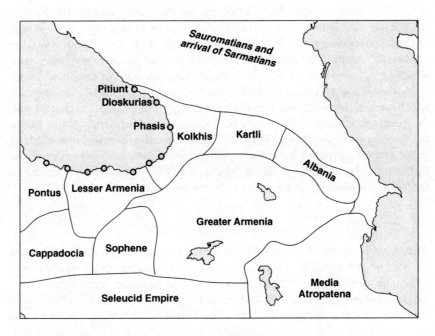

Map 4.3a The early Caucasian kingdoms around 300 BC

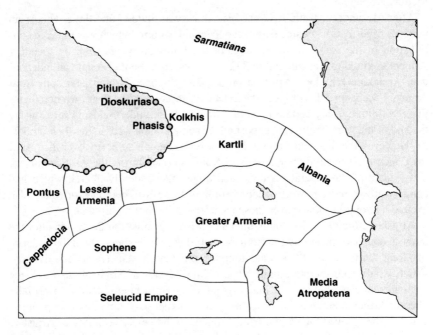

Map 4.3b The early Caucasian kingdoms around 180 BC

suppress the king of Sophene. Tigran II the Great was ruler of Armenia from 95 to 56 BC: he is seen as the most glorious and successful of all Armenian kings and takes credit for uniting Armenia and bringing its empire to its peak. He expanded his territory by annexing Sophene, part of Armenia Minor, Media Atropatena, Media, and parts of Iberia and Albania, and concluded a military and political union with Mithradates VI of Pontus.

The decline of the Seleucids gave rise to a new enemy – the Parthian kingdom, which gradually took over the eastern provinces of the Seleucid Empire in the third century BC. While it showed great interest in the Caucasus, with the exception of a partial success in Armenia, it was not able to make much headway.

Pontus, Rome and Parthia struggle for power in the Caucasus

The kingdom of Pontus originated in the fourth century BC on the southern coast of the Black Sea and soon took in large parts of northeastern Anatolia and Cappadocia. In 104–3 BC Mithradates VI Euraptor annexed Kolkhis to his kingdom and made it one of his provinces. Not much later, parts of Lesser Armenia were included as well. Mithradates and Tigran II the Great of Armenia had much in common. Both wanted to expand their kingdoms, but understood it would be better to cooperate with than to hinder each other. Mithradates therefore concentrated on Asia Minor, the Black Sea coast and Greece, whereas Tigran focused on Parthia, Syria and adjacent countries. In order to strengthen their political and military union, Tigran married the daughter of Mithradates, and this, together with the rapid expansion of the two kingdoms, temporarily ended the advances of Rome and Parthia.

By the end of the second century BC the Roman Empire was in control of a large part of Asia Minor, but it did not show a real interest in what was further to the east until the Roman senate found the expansion policy of Mithradates VI unacceptable. From 89 BC onwards, Pontus and the Roman Empire were in an almost constant state of war with each other. Tigran stayed out of the conflict because he was marching off to confront the Parthians. In 85 BC the Parthians were forced to sign a peace treaty and to hand over a considerable part of their territory to Tigran. As a result of all these conquests, Armenia extended from the Caspian Sea and Kura to the Mediterranean Sea. Tigran built a new capital, Tigranakert, in the region of what is now Diyarbakir in Turkey. In 70 BC the Roman general Lucullus occupied all of Mithradates' territories to the west of the Euphrates, and the defeated Pontian king fled to Armenia to receive protection from his son-in-law Tigran. Tigran refused to extradite Mithradates, and as a result in 69 BC the Romans attacked Armenia, successfully. One year later they went as far as modern Yerevan, but Lucullus had to return to Rome when his troops mutinied. Mithradates reconquered his own land with an army given by Tigran.

In 66 BC Pompey succeeded Lucullus and continued the war against Mithradates, allying himself with the Parthians. While Pompey fought against Pontus, Parthia, aided by Tigran's son – also named Tigran – who wanted to take over from his father as soon as possible, engaged in a war against Armenia.

It did not take long before both Mithradates and Tigran the Great were forced to flee. Mithradates escaped to Kolkhis and travelled to the last of his remaining provinces, the Crimea, where he died three years later. First, Pompey moved deep into Armenia, but before he had the chance to attack the capital King Tigran humbly asked for peace. The Armenian king was forced to pay indemnity and recognize his own son as the king of Sophene – i.e. only a smaller portion of the huge Armenian kingdom. Tigran the younger, who wanted to rule over all Armenia, was not satisfied and carried out secret intrigues, which led to his detention by the Romans. In 65 BC Pompey pursued Mithradates as far as Kolkhis, and once there the Roman general desired to see the places which were famous from Greek mythology. He moved eastward, mainly to gain knowledge of the region and show the might of the Romans. Iberia and Albania put up fierce resistance but were subdued. The entire South Caucasus became part of the Roman Empire, although the local rulers still governed quite independently, especially in the distant and mountainous regions. Rome did not necessarily intend to occupy and control the region because it understood the great cultural differences and that it would probably not succeed. It therefore preferred to install puppet regimes, as in other border regions of the empire. Roman garrisons were present only in the fortified coastal cities, such as Phasis (modern-day Poti) or Sevastopol (the former Greek city of Dioskurias, modern-day Sukhumi). In general, Roman dominion was a time of decay for Kolkhis. There was a lack of political unity and the country was divided into tribal principalities, some of which started to grow more powerful. Kartli and Albania became allies of Rome, which helped the empire keep Armenia in a state of subjugation and to manage the mountain passes whence from time to time nomad tribes launched attacks on the South Caucasus and bordering regions of the Near East.

The Armenian king Artavazd II, who fought for independence from Rome, succeeded in 53 BC with the help of the Parthians, who had turned from enemies into allies. However, with the weakening of Parthia, Armenia was soon forced to recognize Roman sovereignty. Towards the end of the first century BC Parthia started to compete with Rome once more for influence in Armenia and aspired to turn Armenia into its own dependent province. Most of the Armenian aristocracy leaned towards Parthia because of their similar social system, the relatively weak centralized power in Parthia, cultural ties, and mixed marriages. In the early 50s AD Tiridat, from the Parthian Arshakid royal family, gained a foothold in Armenia and a large-scale clash between Rome and Parthia ensued. The two empires eventually reached a compromise which brought Armenia under double dependence: nominally on Rome and de facto on Parthia. In AD 66 the Roman emperor Nero crowned Tiridat I of Parthia – who had been ruling the country since AD 62 – as king of Armenia, but Tiridat had to declare himself dependent on Rome. This was the start of the Arshakid (Arshakuni) dynasty in semi-independent Armenia, which would last until the year 428. Tiridat moved the capital back from Tigranakert to Artashat, which was rebuilt with the help of Nero. Under Tiridat,

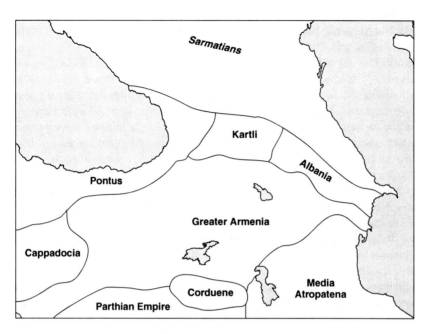

Map 4.4a The Caucasian kingdoms around 85 BC, before the arrival of the Romans

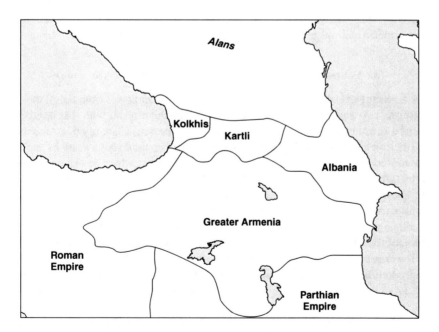

Map 4.4b The Caucasus under Roman and Parthian influence, around AD 220

Armenia was divided into 120 prefectures, each ruled by a *nakharar* (princely lord). But the peace between Rome and Parthia did not last long, and in 114 they clashed again and Armenia was turned into a Roman province.

Kartli (Iberia) did not depend as much on Rome as Kolkhis did, and its king became a 'Friend and Ally of the Roman people'. Initially this dependence was burdensome, but later, taking advantage of the civil wars after the death of Caesar, the Iberians and Albanians revolted against Rome. The Romans were victorious over the Iberian king Farnabas in 36 BC, but gradually the military union between the two countries turned into one based on voluntary agreement and mutual interests. As a result of this union, the Iberian rulers managed to strengthen their country and extend their borders. King Parsman II openly opposed Rome, and in AD 134 he organized an attack of the Alans against the Roman and Parthian vassal states Albania, Media, Armenia and Cappadocia. The Roman emperor Adrianus tried to improve relations, but Parsman refused. Kartli grew even more independent, but Rome tried to maintain the union by sending valuable gifts. Under Antoninus Pius, in the middle of the second century, the Roman influence over Kartli regained strength and Parsman II visited Rome, where he was allowed the rare honour of offering a sacrifice at the capitol, and his statue was erected on the Mars Field. In 189, the Farnabazid dynasty came to an end and was replaced by a pro-Roman Arshakid one, which would rule until 284.

Albania, from its side, began to lean towards Parthia and less to Rome. In the second half of the first century AD (i.e. around the same time that Tiridat ascended the Armenian throne) the Parthian-originated Arshakid dynasty was established and ruled, with a few small breaks, until 510. Albania remained a sovereign state for much longer than Armenia and was not conquered in the early second century AD by the Romans.

The Sassanid and Roman/Byzantine empires struggle for power

The Sassanid state was founded in AD 224, and took over power from the Arshakid Parthians two years later. It replaced the weak Parthian realm with a strong centralized state and unsuccessfully tried to impose Zoroastrianism upon its vassals.

The Roman Empire started to disintegrate in the late third century and its capital was moved from Rome to the old Greek city of Byzantium, which was later renamed Constantinople (modern-day Istanbul). This Greek-speaking Roman Empire is better known in history as the Byzantine Empire.[3] In 313 the Roman emperor Constantine brought an end to the persecutions of Christians and allowed freedom of religion. It was also during those years that Christianity spread among the population of the Caucasus and became the official religion in Armenia and Kartli.

Towards the third century AD the Kolkh tribe lost its power, and the new leading princedom in western Georgia was Egrisi.[4] This kingdom of Egrisi is also known as Lazika in Greek and Roman literature. In the early third century Roman control over the region collapsed as a result of the resistance of the local population, supported by the 'Barbarians' from the north and with help from Sassanid Persia. Still, it did not take too long before the Byzantine Empire regained relative influence over Lazika. In the fourth century, neighbouring tribes (e.g. Apsils, Abasgs, Svans) were subordinated to the Laz king, and soon Lazika controlled all of western Georgia. Lazika in its turn was under the influence of Byzantium and served as an important buffer between the Sassanid and Byzantine empires. The kingdom of Lazika remained a strategic vassal of the latter throughout its existence until the seventh century, with only short periods of Sassanid rule. Later Lazika would be transformed into Abkhazia, a princedom under Byzantine authority.

Kartli apparently became part of the Sassanid state during the reign of Shapur I (240–70), who listed it as one of the lands that paid him tribute. The adoption of Christianity in Kartli in the fourth century had the important consequence of strengthening the union with Rome against the Persians. Still, this union with a weakening Rome could not defend Kartli, and in AD 368 Shapur II invaded Kartli, deposed king Saurmag and put his own relative Varaz-Bakur on the throne. But Saurmag received the support of Rome, and soon Varaz-Bakur was forced into an agreement. The left bank of the Kura and the right bank of the Aragvi were given to Saurmag, while the rest of Kartli was ruled by the Persian protégé. This diarchy did not last very long, and from the second quarter of the fifth century Kartli was a Sassanid vassal state, ruled by the Kartlian king assisted by a *pitiakhsh*, a Persian deputy. The kings kept their seat in Mtskheta, whereas the *pitiakhshs* chose Tbilisi as their residence. In the second half of the fifth century Tbilisi was recognized as the second capital and gradually superseded Mtskheta.

Albania fell under the nominal domination of the Sassanids too, though it retained some autonomy, and its level of development was not as high as that of neighbouring Armenia or Kartli. The Sassanids were interested in Albania because it was the key to controlling the mountain passes of the main Caucasus range and therefore to repelling any attacks by the nomads of the Northern Caucasus (Alans, Huns, etc.). These nomads were a real threat because of their potential alliance with Rome, and thus the Sassanids often hired Albanians to serve in their army. Under Parthian and Sassanid influence, Zoroastrianism spread in Albania; because of the country's geographical proximity to Persia and the latter's stronger political influence, the religion was stronger there than in any other part of the Caucasus. Nevertheless, in the fourth century the Albanian Church was established and headed by an autocephalous catholicos. Gradually, many of the nomad Turkic tribes coming from Central Asia and Siberia intermingled with the Albanians, and in 450–51 the Albanians took an active part in the revolt against the Sassanids. This evoked a more aggressive Sassanid policy, and for two lengthy periods of time royal power was abolished and replaced by a governor (463–88 and 510–629). Caucasian Albania continued its struggle and fully restored independence in 629. From then onwards it was ruled by the Mikhranid dynasty, though it soon had to recognize Arab suzerainty.

The Armenian Arshakid dynasty was an adversary of the Sassanids and turned for assistance to Rome, which had become much weaker by the end of the second century. The Romans suffered one defeat after the other against the Sassanids, and the Armenian king was killed and replaced by a more pro-Sassanid Arshakid. A few decades later, Tiridat III ascended the throne with the help of the Roman emperor. The Sassanids lost a major war against Rome and Armenia in 298, and a 40-year peace agreement was concluded in which Armenia and Iberia were recognized as Roman protectorates. In the fourth century the new aristocracy of *nakharars* took clear shape, but they were less and less willing to pay homage to the king. The Christian Church not only strengthened Armenia's position vis-à-vis the Zoroastrian Sassanids, it also became a good ally of the king when it came to controlling the *nakharars*, who exhibited growing power such that the king could not make any major decisions without the consent of their council. When the fighting between Rome and Persia resumed after the end of the 40-year peace treaty, the king continued his struggle against the *nakharars* under the pretext of the Persian threat. This unsuccessful fight against feudal division led to the temporary capture of Armenia by the Persians. Finally, in AD 387, Armenia was divided after close to five centuries of unity: Byzantium took the western part and Persia the eastern part. The Arshakids were vassals in the Persian part until 428, after which the *nakharars* finally came to power. In the western part, the cultural influence of Byzantium was much stronger than the political, especially through the Christian link. Albania, Kartli and Lazika also approached the Byzantine Empire in order to seek support against the Sassanids, who tried to impose their rule and also Zoroastrianism. This religious struggle led in 451 to the Battle of Avarayr, where the Sassanids defeated the Armenians, who had received support from other Christian Caucasians. Nevertheless, the Sassanids were unable either to assimilate the Armenians or to force Zoroastrianism on the other nations. A large number of Persian–Byzantine wars took place in the period 420–560 and led to a new demarcation between the two empires in 561, but military confrontations did not end until the early seventh century.

The great migration of people

In the third century AD, a mass migration from Middle Asia and Siberia to the west started when one wave of nomads was followed by another. Many of these streams passed through the North Caucasus and left their traces, but they also affected the region south of the Greater Caucasus. Clearly, the great migration of people had a huge impact on the ethnogenesis of the nations in the region.

In the third century AD the Goths, who were forced to move westward under pressure of the Huns, invaded the Sarmatian lands and took over part of their culture, including the techniques of warfare with horses and living in wagons. Some Sarmatian tribes migrated to Central Europe, where they were rapidly swamped by Germanic tribes, whereas others joined the Gothic forces. The Alans, on the other hand, were able to resist the Goths. South of the main Caucasus range, Kolkhis was a victim of Gothic incursions in 253.

When the Huns arrived in the region in the middle of the fourth century, some Alans were assimilated, others escaped to the west – even as far as North Africa –and yet another smaller group settled in the foothills of the Northern Caucasus.

The Savirs (Sabirs), who were possibly of Hunnic origin, lived in the steppes between the Black Sea, the Caspian Sea and the Caucasus Mountains and allied

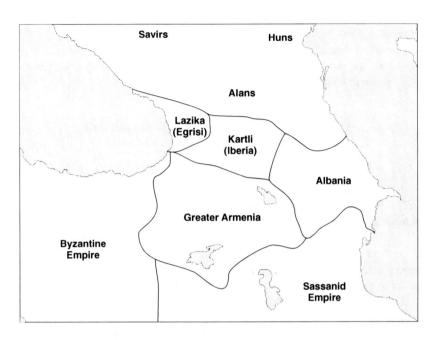

Map 4.5a The political situation in the Caucasus in AD 387

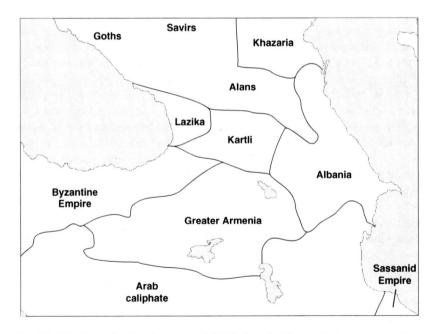

Map 4.5b The Caucasian kingdoms around 650, before the Khazar–Arab power struggle

themselves with Sassanid Persia in the fight against Byzantium. In the first half of the sixth century, they launched several attacks on the South Caucasus; later they switched their allegiance to Byzantium and in 552 invaded Albania. At the end of the 550s the Avars (not to be confused with the modern-day Avars) arrived in the Northern Caucasus and destroyed the Savirs.

Byzantium, Khazaria and the Arab caliphate struggle for power in the Caucasus

The Arab expansion

The Arabs started their expansion soon after the death of the prophet Mohammed in 632. One year later they launched their war against Persia, which was itself in a state of civil war, and in 637 the Sassanid capital was captured.

In 640 the Arabs invaded the South Caucasus and took the Armenian capital Dvin, but they left soon afterwards, taking valuable loot with them. Two years later they conquered all of northern Persia and went as far north as Derbent. The Persian commander in Derbent actually invited the Arabs to help deal with their enemies from the north. Tbilisi was taken in 645, but the Arabs could not conquer Lazika and the mountainous provinces. The Arabs took several attempts to subdue the Armenians and their control started formally in 645. Initially, the Albanian prince Jevanshir had been an ally of his former enemies, the Sassanids, but Persia had become too weak through its wars with Albania and Byzantium. Albania was subjugated and included in the Arab caliphate only after half a century of war (i.e. in 705). From that time the Arabs began referring to the region between the Kura and the Araks as Arran. Gradually the region of Atropatena, the lands south of the Araks, became known as Azerbaijan. The Arabs also ruled for a long time over certain mountainous parts of contemporary Dagestan, such as the region inhabited by the Avars, Dido and Tsez. As a result, at the beginning of the eighth century, the Arabs controlled part of the Northeastern Caucasus and the entire South Caucasus, with the exception of Lazika, which was still under the Byzantines. In general, the domination of the Arabs was commercial rather than political and had a direct effect only on the central regions, where they set up trade activities. The Armenian provinces were granted restricted autonomy, whereas the Iberian and Albanian kingdoms were abolished and reorganized as emirates. In the following years there were continual struggles between the Caucasian leaders and the Arab caliphate. At first the Arabs did not try to spread Islam, but this changed towards the end of the seventh century. The early Islamization, however, proved successful only in Albania and the region of Derbent.

The formation of the Khazar state and the continual struggle with the Arab caliphate

The Khazars, a semi-nomadic Turkic people, arrived in the steppes north of the Caucasus Mountains at the end of the sixth century. Around 650 a Khazar state, led by the Ashina tribe, was formed in the northern Caucasus along the Caspian Sea, and in the following years expanded through the seizure of land belonging to the Bulgars, Magyars, Savirs, etc. Many others, including Caucasian Albania, were forced to pay tribute to the Khazars. By the early eighth century Khazaria stretched from the Dnepr to the Volga in the north to the Caucasus Mountains in the south. It lay on the Silk Road and received most of its income from trade. Semender, in contemporary Dagestan, was the first capital, but after being continually attacked by the Arabs the capital was moved north to Itil in the Volga delta.

The Khazars were powerful allies of the Byzantine Empire, and one Khazar princess even became empress in Constantinople. The Khazars and the Byzantines fought side by side first against the Sassanids and later against the Arabs. In 642 the Arabs arrived in Derbent at the borders of Khazaria, and the following century marked a constant struggle for control over the Caucasus. Between 642 and 737 the Khazars and the Arabs constantly invaded each other's territories. As a result Albania was at times under Khazarian rule and at others part of the Arab caliphate. A sixteen-year Arab–Khazar war broke out in 721 when the Khazars invaded Armenia, but they soon withdrew north of the Caucasus Mountains when they heard of a huge army moving deep into Khazaria. The Arabs indeed captured many Khazarian cities, but retreated to Armenia for the winter. In the following years there were sustained attacks and counter-attacks, with Armenia being the principal battle scene. In 737 peace negotiations were conducted, but at the same time Mervan, the Arab commander, sent troops into Khazaria. The Arabs won a swift victory and the Khazar khagan (emperor) ostensibly converted to Islam. However, the Arabs did not make use of their victory to occupy Khazaria but left the Northern Caucasus, and Khazaria continued to exist.

In the beginning, Khazaria was ruled by a khagan who came from the Ashina clan. After their defeat by the Arabs a dual power structure was set up: the khagan held a representative function, whereas the beg, who was chosen on the basis of proven success on the battlefield, held the real power.

Full religious freedom existed in Khazaria. Originally, most of the population practised traditional Turkic Tengri shamanism, influenced by Confucian ideas from China, but there were large Jewish communities as well. In 730, in the middle of the war with the Arabs, the Khazar khagan Bulan converted to Judaism. The reason for this was probably that the Khazar Empire wanted to remain neutral vis-à-vis the two other empires: on one side there were the Arabs who had forced Islam on the conquered nations and on the other side were the Christian Byzantines. Initially, it was only the upper classes who converted, but it seems that by 950 Judaism had found its way among all classes of society. With the invasions of the Russians, Cumans and Mongols in the following centuries, the Khazars disappeared as a distinct ethnic group.

The fall of Arab authority and the restoration of Byzantine influence

As previously mentioned, the Caucasian states struggled continually with the Arab caliphate and successfully used the hostilities between the Arab and Byzantine superpowers for this purpose. Once the Arabs had lost their authority in the region, Albania split into several principalities. Lazika separated from the Byzantine Empire and was reorganized as the kingdom of Abkhazia in 799. Through the rule of the Arabs, the unity of Iberia had been broken into small separate kingdoms. In 830 Ashot Bagrationi led several military attacks against the Arabs in the south of Iberia and was appointed curopalatus (governor-general) by the Byzantine emperor. By 977 the Bagrationi dynasty – which would remain in power for more than 800 years – ruled over most of Iberia with the exception of the region around Tbilisi, which remained an emirate under Arab control until around 1050. In 1008, all Georgian principalities, in both eastern and western Georgia, were united into a single kingdom. Gradually there emerged a number of Byzantine–Georgian conflicts which ended in 1051 to the advantage of the Georgians.

The Bagratunis, another branch of the Bagrations, re-established Armenian independence in 885, subjugated other Armenian noble families in the following years, and moved the capital to Ani. Their dynasty broke up into several branches in the tenth century, and all of them were conquered by the Byzantines and Seljuks by 1064. As a result, at the end of the tenth century the only areas remaining under Arab control were Shirvan (the northern part of Arran) and the region around Tbilisi. Shirvan, ruled by a shirvanshah, was basically a Persianized dynasty of Arabic origin that lasted from 861 until 1538 and covered a large part of Arran.

The growth of the Kievan Rus and the fall of Khazaria

Towards the end of the ninth century the Kievan Rus emerged to the north of Khazaria. Initially, these two states fought together against the Muslim Arabs, and the Kievan Rus received access to the Caspian Sea. However, once the Kievan Rus became stronger it engaged in war against Khazaria, and in the early tenth century the Khazar–Byzantine alliance began to collapse. With the weakening of Khazaria, the Kievan Rus took over most of the Khazar lands, and Russian settlements arose in the region of the Don River and in the lower reaches of the Kuban. In 965 Prince Svyatoslav conquered the Khazar fortress of Sarkel and built the Russian city of Belaya Vezha, which became a commercial centre for trade between the Caucasus and the Near East. A few years later Itil, the capital, was destroyed. At about the same time the Russian principality of Tmutarakan developed on the Taman peninsula, where traders often gathered at trade fairs. The Kievan Rus and Byzantium joined forces to attack the Khazars, who were eventually fully subdued in 1016.

Thus, the first contacts between Russia and the Caucasus took place as early as the tenth century. The lowlands of the North Caucasus have a lot in common with the south Russian steppes, which contributed to the development of relations between the populations of southern Russia and those of the North Caucasus. Nevertheless, relations were not completely friendly, as nomads often raided the Russian villages and Russians marched into the steppes. Still, by marrying Ossetian, Abkhaz, Georgian and other Caucasian women, the Russian princes attempted to become closer to the Caucasian nations. The Mongol–Tatar invasions brought an end to the bonds of friendship and peace between the Russians and Caucasians and the Russian settlements on the border of the Pre-Caucasus disappeared. It would take more than 200 years before those relations could be re-established.

Alania

The Alans dominated political life in the North Caucasus from the second half of the first century AD. The arrival of the Goths, Huns and other (semi-)nomad tribes led to a loss of power, but Alania did not cease to exist. The Alans in the eastern part of the North Caucasus enjoyed friendly relations with Sassanid Persia, and in the middle of the sixth century these Alans fought alongside the Sassanid forces against Egrisi and Kartli. The Alans in the western part of the North Caucasus were on good terms with Byzantium, but later they became vassals of Khazaria and engaged in several wars against the Arabs. In the early tenth century the Alans gained independence from Khazaria and until the arrival of the Mongols had their own sovereign state. They accepted Christianity but also developed a feudal society. The period from the tenth to the twelfth century was a golden age for Alania.

Pechenegs and Cumans

At the time of this struggle for power between Byzantium, the Arabs and Khazaria the great migration of peoples was still ongoing, and several Turkic tribes moved from Middle Asia to the west. By 870 the Pechenegs (also known as Patzinaks) occupied the steppes of contemporary southern Russia and Ukraine. The weakened position of Khazaria facilitated the strengthening of these semi-nomads. The Pechenegs were constantly engaged in wars with their neighbours, including Kievan Rus, the Byzantine Empire and Khazaria, but were annihilated at the end of the eleventh century.

In the eleventh century, at the end of the great migration, the Cumans (known as Polovtsy in Russian or as Kipchaks in Turkic) invaded the steppes of southern Russia and launched attacks on the Byzantine Empire, the Kievan Rus and the remains of the Pechenegs. The Cuman confederation, which included other ethnic groups, set up an empire from the Dnepr to the Aral Sea. Most of the North Caucasus was part of this confederation of khanates, and the Cumans also meddled in the political life of the South Caucasus. They defeated the Kievan Rus in the twelfth century, but were slain themselves in 1238 by the Mongols. Most Cumans fled to Eastern Europe, and the ones who remained formed part of the Golden Horde.

Seljuk domination over the South Caucasus

In the middle of the tenth century, the Seljuk house of the Oghuz Turks moved from the north of the Aral Sea to Persia, where they adopted the Persian language and

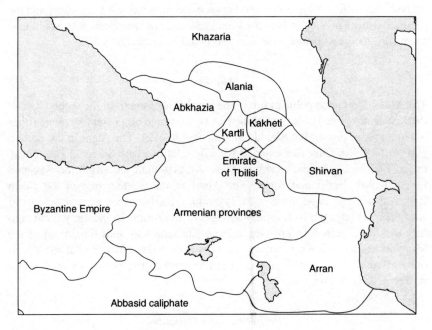

Map 4.6a The new Caucasian kingdoms, around 950, before the fall of Khazaria

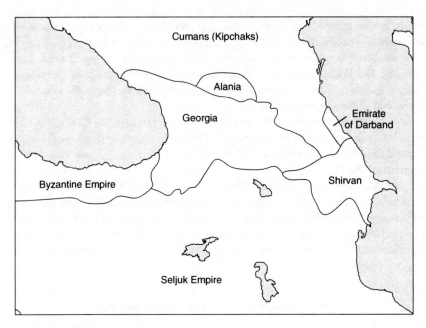

Map 4.6b Unified Georgia, wedged between the Cumans, the Seljuks and the Byzantine Empire in 1122

culture. The Seljuks were involved in a power struggle in the region and gradually built up their own state: by 1040 they possessed a huge nomadic empire, including most of Central Asia and Persia. Under Sultan Mehmed Alp Arslan, the Seljuks aimed to invade and crush the Byzantine Empire. Alp Arslan first moved through the South Caucasus, which he added to his empire in 1064–8. The Caucasian states were able to retain a high degree of autonomy but had to pay annual tribute to the Sultan. The Byzantine Empire was invaded several times from 1068 onwards, and its defeat in 1071 at the Battle of Manzikert meant that the Turks had the upper hand in the Middle East. In 1077 the Seljuk Empire split, and the (Seljuk) sultanate of Rum thereafter exercised nominal control over the South Caucasus.

In 1089 the 16-year-old David IV took over the throne of Georgia and inherited a country that had been devastated by Seljuk invasions, internal wars and earthquakes. He managed to centralize the state administration, form a new army and gather feudal lords loyal to him. King David gradually expelled the Seljuk Turks from Kartli, and he also refused to pay tribute to them. These actions encouraged the Georgians, and in the following years more and more territory and cities were freed from Seljuk rule. In 1118–20 David resettled 40,000 Kipchak families from the North Caucasus in Georgia, each of these families being required to provide one warrior and a horse. These easily integrating Kipchaks also served to revive the weak economy. In 1120–21 Georgian troops were able to take control of a considerable amount of territory in present-day Azerbaijan and Georgia. The decisive victory against the Seljuks took place at the Battle of Didgori in 1121, and one year later Tbilisi was finally taken, after having been under Seljuk rule for half a century. David IV also developed the social and cultural life of his people and is hence better known as David the Builder (David Aghmashenebeli).

Around 1080, Armenians founded the kingdom of Cilicia in the Mediterranean coastal region in the southeast of contemporary Turkey. It became a strong supporter of the European crusaders and, in order to resist the Seljuks, an ally of the Mongols. The kingdom ceased to exist in 1375 after the Egyptian Mamluks invaded the region.

In 1136, when the power of the Seljuk Empire was already considerably weakened, the sultan appointed an *atabek* to rule over the remainder of the South Caucasus and northern Persia. Gradually these *atabeks* turned against the Seljuks and also fought against the Georgians, who were expanding their kingdom. This *atabek* state collapsed in 1225, with the Mongol conquest of the region.

The golden age of feudal Georgia (1122–1220)

David the Builder's policy continued under the reign of his son Demetre I and grandson Giorgi III. The Georgian kingdom expanded and several Armenian cities were incorporated. This expansion went hand in hand with certain political marriages: Giorgi III married the daughter of the king of Alania, his sisters married the sultan of Rum and the prince of Kiev, and his daughters married the son of the Byzantine emperor and the prince of Suzdal.

Tamar, a daughter of Giorgi III, was the first female to become queen. She married Prince Yuriy Bogolyubskiy from Suzdal in 1185, but that marriage broke down after two years. Bogolyubskiy led a rebellion of western Georgian feudal lords against his former wife in 1191, but was crushed. In 1189, two years after her divorce, Tamar married again, this time the Ossetian prince David Soslan. During this period the Seljuk Turks launched numerous attacks on Georgia, but the Georgian forces won two major battles, in Shamkhor (1195) and Basiani (1203). In 1204 Tamar invaded Trebizond (contemporary Trabzon in Turkey) and founded the kingdom of Trebizond, which became a vassal of Georgia.

During the reign of Tamar, who is a saint in the Georgian Orthodox Church, Georgian power reached its zenith. Georgia not only embraced a huge part of the land between the Black Sea and the Caspian Sea – including the territories of modern-day Armenia, Azerbaijan, the Northern Caucasus, the north of Persia and northeastern parts of Turkey – it also made other neighbouring states its vassals. This was also a golden period in terms of culture, and during the reign of Tamar Shota Rustaveli wrote his famous poem *The Knight in the Panther's Skin*.

King Giorgi IV Lasha succeeded his mother after her death in 1213, and Georgia became the major political and economic feudal monarchy in Asia Minor and the Caucasus. This golden age was brought to an end by the Mongol invasion of 1220. Giorgi IV Lasha died in 1223 and was succeeded by his sister Rusudan.

In the twelfth and thirteenth century, some of the Armenian nobility joined the Georgians and were able to take back a number of Armenian cities, such as Kars, Ani and Dvin, particularly under the reign of Giorgi III and Tamar.

The Caucasus under the Mongol-Tatars

The first invasions

In the early years of the thirteenth century, Temüjin Borjigin, better known as Genghiz Khan, united disparate nomad tribes in Mongolia and captured northeastern China and Central Asia. In the following years he set up one of the largest empires history would ever know. The Mongol Empire was initially one large realm, but gradually it fractured: the Golden Horde (Altyn Orda) was founded in 1243 by Batu Khan, the Hülegü Ulus or Il-Khanid state was formed in 1256, the Chagatai Ulus separated in 1266 and the remainder became known as the Yuan dynasty.

In 1220 Genghiz Khan sent out Jebe and Subedei, two of his best generals, together with 20,000 cavalry, to carry out a reconnaissance mission to study the roads to the west. They also went in pursuit of the shah of Khwarazm, who had fled from Central Asia and raided the Caucasus, but would die soon after in obscurity. The Mongols entered Armenia from the southeast by crossing the Araks, moved towards the north and invaded and looted Georgia in January 1221, and then moved through the mountains to the plains of Dagestan and Chechnya. In 1222 they arrived in Alania. Initially, the Alans and the Cumans had formed a military union, but the Cumans broke it at the request of the Mongols. The Alans

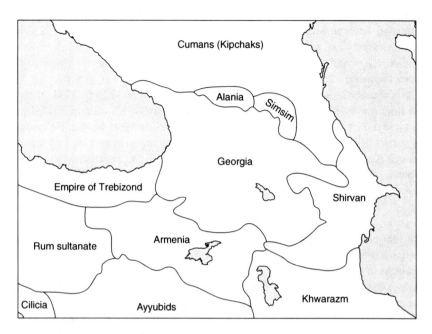

Map 4.7a The golden age of Georgia, around 1200

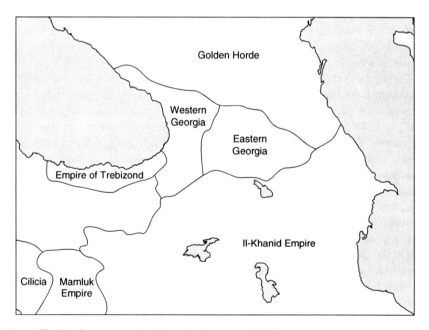

Map 4.7b The Caucasus under Mongol rule, around 1300

were soon defeated, but the Mongols started hunting the Cumans. Although the latter had become allies of the Kievan Rus, both were defeated in 1223. No administration was set up yet, but all this time Mongol administrators drew detailed maps and set up an intelligence network, which was to help with the future inclusion of the region into the empire.

A new assault on the South Caucasus took place from 1225 to 1231, though this time not by Mongols. Jalal ad-din, the new shah of Khwarazm, raided and devastated the region, just like his father had done a few years before. He crossed the Araks River with his ethnically diverse army of mercenaries and moved through Armenia to Georgia. A large part of the Christian population was exterminated, and much loot was captured.

The Caucasus as part of the Mongol Empire

The real conquest and installation of a Mongol administration in the Caucasus started around 1234 under the leadership of General Chormaqan. The constant invasions had left the Caucasian forces weaker, both physically and mentally, and made it easy to conquer their lands. The Mongols carried out their raids during summer and spent the winters in the warmer regions of Mughan, in the southeast of contemporary Azerbaijan. The northern part of Armenia had already been subjugated by 1234, partly by military force and partly through treaties. In the following years Georgia and Arran were subdued, and the conquest of the territories south of the Kura River was finalized in 1240. Part of Georgia between the Kura and the main Caucasus range was still under the rule of Queen Rusudan, who had fled Tbilisi. However, in 1243 she was forced to become a vassal of the Mongol khan, to pay annual tribute and to help with military forces if needed, but the Georgian kingdom as such was not abolished by the Mongols.

During the first years of Mongol domination, life did not change that much in the South Caucasus, as most of the local rulers remained in place and several princes were made generals in the Mongol army. This situation changed dramatically in 1243, when permanent formal taxes were imposed and collected in a brutal manner. This resulted in several uprisings (especially in 1248–9 and 1259–61), which were all crushed and resulted in even more suffering. At first the South Caucasus formed a single administrative unit, but in 1256 the Il-Khanid Mongol state, in which the South Caucasus was included, was established. Georgia, however, was a special case. In 1247 both the son of Giorgi IV Lasha and the son of Rusudan had been affirmed as kings of eastern and western Georgia respectively.

The conquest of the North Caucasus took place almost simultaneously with that of the South Caucasus. In 1235 Ögödei Khan (son of Genghiz Khan) ordered some of his troops to head west to invade Russia, and in 1237 part of these moved towards the Northwestern Caucasus. They first crushed the Adyghe tribes and then completely destroyed the capital of Alania, Magas (1239), before going further east to take Derbent and Avaria. By 1240 almost the entire Northern Caucasus was under their control. Only the Alans, the Nakhs (ancestors of the

Chechens and Ingush) and the Dagestanians, together with some Kipchaks who had escaped to the mountains, retained their sovereignty and would continue their struggle in the following decades. The Mongols in fact did not go far into the mountains, but blocked the valleys instead. The North Caucasus became part of the Golden Horde, but its mountainous regions were never under the full control of the Mongols.

In the early 1260s, relations between the leaders of the successor states of the Mongol Empire deteriorated. This was the case especially between the shamanist Hülegü, the ruler of the Il-Khanid state (which included the South Caucasus), on the one hand, and the devout Muslim Berke, khan of the Golden Horde (which included the North Caucasus), on the other: Berke would invade the South Caucasus and Hülegü would move with his army to the North Caucasus. This struggle between the two states continued for many decades, and towards the end of the 1280s the Golden Horde received support from the Muslim Mamluks from Egypt and Muslim Turks in Asia Minor. As a result the Il-Khanid state lost power and the South Caucasus was left in political chaos. Eastern Georgia was liberated in the 1320s by King Giorgi V, who also annexed western Georgia and Samtskhe. From then on Georgia began a revival, but only until the arrival of Tamerlane. Armenia and Arran, on the other hand, fell under the influence of two nomadic Mongol clans: the Chobanids (or Chupanids) and the Jalayirids. Initially, the Chobanids emerged as victors, but in 1357 the Golden Horde overran Arran and put its own governors in place. While in the following years the Jalayirids were able to drive the Golden Horde out of the South Caucasus and control the region, in 1374 the Jalayrid federation of tribes split and, as a result, several tribes warred for power.

The Timurid invasions

Pestilence broke out in the Caucasus in the fourteenth century, but shortly afterwards another evil hit the region. At the same time as power struggles shaped the political life of the Caucasus there arose another Mongol leader: Timur Barlas, better known as Timur the Lame (corrupted to Tamerlane) because of an arrow wound to his leg. By 1383 he and his huge army of mercenaries had started on the conquest of Persia and moved closer to the Caucasus. Khan Tokhtamysh of the Golden Horde, an enemy of Timur, noticed the problems in the South Caucasus and in 1385 launched a massive raid on Arran and Armenia. Timur invaded the Caucasus for the first time in 1386, ravaging Armenia and Georgia. One year later he attacked Arran, and during the following years he raided and looted the region regularly. Georgia, for example, was invaded eight times, but was never fully subdued. Timur's toughest battles probably took place in 1395, when he pursued Tokhtamysh through the South Caucasus into the Chechen plains and finally defeated the Golden Horde. He continued by attacking the allies of the Golden Horde and, after a series of adventures on the territory of contemporary Karachay–Cherkessia, Kabardino–Balkaria and North Ossetia, prepared for an attack on the state of Simsim. Simsim, the only recorded attempt by the Vainakh to establish statehood, was devastated.

Miran Shah received control of the Caucasus after his father Timur died in 1405, but he himself died two years later. Timur's invasions were probably the most brutal, soulless and destructive that the Caucasus had ever experienced, and in the end he did not even leave a real empire.

The free communities

In the thirteenth and fourteenth centuries free communities arose around larger settlements in the mountains of modern-day Dagestan and Chechnya. They were ruled by a community assembly and were able to remain beyond the control of the Golden Horde. Gradually many of these communities formed alliances, and during the following centuries became incorporated in the Dagestani khanates.

Three superpowers compete for supremacy over the Caucasus

The fall of the Timurid Empire and the Golden Horde

After the death of Timur and his son, the Caucasus became a zone of interest for those who had previously been enemies of Timur. The Turkmen Horde of the Black Sheep (Qara Qoyunlu) took control of Arran, which was subdivided into small khanates. The Horde of the White Sheep (Ak Qoyunlu), which had already taken over Armenia after Timur's death, overran the Black Sheep emirate in 1468. The Georgian kingdom, unable to flourish, became surrounded by Muslim states, especially after the Ottomans defeated Constantinople in 1453. It soon disintegrated, and at the end of the fifteenth century it was divided into the Kartli, Kakheti and Imereti kingdoms and the Samtskhe princedom. In the following decades the principalities of Odishi, Svaneti, Guria and Abkhazia broke away from the Imeretian kingdom.

The Golden Horde was hit by civil war in the 1440s, and as a consequence the Kazan, Astrakhan and Crimea khanates separated from the Golden Horde. Two states grew stronger and were able to fill the vacuum after this decline. First, Muscovy, which had come to power after the decline of the Kievan Rus, broke away from the rule of the Golden Horde in 1480. Tsar Ivan IV the Terrible conquered Kazan in 1552 and Astrakhan two years later. The Ottoman Empire was the second state to make use of the weakness of the Golden Horde and expanded its influence in the Black Sea region. In 1475 the Crimean khan became a vassal of the Ottomans, and the Crimean khanate went on to become the longest-lived successor state of the Mongol Empire; it was finally annexed by Russia in 1783.

The Safavid Empire versus the Ottoman Empire

In the early fourteenth century Sheikh Safi ad-din established a Sufi order called Safaviyeh in Persian Azerbaijan, and gradually the Safaviyeh gained political

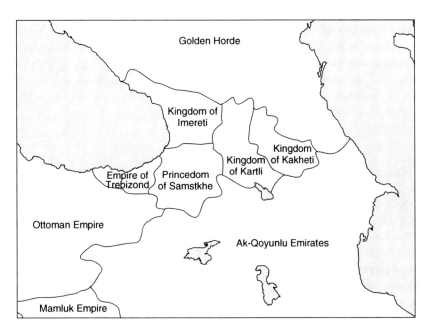

Map 4.8a Fragmented Georgia and the supremacy of the Ak-Qoyunlu in 1468

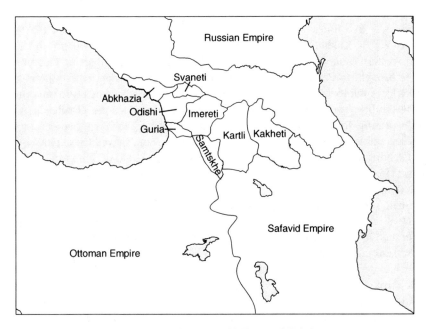

Map 4.8b The new political set-up after the 1639 Treaty of Zuhab

and military power. In 1501 the fifteen-year-old Ismail I, who led the Safaviyeh, received support from the Qizilbashi, or Redheads (extremist Shiite militant groups), and seized control of the region from the weakened Sunni White Sheep emirate. Ismail I became the shah of a new Persian kingdom in 1502, after nine centuries of Arab and Mongol rule, and declared Tabriz the capital. Initially, the official language was Azerbaijani, but over the course of the years the Safavid dynasty – which was in fact Turkic – lost its Azerbaijani character. Ismail I expanded his territory during the following decade to include the Southern Caucasus, Persian Azerbaijan and most of Iraq. He created a feudal theocratic dynasty and made Shia Islam the official religion, thus separating the Azerbaijanis from the Sunni Ottoman Turks. Although this explains why Azerbaijan and Iran follow Shia Islam, it is important to note that, in the middle of the nineteenth century, half of the population of contemporary Azerbaijan was still Sunni.

The Ottomans felt threatened in eastern Anatolia by the rise of the Safavid Empire and Shia Islam. Thus in 1514 the Ottoman sultan Selim I invaded historic Armenia – which had been captured by Persia in 1472 – but the Safavid army was not ready for a war with the Ottomans and withdrew. The Ottoman forces pushed deeper into Armenia, crushed the Persian army at the Battle of Chaldiran and captured Tabriz, the capital of the Safavids. However, the Ottomans withdrew one week later because they did not want to winter there. The Ottoman–Persian war continued for another 40 years and ended in 1555 with the Treaty of Amasya, which stipulated Persia's loss of most of eastern Anatolia and Armenia. The Georgian kingdoms, which had been raided and plundered five times during the 40-year war, were divided between the two rivals: Kartli, Kakheti and eastern Samtskhe fell under Persian influence, Imereti and western Samtskhe under Ottoman influence. Large numbers of Georgians were brought to Persia – especially to the region of Fereidan, where there still are a large number of Christian Georgians – where they became more important in the military aristocracy[5] and even threatened to replace the Qizilbashi. The Safavid king Tahmasp understood the vulnerability of Tabriz – it had been conquered and left a number of times during the war – and moved the capital south to Qazvin. A new war started in 1578, following the death of Tahmasp, and the Ottomans took most of the Southern Caucasus (even up to Derbent) and Persian Azerbaijan.

Shah Abbas the Great, who in turn moved the capital to Isfahan, understood the relative weakness of his own army and signed a peace treaty in Constantinople with the Ottomans in 1590. He immediately started to reform his forces along a European model with the help of an English general, Robert Sherley: mercenaries were recruited and artillery was introduced. By 1603 Shah Abbas felt his army was strong enough to force the Ottomans out of Persian Azerbaijan and the Southern Caucasus, which he finally achieved by 1622. He was seen as a liberator by many of the local population, who had suffered from high taxes and religious persecution.

In eastern Georgia, however, the population revolted almost constantly against Abbas I and his successors, but the Safavids often replaced the local kings, who had to convert to Shia Islam. With the Treaty of Zuhab of 1639, the Ottomans surrendered all of the Southern Caucasus apart from western Georgia, and a border was drawn between Persia and the Ottoman Empire – dividing historic Armenia and leaving only a few self-governed principalities – which held until 1914. After the death of Abbas I in 1629, Persian influence in Kartli increased. Kakheti, on the other hand, showed more resistance, and its king, Teimuraz, sought Russian and Ottoman support to unite eastern Georgia. The support never came, and finally Rostam Khan, the king of Kartli, invaded and was appointed king of Kakheti as well. The Kartlian kings, sharing good relations with the Safavids, still cherished the idea of an independent Georgia and asserted every opportunity that arose, especially in the eighteenth century.

Whereas initially the main enemies of Safavid Persia were the Uzbeks and Ottomans, the Afghans and Russians also became a real threat towards the end of the seventeenth century. The Afghans assaulted Persia in 1722 and captured Isfahan, which meant the fall of the Safavid dynasty. The Ottomans attacked the Persians one year later, seizing control of eastern Georgia, whereas the Russians conquered the Caspian coastal region. Persia reasserted itself very briefly under Nadir Shah Afshar (1736–47), who was able to gain back most of the lost territories, including those in the Caucasus, but in the process of his many wars he bankrupted the state. During the 50 years following Nadir Shah's assassination, most of the Southern Caucasus was virtually independent.

Renewal of Russian–Caucasian relations

The collapse of the Golden Horde and the foundation of a Russian centralized state favoured new Russian–Caucasian relations towards the end of the fifteenth century. Several Caucasian rulers sought protection from the Russian tsars against Ottoman expansion in the Black Sea region. Russia's relations with the Ottoman Empire worsened as the former obtained an outlet to the Caspian Sea and moved its border to the rivers Terek and Sunzha. Russia's influence in the North Caucasus was consolidated even more in 1557, when Kabarda became a Russian protectorate under Prince Temryuk, whose daughter Maria married Ivan IV the Terrible four years later. Through its important strategic strongholds and the support of the local rulers, Russia was very successful in opposing Ottoman expansion in the Northern Caucasus. Many Christian nations that had suffered from pressure from Muslim states, especially Ossetians, Georgians and Armenians, met this Russian advance with great enthusiasm. Russia tried to expand its influence in the region through political and economical means, but also through military conquest. In 1604 it tried to break through Dagestan but was defeated by the Dagestanians and Ottomans. The North Caucasus was spared any major war for the following 150 years, and many communities, including in Chechnya and Dagestan, voluntarily recognized the supreme power of Russia but remained independent.

The inclusion of the Caucasus in the Russian empire

A new stage in Russian–Caucasian relations developed in the early eighteenth century through increased political and military activity by Russia, which intensified the burden on the Caucasian people. The North Caucasian Caspian shores and the South Caucasus were conquered first, followed by the main mountain massif. It is, however, important to realize that there was a difference between the inclusion of these territories in the Russian Empire and the establishment of a tsarist administrative apparatus in the region; it often took many years after the region was conquered for it to be under direct central rule. Nevertheless, Soviet and Russian literature describes this process as voluntary.

Making use of the weakness of the Safavids, the Russian tsar Peter the Great launched his 'Persian Campaign'. He took the Caspian coastal region of Dagestan without much effort in 1722 and captured Baku one year later. His troops also landed on the southern Caspian shores in the Persian provinces of Gilan and Mazanderan. Because he was aware that the Ottoman sultan was also looking at the region, Peter the Great understood that this was his chance to advance in the Caucasus. He feared that once the Ottomans had taken the entire Southern Caucasus, up to the Caspian Sea, Russia would have lost its opportunity to take its share of the region. Still, the Russian tsar did not want to provoke a war with the Ottomans, who took Tbilisi in the summer of 1723. A year later the Treaty of Constantinople was signed between the two empires. Russia kept most of the Caspian border region, whereas the Ottoman Empire obtained the recognition of its influence in the Caucasus. During this time the Safavid Empire gained strength, and in 1735 Russia signed the Ganja Treaty, which stipulated that it had to retreat from all the lands it had conquered in 1722–4, including Baku, Derbent and Dagestan.

The Ottoman Empire was not pleased with the Ganja Treaty and directed its forces to Dagestan. Russia reacted by sending troops to the Crimea, and soon war between the two powers erupted, not only in the Caucasus but also in Europe. Initially Russia was the stronger, but it was forced to sign a peace treaty in 1739. The Treaty of Nissa declared Kabarda to be neutral territory, i.e. as a buffer zone between Russia and the Ottoman Empire. Instead of solving any dispute, this treaty actually aggravated the Russian–Ottoman rivalry in the Caucasus and the Crimea. During the following two decades the Ottomans continually carried out devastating raids on the Northwestern Caucasus and gained control over the Adyghe tribes. In the mid-1760s the Russian government decided to continue its advance in the Caucasus and expanded its ties with Kabarda, Ossetia and Georgia, thereby violating the Nissa Treaty. In 1768 a new Russian–Ottoman war erupted, in which the Ottoman army was defeated. The Treaty of Küçük Kaynarca in 1774 eliminated the restrictions of the Nissa Treaty: Ottoman rights were severely limited, and Kabarda, Ossetia and Ingushetia were transferred to Russia. Ingushetia had been integrated into the structure of the Russian Empire in 1770 and was followed by North Ossetia four years later. Other wars erupted later in

1770 – 1825: Ossetia, Ingushetia
1783: Crimean Khanate
1801: Kartli–Kakheti
1803: Dzharo-Belokan Dzhamaats, Megrelia
1804: Imereti, Guria, Ganja Khanate, Ilisu Sultanate
1805: Shirvan Khanate, Sheki Khanate, Karabakh Khanate
1806: Derbent Khanate, Quba Khanate, Baku Khanate
1810: Abkhazia
1813: Talysh Khanate
1817: Northern Chechnya
1819: Eastern Dagestan
1828: Nakhchivan Khanate, Yerevan Khanate
1829: North Black Sea Coast, Samtskhe-Javakheti, Karachay
1833: Svaneti
1840 (approx.): Pre-Kuban
1859: Chechnya and Western Dagestan
1864: Circassia
1878: Batumi, Kars, Ardahan regions

Map 4.9 The inclusion of the Caucasus in the Russian Empire between 1770 and 1878

the century, and in 1783 Russia was able to defeat the Crimean khanate and obtain full control over the northern coastal regions of the Azov and Black seas.

After the death of Nadir Shah eastern Georgia became quasi-independent, but its king, Irakli II, understood the need for Russian protection. Russian–Georgian relations intensified and trade between the two boomed. As a result of this the Treaty of Georgiyevsk, signed in 1783, made Kartli–Kakheti a Russian protectorate. The foundation of the fort and city of Vladikavkaz in 1784 was crucial for the important Georgian military highway and for maintaining relations with the lands south of the main Caucasus range. Although the Ottomans tried to stage another military campaign in eastern Georgia, they were unsuccessful. The situation in western Georgia, which had been under Ottoman influence for centuries, was a little different. Under the terms of the Küçük Kaynarca Treaty, Imereti, which had rendered tribute to the Ottomans since 1555, was now freed from its obligation.

The Cossacks as a tool for securing Russian influence

In the mid-fifteenth century, peasants dissatisfied with the worsening living conditions formed independent, self-governing military communes to fight against the Turks and the Tatars. This was the start of the Cossack movement, which took shape in the regions of Zaporozhye (in Ukraine) and Don (in the south of·Russia) and moved gradually into the North Caucasus. The Cossacks, who were mainly Russians and Ukrainians but also incorporated other ethnic elements, were devout Christians and saw it as their task to defend their land from the Muslims. This became particularly important when the Crimean khanate came into existence, when Byzantine Constantinople was conquered in 1453, and when the Ottoman Empire threatened the Christian states.

The Russian tsar started making use of these Cossacks in the middle of the seventeenth century because of their vast military experience, and this would become key to the Russian advance in the Caucasus. The Cossacks were released from the Peasant Law and colonized and defended the newly acquired Russian territories. By the time of Peter the Great almost all of them were in the service of the tsar. They not only played a major role in the expansion of the Russian Empire, they were also instrumental in the protection of its borders. They lived on the defence lines and built up fortresses – Mozdok, Groznyy, Kizlyar – which are now among the main cities in the North Caucasus.

Starting in the middle of the nineteenth century, the Cossacks experienced a golden age on account of the stability on Russia's borders. By the beginning of the twentieth century there were between 4 and 5 million of them, divided into eleven geographically organized Cossack *voiska*, or hosts. The three largest hosts – the Don Cossacks, the Terek Cossacks and the Kuban Cossacks – were active in the North Caucasus. The Cossack communities were headed by an *ataman* and founded many *stanitsy*, or settlements, in the steppes north of the Black and Caspian seas. Because of their loyalty to the tsar, the Cossacks refused to accept the Bolsheviks, and many later fought alongside the White Army against the new

Soviet government. As a form of punishment, over 70,000 Cossacks were removed to Siberia and the Cossack administrative units were liquidated.

The Qajar threat and inclusion of the South Caucasus in the Russian Empire

In the early 1790s the threat to the Caucasus did not come as much from the Ottoman Empire as from Persia, where Aga Mukhammed Khan, of the Qajar dynasty, had taken power and tried to restore the country's borders to what they had been during the Safavid era. He started his conquest of the South Caucasus in 1795 and, having taken the Yerevan and Karabakh khanates, headed for Tbilisi, which he took in a few days after killing thousands of people. The response of Yekaterina II of Russia was to send her troops to assist Irakli II of Georgia, and in the following months Russia gained control over most of the South Caucasus, including the Caspian coastal region. The fragmentation between some 20 khanates in the Azeri-inhabited areas made it easier for Russia through its divide and rule policy to emerge as a superpower in the region. Yekaterina II died in 1796 and was replaced by Pavel I, who had a different approach to the Caucasus. His idea was to establish a pro-Russian South Caucasian federation which would be strong enough to defend itself, allowing Russian forces to leave the region. Aga Mukhammed Khan made use of this change in Russian policy and once more directed his troops towards the region. However, soon after this he was killed, and Russia decided to withdraw from its last bases in Georgia. The death of Irakli II was another factor which complicated the situation in the South Caucasus. Giorgi II again asked Russia for military assistance in 1799, but died a year later. Pavel I, who had changed his policy again, used this situation in 1801 to proclaim the incorporation of Kartli–Kakheti into the Russian Empire. This annexation was the beginning of the colonization of the South Caucasus. Imereti became a Russian protectorate in 1804 and was included in the Russian Empire six years later. Thus, after more than three centuries of division, Georgia was united again, this time thanks to the Russians.

Persian and Ottoman recognition of Russia's domination of the Caucasus

The First Russo–Persian War began in 1804, when Russia refused to remove its troops and administration from Georgia and the Persian shah Abbas-Mirza invaded the khanates of the South Caucasus. The Russians proved to be stronger and were soon able to drive the Persian troops back and conquer half of eastern Armenia. Two years later the Ottomans also declared war on Russia, but they experienced many setbacks and in 1812 signed the Bucharest Treaty, recognizing Georgia, Imereti, Samegrelo and Abkhazia as Russian territory. In 1813 Persia was forced to sign the Gulistan Treaty, confirming the supremacy Russia had gained over Dagestan, Georgia and the Karabakh, Ganja, Sheki, Shirvan, Quba, Derbent, Baku and Talysh khanates.

Having prepared for over ten years, in 1826 Shah Abbas-Mirza again crossed the Araks with his troops and besieged the fortress of Shusha, capital of the Karabakh khanate, but his victory did not last long. During this Second Russo-Persian War the Russians conquered all the lands north of the Araks River. The Treaty of Turkmenchay in 1828 gave the large khanates of Nakhchivan and Yerevan to Russia and made the Araks the border between the two empires. The Turkmenchay Treaty also demarcated a borderline between two Azeri-inhabited regions (i.e. North and South Azerbaijan), and the Russian authorities even encouraged Muslims to leave the Russian Empire in order to settle Armenians there instead. Some 40,000 Armenians left Persia and moved to the Russian Empire.[6]

Russia's initial policy was to establish three Christian states on the territory of the South Caucasus: a revived Albania, Armenia and Georgia. However, after signing the Turkmenchay Treaty, plans changed concerning the restoration of Albania. Instead, Russia finally opted for the Armenization of the remainder of the Albanians, which also included the abolition of the Albanian autocephalous church.

The last Russian–Ottoman war (with the exception of the confrontation during the First World War) took place in 1877–8, when the Russians tried to liberate the Orthodox Christian Slavic people of the Balkan peninsula from the Ottomans. The Caucasus was affected by the outcome, since he Treaty of San Stefano stipulated that the regions of Batumi, Ardahan and Kars had to be handed over to the Russians.

The Caucasian War

Most of the North Caucasians were not enthusiastic about the Russian policy towards their region, and the aggression of the Russians led the indigenous people, whose traditional way of life was at stake, to revolt. The main centres of resistance against the Russian tsar were in Chechnya and the mountainous area of Dagestan in the east, and the Abkhaz-Abaz and Cherkess peoples in the west. The Ossetians and Ingush remained loyal to the tsar.

Although it is generally accepted that the start and end dates of the Caucasian War are 1817 and 1864 respectively, the conflict between Russia and the North Caucasian highlanders should be seen in a wider context. Discontent among North Caucasians started much earlier and took its organized form under Sheikh Mansur in 1783. Two years later, almost the entire North Caucasus was in a state of revolt, which the Russians answered with punitive expeditions. In 1791 Sheikh Mansur was captured by the Russians in Anapa.

The Caucasian War proper started in 1817, when General Yermolov implemented his subjugation plan by making regular incursions into the mountain regions: he cut wide openings in the forests, constructed roads and set up defence lines of fortresses. In the following years the Sunzha line was heavily fortified and attacked by Chechens and Dagestanians. Yermolov was replaced in 1827 by General Paskevich, who returned to the tactic of undertaking punitive campaigns, but he kept the defence lines. Towards the end of the 1820s Muridism developed in Dagestan and spread to Chechnya. This religious movement did not call only for *ghazawat* or *jihad*, but also for the creation of a theocratic state, i.e. an imamate. Not all Caucasian ethnic groups participated in the war, however, and some were even hostile towards Muridism. The Ossetians were Christians, Islam did not play a central role in the life of the Kumyks and Kabardians, and the Ingush and Avars had a pro-Russian stance, but despite this an imamate was founded in 1828. In 1837 Shamil, the third imam, was able to increase his authority by successfully crushing a Russian military expedition. Two years later war erupted again, and in 1846 odds changed for the Murids. In spring 1853 Shamil had to leave Chechnya and Dagestan. The start of the Crimean War (1853–6) gave a new stimulus to the *ghazawat* of the highlanders, especially in the western part of the Caucasus, because both wars involved Muslims against Russia. When the Muslim Ottomans tried to conquer Tbilisi in 1854, Shamil and his Murids occupied Tsinandali, which was only 60 km away. The Murids were driven back by the Russians, and the Ottoman defeat one year later took away all hope. Russia continued its efforts to drive the Murids out of the North Caucasus and finally, in the summer of 1859, Shamil was captured and the rebellion was ended.

After the defeat of Shamil, the only peoples in the Caucasus who had not been subdued were the Circassians (Adyghe, Cherkess and Kabardians), the Abazins and the Ubykhs. In the following years Russia carried out an operation of demographic warfare which in contemporary international law would be considered as genocide or ethnic cleansing. By conquering villages, killing or expelling its inhabitants (including forced migration to the Ottoman Empire) and giving the lands to Russian and Cossack settlers, the tsarist regime aimed to end the war and consolidate their hard-won territories, a policy already decided upon in 1808. Most Cherkess capitulated in 1859, but the Adyghe intensified their struggle in 1862. On 21 April 1864 General Evdokimov's troops crushed the Ubykhs, who had formed the last outpost of opposition. This date is also seen as the official end of the Caucasian War. This did not mean that all people quietly accepted their fate; on the contrary, many revolts took place in Chechnya and Dagestan in the following decades.

The forced migration and hijra of North Caucasian people to the Ottoman Empire

During the period 1859–1920, an estimated 2.5 million Caucasians left their homeland and migrated to the Ottoman Empire, half of them by sea, the other half over land. The truth about this historic event is not entirely clear, but it was probably the result of a combination of motives. The first of these was the tsarist reaction to the Caucasians' desire for independence, i.e. they were forced to resettle. Second, there was an internal call for *hijra*. *Hijra* is a population movement triggered by the unwillingness of Muslim communities to live under non-Muslim rule. This was also closely related to the Ottoman influence on the North Caucasus and stories of Northeast Caucasians who had successfully established themselves in the Ottoman Empire. Furthermore, some members of the Adyghe aristocracy were unhappy with the abolition of serfdom in 1861 and decided to emigrate, together with their dependants. Following the migration of these Caucasians, Russians were resettled in their lands.

At the same time, Ottoman emissaries promoted resettlement to the Ottoman Empire. In the period 1859–64, as many as 1.5 million so-called *mahajirs* (religious migrants) were either violently evicted or left voluntarily. According to many historians, half of them died of disease, starvation or drowning, and many others died or were sold as slaves on their arrival. Only a very small percentage of the Circassians stayed in the Caucasus, and they were resettled to the plains. Both the brutality of the Russians and internal calls for this *hijra* resulted in a wave of panic and the emigration of tens of thousands of other Muslim peoples from the Caucasus. Two-thirds of the Nogays, the last Turkic nomads, who had suffered greatly after the Russian annexation of the Crimean khanate in 1783 and who lived mainly in the Kuban area, abandoned the region. Tens of thousands of Chechens, Ubykhs, Abkhazians, Abazin and Laz followed their example. However, it was not only the Caucasus that was affected by the forced migration and *hijra*: hundreds of thousands of Crimean Tatars, Bosniacs, Pomaks and Balkan Turks from other parts of the Russian Empire left their native lands for the Ottoman Empire. This mass migration continued until 1920, but reached its peaks during the years 1859–65, 1877–8 and 1890–1908. Most migrants settled first at the Russian–Ottoman border and later in Anatolia. Many others moved on to Syria, Jordan or Egypt. It is important to stress the successful settlement policy of the declining Ottoman Empire, which already found itself in a difficult situation without these immigrants.

Russian administrative reforms

The administrative reforms of the 1860s and 1870s, which were needed to put the country on a par with the rest of Europe, constituted the final phase of the integration of the Caucasus into the Russian Empire. Initially, the reforms of Tsar Aleksandr II took place only within the ethnic Russian territories, but his son Aleksandr III extended them to the rest of the empire. These were not the only changes, as at the same time there were the beginnings of industrialization and Russification.

By far the most important reform was the abolition in 1861 of serfdom in the Russian-populated territories. When the mountain people found out about these changes, they pushed for similar reforms – to the dissatisfaction of their feudal lords. In 1866 a special Committee for Serf Issues was created in Tbilisi, and in the following years serfdom was abolished in the entire Caucasus. Slavery, which had existed in Dagestan, was also eliminated between 1866 and 1868.

The South Caucasian viceroyalty, consisting of several guberniyas (provinces) and oblasts, and the Stavropol province were under civil administration, whereas the mountainous people were under the supervision of the military. Dagestan had a more complex administrative system, which was different for the cities, the Cossack territories and the mountain regions. From 1860 onwards the entire North Caucasus was divided between the Stavropol Guberniya and the Kuban, Terek,

Map 4.10 The Russian administrative division of the Caucasus at the end of the nineteenth century

Dagestan and Black Sea oblasts, each further subdivided into okrugs. As a result, all feudal properties (mainly khanates) in the Dagestan Oblast were abolished in the period 1858–67. The tsar understood the need for representative government, and hence in 1864 local government was created in the form of a so-called *zemstvo* system, but this was not really introduced in the mountain regions.

Reforms to the judiciary and the legal system took place in 1864, but it was a few years before these affected the Caucasian people. Among the mountain nations *adat* and Sharia remained in use, but imperial legislation was employed in cases where the former failed to provide a solution.

It is also meaningful to place this Russian colonial period in broader historic perspective. At the same time Americans were conquering the western part of what is now the United States and slaughtering the indigenous population.

A first Russian revolution took place in 1905, starting in St Petersburg and gradually expanding to other industrial centres and major cities of the empire. Inter-ethnic tensions grew among Azeris and Armenians, and there were clashes between them throughout the Caucasus, but mainly in the Baku area and in Nakhchivan, Nagorno Karabakh and Ganja.

The situation of the Armenians in the declining Ottoman Empire

For a period of three and a half centuries the Armenians had enjoyed many privileges and been appointed to high positions within the Ottoman administration. They were very loyal to the empire and lived in harmony with the Turks. However, after the multi-ethnic Ottoman Empire weakened in the 1800s and lost several wars against Russia and its other enemies, several discriminatory laws against non-Muslims were established. Simultaneously, its decline led to a growth of nationalism among the minorities within its borders. The independence of other Christian nations, such as Greece and Romania, led to Armenian dreams of their own state. A series of massacres was carried out on the order of Sultan Abdul Hamid II during the period 1894–6 and resulted in the deaths of between 100,000 to 300,000 Armenians, and many smaller incidents took place in the following years. A group of nationalist reformists known as the Young Turks wanted to prevent the further decline of the Ottoman Empire, and in 1913 a triumvirate staged a coup. Their aim was to create Turan, a state comprising all Turkic people which would extend as far as Central Asia. However, the Christian Armenian state lay in the path of their intended expansion.

From Russian Empire to Soviet Union

The start of the First World War

The First World War broke out in July 1914, and soon Russia became involved. After suffering great losses against the Germans in the west, Russia had to cope with another enemy in the south. Ottoman forces led by their supreme commander, Enver Pasha, invaded the Caucasus in October 1914 with the aim of reaching Baku, where they would capture the oilfields and move further into Central Asia and Afghanistan to threaten British India. The Russians drove them back and launched their own advance towards Erzurum, some 100 km deep into the Ottoman Empire. Turkish forces began a counter-offence but incurred huge losses, mainly through the winter cold and exhaustion rather from actual fighting. Also the Turkish troops that had occupied Tabriz in neutral Persia were driven back by a Russian retaliation. Russian forces launched a new assault on Turkish Armenia in spring 1916 and soon controlled part of the southern Black Sea coast. Grand Duke Nikolay, the Russian commander, was ready for a major offensive in the spring of 1917, but due to the February Revolution – which had led to the abdication of the Russian tsar and the installation of a parliamentary government – he was forced to abort his plans and the Russian army fell apart. Gradually, the Russian forces withdrew from the Caucasus.

The Armenian genocide

Armenian sources claim that up to 1.5 million Armenians lost their lives between 1915 and 1922 in what is now controversially labelled the Armenian genocide. The Turkish authorities do not wish to recognize the events as genocide and refer to them as the results of a war in which both sides lost casualties and where Armenians were removed from the war zone. Indeed, it should not be forgotten that Armenians also perpetrated atrocities against the Turks. The world war, the support given to the Russians by the Armenians, and certain Armenian hostilities to Turks formed the ideal pretext for the Young Turks to advance with their plan to drive them out. On 24 April 1915, several hundreds of Armenian leaders and intellectuals were murdered in Istanbul. All Armenians were required to surrender their arms, and Armenians serving in the Ottoman army were placed in labour battalions where few survived. Other Armenian men were arrested and killed. Women, children and the elderly were ordered to move away from the war zone, but in reality many of them were sent on a death march. Some three-quarters of them died while trudging through the desert without water or food. Many others died in concentration camps, which were similar to those used a few decades later by Nazi Germany. Although Western countries reacted to this and issued warnings that the authorities would be held responsible, the Ottomans did nothing to curb their atrocities. Temporary relief came when Russia occupied some Armenian villages, but this changed after their withdrawal in 1917.

From the October Revolution to the independence of the South Caucasian states

Following the February Revolution in Russia a Menshevik administration was installed in the South Caucasus which the local political elite was happy to accept. The October Revolution worsened the situation and Russia fell into a state of civil war. Since they were not willing to recognize the Bolshevik central authority, they set up an independent Transcaucasian Commissariat on 15 November 1917 (the Baku area formed an exception and was in the hands of the Bolsheviks). Newly established Georgian-Armenian forces took control of western Armenia from the departing Russian troops, but the Azerbaijanis did not wish to take up arms against their Turkish brethren. On 3 March 1918 Lenin signed the Treaty of Brest–Litovsk, which annulled some of the conditions of the 1878 Berlin Treaty and stipulated that the Kars, Ardahan and Batumi districts had to be returned to the Ottoman Empire. Soon Turkish troops advanced and, in accordance with the treaty, in April 1918 took control of western Armenia and Adjara. On 22 April an independent Democratic Federative Republic of Transcaucasia was proclaimed in the South Caucasus, but five weeks later it was abolished because interests were too divergent. Georgia was oriented towards Germany for a secure and prosperous future, Azeri politicians sided with the Ottomans, and Armenians tried to get British and Russian support.

On 26 May 1918, a few hours after the abolition of the federation, Georgia declared independence and immediately became a German protectorate in order to avoid becoming a Turkish colony. Shortly afterwards German troops arrived in Georgia. Azerbaijan declared independence on 28 May, but did hold Baku and thus took Ganja as capital. The same day, at the Battle of Sardarapat, the Armenians defeated the much larger Turkish forces and declared independence. A few days later Azerbaijan and Turkey signed a Peace and Friendship Agreement, which led to the establishment of a Turkish Military Mission in Ganja. In the following weeks various battles took place between Azerbaijani and Turkish troops on the one hand and the Communist Baku Soviet on the other. And the British armed forces also entered the region: they took control of several oil fields and entered Baku in July and August, but were expelled by the Azerbaijani and Turkish army on 15 September 1918.

The end of the First World War

The Ottoman Empire withdrew from the First World War on 30 September 1918, and British troops gradually replaced the evacuated Turkish forces. The armistice of 11 November 1918 finally put an end to the war. Alongside the British governorship there was a pro-Turkish Southwest Caucasian Democratic Republic in the Kars province that wanted to take over parts of Armenia and Georgia. However, after various clashes the Kars province was put under Armenian rule.

The end of the war did not mean peace for the South Caucasus. A war between Armenia and Georgia in the Javakheti region was fought in November–December 1918 and clashes occurred in Karabakh in 1920. The Treaty of Sèvres (10 August 1920) called for Ottoman compensations to Armenia, whose independence it had to recognize. The treaty was never implemented, and was replaced three years later by the Treaty of Lausanne, which did not even mention Armenia. Turkish troops entered Kars in October 1920 and took it without much problem. In fact they did not stop there, but moved beyond the border of 1878. But on 2 December 1920 Armenia and Turkey signed the Treaty of Aleksandropol (Gyumri), which restored the old border.

Turkey and Soviet Russia understood the need for friendly relations and on 16 March 1921 signed the Treaty of Moscow and also confirmed the cession of Ardahan, Kars and the southern portion of the Batumi district. This strange alliance between Turkey and Bolshevik Russia was thus detrimental to the Armenian cause. Seven months later the Treaty of Kars (between Turkey and the three Socialist Soviet Republics in the South Caucasus) confirmed the border as defined in the Treaty of Moscow.

The triumvirate of the Young Turks, which had been responsible for the genocide and had fled to Germany in 1918, was sentenced to death in absentia the same year. Nevertheless, the killings and deportations continued until 1922 under the first years of rule of Kemal Atatürk.

The Civil War (1917–21) and the creation of Soviet Socialist Republics

The October Revolution was not welcomed by all levels of society, particularly among army officers and Cossacks. As a result a situation of civil war emerged, in which several smaller forces fought against the Bolshevik Red Army. During the first months of 1918 the North Caucasus witnessed the foundation of several Bolshevik Soviet Republics, especially in the Russian-populated areas, all of which merged into the North Caucasian Soviet Republic that July. Several North Caucasian peoples, on the other hand, were interested in independence, and in May 1918 they created a Mountain People's Republic, which separated from Russia. However, the region was soon recaptured by troops from the North Caucasian Soviet Republic.

The counter-revolutionary White Volunteer Army, led by the nationalist General Denikin and supported by many Cossacks in the North Caucasus, received support from the Allies after the end of the First World War. By early 1919 Denikin had taken control of most of the North Caucasus, which led to the dissolution of the North Caucasian Soviet Republic. As a rebellion against the White Army, a North Caucasian Emirate was founded by Uzun Haji and comprised the mountainous areas of Dagestan and Chechnya.

During summer 1919 the White Army lost strength and over the following two years the Bolshevik Red Army gradually brought the entire Caucasus back under its authority. By March 1920 the White Army was largely defeated, opening the way to the South Caucasus, which had been under Menshevik influence. The Soviet Socialist Republic of Azerbaijan was established on 28 April, the Soviet Socialist Republic of Armenia came into being on 20 November 1920, and the Soviet Socialist Republic of Georgia came into existence on 25 February 1921. Over the following months a number of autonomies (e.g. Abkhazia, South Ossetia, Nagorno Karabakh) were created. The Soviet Socialist Republics were considered to be independent, but this was not the case in reality. Their territories were occupied by the Russian army and every decision was taken in Moscow. The three republics united on 12 March 1922 in the Federative Union of Soviet Socialist Republics of Transcaucasia, which on 13 December that year was renamed the Transcaucasian Soviet Federative Socialist Republic (TSFSR) – one of the four founding components of the Soviet Union on 30 December 1922. The TSFSR was dissolved on 5 December 1936, and as a result three Soviet Socialist Republics in the South Caucasus obtained the status of union republics.

Because they had been promised self-determination and a high degree of autonomy, most North Caucasian peoples had joined the Bolsheviks. In November 1920 the Dagestan Autonomous Socialist Soviet Republic (Dagestani ASSR) was created. A few days later a Mountain People's Autonomous Socialist

Soviet Republic (MPASSR) was established, taking in the territories of six ethnic groups: Chechens, Ingush, Ossetians, Cherkess/Kabardians, Balkars and Karachays. Initially, Sharia and *adat* were acknowledged as constitutional law, which indicates the support for autonomy these groups initially received from Moscow. However, it did not take long before euphoria had to make room for pessimism. Gradually autonomies were granted which reduced the size of the MPASSR. In January 1922 the Karachay–Cherkess, Kabardino–Balkar and Adyghe autonomous districts were created, and these were followed in November by the Chechen autonomous district. The Mountain Republic was finally dissolved in July 1924, a few months after the Soviet Union had been created, and resulted in the Ingush and the North Ossetian autonomous districts. Different ethnic groups were put together in one autonomy (e.g. Karachay and Cherkess), and similar ones were divided (e.g. Karachay and Balkar). This demonstrated again the divide and rule strategy of the Soviet authorities in order to control the region. The constant change in territorial borders continued during the first decades of the existence of the Soviet Union.

With Bolshevik support, the Persian Socialist Soviet Republic (also known as the Soviet Republic of Gilan) was set up in May 1920 in the north Persian province of Gilan. But disagreements soon arose within the leadership of the republic, and in 1921, after it had achieved an agreement with the British, the Soviet Union decided not to support it any more. The same year the Russo-Persian Friendship Treaty was signed, with the result that Soviet troops, who had arrived in pursuit of the White Russian General Denikin, retreated from Persian soil.

The Caucasus as part of the Soviet Union

Repression and the administrative-territorial changes of the 1920s–1930s

The reconquest of the Caucasus and the establishment of Bolshevik Soviet regimes did not result in the population and local political elite being satisfied with the situation. Until 1924 there were many anti-communist uprisings in the South Caucasus, especially in Georgia, but all of them were suppressed. In order to get a better grip on the population in the Soviet Union and to improve the economic situation, which lagged behind that in Europe, the Russians instituted a massive number of changes, and not only in the Caucasus.

Principal among these, and aimed at creating a 'Soviet nation', were the attempts to Russianize and Russify all aspects of life. These efforts were often very brutal and offensive in the Caucasus. Arabic script was forbidden and the Latin and Cyrillic alphabets were used instead, old school books were destroyed, and schools were forced to teach in Russian. Historical facts were distorted and falsified in order to create the impression of centuries-long friendly relations between Russians and the Caucasian nations. For example, the inclusion of the Caucasus in Russia was described as voluntary, and rebellions, such as the one led by Shamil, as having been sponsored by foreign capitalist countries.

Second, to create a loyal Soviet nation it was necessary to reorganize the ethnic composition of the autonomies and eliminate anti-communist forces: this was realized through deportations, forced resettlements and executions which affected almost every family. Thousands of people were imprisoned or deported because of their wealth, an anti-communist attitude, treason, spying or being an agent of an imperialist power. In many cases accusations were false and trials were a sham. This repression was most brutal under Stalin; it escalated in 1934 and reached its peak in 1937–8. Ethnic Russians were resettled in the autonomies in order to increase the percentage of Russians, people living in the mountains were forcibly moved to the lowlands, and nomads were obliged to settle. Religion was also the subject of repression. Thousands of mosques and churches were destroyed, madrasas (religious schools) were abolished, and religious leaders were persecuted.

The political leadership of the USSR understood the need for economic reforms in order to compete with the booming industrialization of the West. As a result, private land was abolished and every aspect of economic life was placed in the hands of the government. Huge processes of industrialization and collectivization were begun in the second half of the 1920s, including several five-year plans aimed at transforming the USSR into an economic superpower. However, this did not prevent famine, and in 1932–3 up to a million people died of hunger in the North Caucasus alone. At the same time the social sectors developed through the building of hospitals, schools and universities.

The Great Patriotic War

The Second World War is known to the former Soviet Union as the Great Patriotic War, in which an estimated 26 million Soviet citizens died. The Caucasus held an important position in Hitler's strategy, since it would have provided Germany with fuel from its large oil and gas deposits and made it independent from other countries. At that time some 90 per cent of petrol, diesel and kerosene for the Soviet forces came from Azerbaijan. Furthermore, control of the Caucasus was part of the bigger Edelweiss plan, the aim of which was to capture the Middle East and India. At the beginning of July 1942 Hitler and his advisors were convinced that the USSR had lost the war. Germany planned to burst through Groznyy in the east and reach Baku via the Caspian. In the centre, they would take Vladikavkaz and break through to Georgia via the Georgian military highway and other mountain passes, and from there go on to the Black Sea. The series of military actions that took place in the North Caucasus between the German A-troops and the Soviet North Caucasian front and Transcaucasian front are known as the Battle for the Caucasus.

This battle started on 25 July 1942 when German troops crossed the lower Don River after taking Rostov-na-Donu. In the following weeks the German troops advanced quickly through the Don and Kuban steppes and captured Stavropol, Krasnodar, Maykop, Cherkessk, Nalchik and Mozdok. However, no oil could be pumped from Maykop because the Soviets had destroyed the oil fields before leaving. On 21 August the German Edelweiss division planted the Nazi flag on Mount Elbrus. This had no strategic value per se but rather was intended to undermine the confidence of the Soviet troops. The North Caucasian front was defeated, but in September 1942 the Transcaucasian front was able to build up its impenetrable defence along the main Caucasus range and the Terek River, thus blocking the way to the Chechen oilfields and mountain passes to the South Caucasus. The front line was stabilized from the southern outskirts of Novorossiysk to Goryachiy Klyuch, through the passes of the main Caucasus range to Alagir and the northern outskirts of Vladikavkaz, and thence to Malgobek, Ishcherskaya and Achikulak. With the exception of a small German invasion in Abkhazia, there was no military action in the South Caucasus or Dagestan.

In January 1943 the Soviets launched counter-attacks and liberated Mozdok, Malgobek and Nalchik. Having lost the Battle for Stalingrad on 2 February 1943 Nazi Germany decided to pull its A-troops out of the Caucasus, and on 22 April most of the Caucasus, apart from some of the Black Sea coast, was freed. The Battle for the Caucasus ended on 9 October 1943, when the last German troops withdrew from the Taman peninsula.

In order to secure British oilfields and to ensure supply lines for the Soviet forces, both the United Kingdom and the Soviet Union invaded Iran, which was neutral but seemed to be close to Germany. The Anglo-Soviet invasion, code-named Operation Countenance, started on 25 August 1941, when the British forces invaded from the Persian Gulf and the Soviet army from the north and across the Caspian Sea. Iran was entirely and effectively taken by 17 September and divided between the two victors for the period of the war. Four months later a tripartite agreement was signed where the Iranians had to provide non-military assistance to the Allies. The British forces left soon after the Second World War ended, but the Soviet troops in northwestern Iran refused to withdraw and backed pro-Soviet separatist regimes in the region. As a result, the People's Republic of Azerbaijan and the Kurdish People's Republic (the Republic of Mahabad), two short-lived Soviet puppet states, were set up late in 1945. The Soviet troops withdrew in May 1946 after promises of oil concessions, which, however, were soon revoked.

The deportations to Central Asia and Siberia

One of the most dramatic and traumatic events for the Caucasian population, mainly in the North Caucasus, was the deportation in the 1940s of approximately 1 million people. Deportations and forced resettlements were definitely nothing new in Russian and Soviet history: Russians had been moved to the Caucasus during colonization, Adyghe groups were relocated to Turkey in the 1860s and Cossacks had been exiled after the victory of the Red Army.

A new wave started in 1937, when Stalin felt that the Soviet Union might become engaged in a war. He therefore ordered the deportation that year of the Kurds (1,300 people) and the following year of Iranians (6,000) from the border zones in the Armenian and Azerbaijani SSRs to Central Asia. In the autumn of 1941, all citizens with German roots in the Caucasus (240,000) and the western part of the USSR had to leave for Central Asia and Siberia. Other minorities, such as Greeks, Crimean Tatars and Romanians, were deported in spring 1942.

After the German troops left the Caucasus, several Caucasian peoples were deported on account of their alleged support for and collaboration with the Germans, participation in criminal gangs, or resistance to the Red Army. The first to be deported were the Karachay. Some 500 people were removed in the summer of 1943 and 63,000 more followed in November. Close to half a million Chechens and Ingush were deported on 23 February 1944. Somewhat less tense was the deportation of 37,000 Balkars, which began on 8 March 1944 and was spread over several days. The autonomy of all these deported peoples was cancelled and their territories were divided among neighbouring administrative units. However, this was not the end. Because of the possibility of a war with Turkey, potential allies of the Turks had to be removed from Georgia. Some 85,000 Meskhetian Turks, 8,700 Kurds and 1,400 Hemshin were transported to Central Asia on 31 July 1944. People belonging to these nations but serving at the front were also removed. As a result, artificial national minorities arose in Central Asia and Siberia. They were not allowed to leave their new settlements and simply had to learn to cope with their new geographical and climatic settings.

The transport to Central Asia and Siberia took place mainly by train in cattle wagons with no sanitary arrangements. Disease soon took hold, and many people died from cold and starvation before the end of the long journey. In the first few years after their arrival many more died because they could not deal with the new situation. Estimates of the number of people who met their deaths in the first five years after being forced to leave their homes vary from between 20 and 30 per cent.

From 1954 onwards, some of the deported people travelled illegally to their homelands, and in 1956 Khrushchev gave a secret speech at the twentieth congress of the Communist Party in which he condemned the deportations as a violation of Leninist principles. That same year most of the nations were allowed to return to their native lands, though they did not receive full rights. As a result, Ingush could not go back to the Prigorodnyy Rayon, where Ossetians had taken up residence, and Chechens could not return to the Aukhovskiy Rayon, where Laks had been forced to settle. Some of these issues remain unsolved to this day and have the potential for conflict – for example the Ingushets against the Ossetians, the Cherkess against the Karachay and both of these against the Cossacks, and the Chechens against the Laks. Nor did the indigenous people have political control in the re-established autonomies. Although restrictions on free movement were eased in 1956, the Meskhetian Turks were not allowed to return to Georgia until 1966. The Georgian authorities were not very welcoming, but Azerbaijan accepted many of them. The Meskhetians who stayed in the Ferghana valley in Central Asia were exiled a second time in 1989, when a pogrom took place against them in Uzbekistan.

From perestroika to independence

Mikhail Gorbachev became the secretary-general of the Soviet Union in 1985 and started the programmes of glasnost (political openness) and perestroika (economic restructuring). These allowed for private ownership in some sectors, a greater freedom of speech and multi-candidate elections. However, it led to an uncontrollable situation in which the media also covered the negative aspects of life in the Soviet Union and where the state lost control over its satellites in Eastern Europe. It also resulted in the rise of nationalist and pro-independence movements in the non-Russian entities of the Soviet Union, such as in the Baltics, the Caucasus and Central Asia.

On 17 March 1991 the results of a union-wide referendum, which was boycotted by Georgia, Armenia, Moldova and the Baltic states, showed that 78 per cent of voters were in favor of the retention of a reformed Soviet Union. On 9 April the Republic of Georgia declared independence, but this was not recognized by the Soviet Union. The union republics were supposed to sign a new union treaty on 20 August, but on 19 August a coup was launched against Gorbachev in order to prevent this. Boris Yeltsin rallied mass opposition, and on 21 August the coup collapsed. After this, the calls for self-government became stronger and the Soviet leadership was forced to recognize the independence of the new republics. Azerbaijan declared on 30 August and Armenia on 23 September. The Soviet Union was officially dissolved on 8 December 1991.

5

CONFLICTS

The Caucasus is not only the bridge between Europe and Asia, it can also be the battleground between them. It is no wonder that the region has been and still is plagued by wars and conflicts. The large number of ethnicities and religions means that there is great potential for inter-ethnic strife, especially where national and ethnic identities are strongest. Interestingly enough, though, most of the Caucasian people acquired their ethnic identity only after the Russians conquered the region in the eighteenth and early nineteenth century. Before that they would consider themselves as, for example, a mountain people or a Muslim people. Many ethnic groups desire to avail themselves of their right to self-determination, which is in conflict with preserving the territorial integrity of the state in which they live. The nationalist and ethnocentric rhetoric of certain leaders – which serves mainly to enhance their own political power – adds even more fuel to the fire. However, ethnic backgrounds are not the only cause of conflict. Experience has shown that different nations can live together peacefully as long as the economic situation is favourable: Switzerland provides a good example. But the economic decline and chronic socio-economic problems of the past two decades have seriously aggravated the potential for conflict in the Caucasus. Finally, one should not forget the influence (or the perception) of history on the current wars and conflict potential. Many are the heritage of the Russian and Soviet divide and rule policy. While some ethnic groups were split, others received a high degree of autonomy, and yet others were deported by the Stalinist regime. After the collapse of the Soviet system each ethnic group struggled for their autonomy. For example, those who had been deported wanted to repossess the regions they had lost during their period of exile (e.g. the conflict between the Ingush and Ossetians over the Prigorodnyy Rayon, the Cherkess against the Karachay, and both of these against the Cossacks, and the Akkin-Chechens versus the Laks). Others – for example in Abkhazia, South Ossetia and Nagorno Karabakh – wanted to establish independence. Only four conflicts (those in Chechnya, Abkhazia, South Ossetia and Nagorno Karabakh) have received wide international attention, but many more clashes have occurred. However, these conflicts were nothing new, as there had been a lot of violence – mainly unreported – during the Soviet era.

The media (and sometimes other actors) are fond of giving conflicts a religious character; stories about Islam versus Christianity seem to sell copy. In order to make them easy to understand, some seek to simplify the roots of the conflicts in the Caucasus as religiously motivated. However, just because belligerents belong to different religions does not mean the conflict per se is religiously motivated. While none of the present conflicts in the Caucasus is about religion, religion has often – successfully – been exploited in order to influence public opinion and mobilize the people. Probably the best example of this is the war in Chechnya, where the Islamic factor was misused to whip up opposition against the Christian Russian 'occupier'. In fact, many of the conflicts have been taking place among people of the same or a related religion – for example Ossetians or Abkhaz against Georgians, Karachay versus Cherkess – and many strategic alliances actually go far beyond religious divisions: Iran and Armenia have a strategic partnership, Georgia enjoys prosperous relations with Turkey, but there are animosities between Azerbaijan and Iran.

Wars in the Caucasus have been many and bloody. Atrocities were committed on all sides, often because troops were not disciplined and commanders acted in their own interests. In addition political and military interests did not always coincide. For example, in the early 1990s there were many different armed factions in Georgia, such as the official National Guard, the White Eagles, the White Falcons, the Black Panthers, the Kutaisi National Guard and the Merab Kostava Society. Many of these groups had only 50 to 200 men, and they did not coordinate their activities with others. Some were loyal to the president, others to the opposition, and yet others to mafia-affiliated organizations. This meant that there were violations of ceasefires, hostage-takings, the targeting of civilians (infants being decapitated, women being raped, men being executed in front of family members) and looting. There were and still are people who took advantage of the anarchy caused by the conflicts, and who do not want those conflicts to be solved. The unsettled status helps their criminal activities, which are often centered on smuggling.

Over the past few years both Russia and the United States have been accusing each other of meddling in the political affairs and hostilities in the Caucasus. Russia claims it has only 'interests' in the region and tries to act as a buffer between the Islamic world and the West, whereas the US argues that American foreign policy includes spreading democracy in the Caucasus. However, several Caucasian republics and autonomies are unhappy with foreign interference – especially Russian – in their internal issues and conflicts. Russia, which claims to have the exclusive right to be guarantor of peace and stability in the former Soviet republics, has several peacekeeping operations in the Caucasus. Many see this as a Russian instrument of preserving influence in the CIS. As an aside, the term 'peacekeeping' and the Russian concept of *mirotvorchestvo* (better translated as 'peace*making*') do not fully coincide; the latter covers a broader range of activities other than pure peacekeeping as understood in the UN and international context. At the same time, Russia has been accused – although this has never been 100 per cent proved – of siding with certain warring parties and is in fact purposely destabilizing the Caucasus. For example, during the 1992–3 war, the Abkhaz troops were armed with T72 tanks, Grad rocket launchers, Sukhoi fighter planes, and other heavy equipment that they had not possessed before the war. Whatever the truth of this, it is a fact that without a positive attitude from Russia there cannot be any long-lasting peace or stability.

The Chechen wars

The Chechen wars (1994–6 and 1999) have been the most disastrous, destructive and cruel wars on the territory of the former Soviet Union. While the Russian army initially considered it would take only a few days to restore order in Chechnya, these wars resulted in the deaths of more than 100,000 people and the complete destruction of the capital Groznyy. The situation is still not fully calm and there are still frequent small fights between the Russian forces, rebel groups and others involved. The situation is extremely complex because the conflict is not just between 'the Russians and the rebels', as is often depicted in the media. In order to understand the attitude and reactions of the Chechen people, it is of utmost importance to take into account the trauma of the 1944 deportation and the meaning of the social structure (*teips*).

After the re-establishment of the Chechen–Ingush ASSR in 1957, the republic was ruled by a Russian leader. In 1989 Doku Zavgayev became the first Chechen chairman of the Supreme Soviet of the Chechen–Ingush ASSR. He allowed the publication of independent newspapers and journals, and in 1990 political parties, other than the Communist Party, were founded. The two main political groupings were the Vainakh Democratic Party, led by Zelimkhan Yandarbiyev, and the Chechen Pan-National Congress, an alliance of several nationalist factions headed by Dzhokhar Dudayev. Major-General Dudayev had been one of the few Chechens to reach a high position in the Soviet Union. He belonged to the rather insignificant Yalkhoro *teip*, and thus the Congress did not fear one specific *teip* would dominate their movement. A few days after his election as chairman in November 1990, Dudayev demanded the proclamation of Chechnya's independence – which the Supreme Soviet of Chechnya–Ingushetia complied with – in order to raise the status of the ASSR to that of a union republic. A few months later Dudayev invited several influential people to join a radical wing of the Congress, which soon took control of the movement and enjoyed strong popular support. On the one hand the Ingush population was left out of all these political events, but on the other hand Dudayev urged for closer cooperation among the North Caucasian nations, and even proposed the re-establishment of the Mountain Republic which had existed from 1920 to 1924.

The 19 August 1991 coup against Gorbachev also had an effect on Chechen politics. Whereas Zavgayev did not take sides, Dudayev condemned the coup and expressed his support for Yeltsin, who had defied the perpetrators of the coup, and as a result he received support from influential politicians in Moscow. During the following weeks, strikes and demonstrations took place in Chechnya. On

6 September the Supreme Soviet of the Chechen–Ingush ASSR was dissolved and Zavgayev resigned. Dudayev seized power and a provisional council was set up. Dudayev was elected president on 27 October 1991, and six days later he proclaimed the independence of the Chechen Republic. This led to tensions not only with Moscow but also with the Ingush, who were not represented in the Congress. The Ingush–Chechen problem was solved peacefully, as an Ingush Republic, which remained part of the Russian Federation, was formed on 4 June 1992. But Yeltsin did not recognize Chechen independence: he declared a state of emergency, sent troops to Chechnya and ordered the arrest of Dudayev. The latter organized a personal guard, composed of escaped prisoners. His troops occupied the airport and Russian interior ministry troops were forced to leave. However, contrary to Russian law, the state of emergency had not been approved by the Duma and two days later it was cancelled. Consequently the Russian troops were pulled out of Chechnya and the humiliated Yeltsin decided to use an economic blockade to bring Chechnya back under his control.

In the following months, while Dudayev developed the Chechen state, he lost some popular support on account of the economic decline, which went hand in hand with a rising level of crime, a flourishing black market and trade in arms. First, there was the Russian embargo, but then in 1992 Georgia closed its border with Chechnya after Dudayev had granted asylum to the ousted President Gamsakhurdia. Second, some 150,000 Russians, among whom were many skilled and qualified people, left Chechnya, which resulted in a fall in industrial and agricultural output. Soon Dudayev was also criticized both for his authoritarian and military-style rule and for his lack of economic skills and neglect of economic problems. Gradually tensions rose between the parliament, which wanted to negotiate with Moscow, and the Chechen president, who opposed talks with Russia and wanted to reduce the power of parliament. Demonstrations calling for Dudayev's resignation emerged in April 1993 and were answered by the dissolution of parliament and the imposition of a curfew. But the demonstrations continued, and Dudayev closed the constitutional court which had ruled the dissolution of parliament unconstitutional. Gradually, tensions led to both sides taking up arms.

During this period of Chechen 'independence' (1991–4) several attempts had been made to set up negotiations between Dudayev and the Russian leadership. Although Dudayev was initially willing to meet Yeltsin, the two men remained deadlocked and no negotiations ever took place. As a result, Russia increased its support for the opposition. One of the main opposition leaders was Omar Avturkhanov, who had never accepted Dudayev and who formed a provisional council assisted by contacts with Moscow in December 1993. Most other members of this provisional council were former allies of Dudayev. Initially, because of mutual suspicion, the different opposition groups did not coordinate their efforts, and as a result they were not able to take Groznyy and oust Dudayev. After four months of civil war the opposition united its forces in September 1994 and received strong military support from the Russian defence ministry, armed forces and FSB.

On the morning of 11 December 1994, some three years after the Chechen declaration of independence, Russian forces started a military invasion of Chechnya from the west, north and east. The aim was to encircle Groznyy but leave a passage to the south so that rebel forces would be forced to retreat to the mountains, where they could be isolated and eliminated. However, the numerically larger but basically unmotivated and untrained Russian troops were hindered in Ingushetia and Dagestan and experienced fiercer resistance than expected from the Chechens, whose morale was high. The corridor in the south was used unhindered by the rebels for transport of troops and weapons. Instead of an estimated two hours, it took two weeks for the Russians to reach Groznyy. On New Year's Eve they attacked the city from four directions, but only one detachment reached the centre. The problem was that the Russians tried to invade Groznyy with tanks without infantry protection and thus were easy targets for the small and extremely mobile groups of Chechens. After this failure, Moscow used heavy artillery and air strikes, and after several months, marked by a high number of both military and civilian casualties, was able to control the lowlands and the capital. The Chechen resistance fighters moved into the mountains and operated from there until a military accord was reached on 30 July 1995. The accord was never fully implemented, but the temporary ceasefire allowed the Chechen fighters to travel almost freely throughout Chechnya and regroup. While tensions grew, the Russians were still able to hold elections, which put Zavgayev officially back into power. After an increasing number of incidents, a new Russian offensive took place in March 1996. In April Yeltsin ordered a withdrawal and peace negotiations, probably because he knew he would not be re-elected unless he ended this unpopular war. Although negotiations took place, the war continued, and on 16 April Dudayev was killed in a helicopter attack.

Yandarbiyev, the founder of the Vainakh party and later the main ideological influence on Dudayev, took over the leadership of the rebel government and continued the struggle for independence. A ceasefire was signed on 30 May but was not maintained for very long: on 6 August the militant Islamist Shamil Basayev, with some 1,500 fighters, launched an attack on Groznyy and took the entire city in about a week. Yeltsin appointed General Lebed as his personal envoy in Chechnya to negotiate with Aslan Maskhadov, who headed the negotiations from the Chechen side. The legitimate Chechen government, led by Zavgayev, was not included in these negotiations. A ceasefire came into effect on 23 August 1996 and an agreement, leaving Chechnya with de facto autonomy, was reached in Khasavyurt eight days later. This First Chechen War had led to the deaths of between 45,000 and 60,000 people and largely devastated Groznyy, but, with the exception of some clashes in Dagestan and one major incident in the Stavropol Kray,[1] it had not spilled over to neighbouring regions.

In December 1996, a few months after the signing of the Khasavyurt agreement, the Russian military units withdrew from Chechnya and in February 1997 Aslan Maskhadov was elected president of the republic. Over the following months many officials, soldiers and humanitarian aid workers, as well as ordinary people, were kidnapped. In many cases a ransom was demanded, but in many others the person was never heard of again. Often families had to scrape money together in order to buy back a dead body and bury it in a fitting manner – a matter of major importance in Islam. Even now, kidnappings occur regularly in Chechnya and Ingushetia.

In August and September 1999 a group of a few hundred armed men twice crossed the border from Chechnya to Dagestan with the aim of setting up an independent Dagestani state. In both cases the Russians were able to repel the aggressors with air and artillery strikes. During the same period several terrorist attacks occurred in Dagestan, Moscow and Volgodonsk (in the Rostov Oblast), killing almost 300 people and injuring many more. The Russian authorities linked the explosions to Chechen and Dagestani extremists, but produced little evidence for their allegations.

In order to gain control over the situation in the Northeastern Caucasus, the Kremlin decided to create a security zone between Dagestan and Chechnya and to exterminate the rebels. Because a ground invasion would lead to many casualties, a large air campaign with minor incursions of ground troops was started on 23 September 1999. This was the start of the Second Chechen War, and a few days later Prime Minister Vladimir Putin declared the illegitimacy of Maskhadov and his parliament. Ground forces advanced and captured the north of Chechnya. After only a few weeks Russian troops held half of the territory of Chechnya and Groznyy was fully blockaded. The elimination of armed groups in the capital started in early December 1999, when the entire population, which had suffered tremendously from the heavy bombardments, was told to leave the city. Everyone remaining would be considered as an enemy combatant. Between 15,000 and 50,000 of the original 300,000 inhabitants stayed behind.

In the following weeks Russian ground forces tried to capture the city block by block, but met stiff resistance from the rebel groups. By early February the Russians had gained control over half of the city, and thousands of rebel fighters tactically retreated from Groznyy into the mountains, from where they continued a guerrilla war. In the following months Russian aircraft bombed the suspected strongholds of the estimated 8,000 rebels, and ground troops moved into the mountains for their final offensive. Fighting in the mountains was not as easy as had been expected and resulted in many casualties from both ambushes and hit-and-run attacks. In spring 2002 President Putin claimed the war was over, but although Russians occupied most of Chechnya, they were not really in control. That year many refugees were forced to return to the ruins of their houses. Millions of dollars were allocated and sent to Chechnya for reconstruction work, though not much was achieved until 2005.

Since the official end of the war in Chechnya, violence has spread over greater parts of the North Caucasus, and there have frequently been fights between rebels and federal troops as far away as Kabardino–Balkaria. Furthermore, extremists have abandoned conventional warfare and taken up terrorist tactics, the most important being the hostage-takings in the Nord-Ost Theatre in Moscow and school number 1 in Beslan. The Second Chechen War resulted in over 60,000 dead, most of them civilians, and also led to more than 250,000 people being internally displaced.

The conflict over Nagorno Karabakh

The violent conflict over Nagorno Karabakh (Artsakh in Armenian; Yuqari or Dagliq Qarabag in Azerbaijani) lasted from 1988 until 1994 and resulted in 20,000 dead and some 1 million IDPs and refugees. To this day, no solution has been reached, and the crisis has the potential to flare up again. Armenians currently occupy Nagorno Karabakh and the surrounding region (i.e. approximately one-fifth of Azerbaijan's territory) and only a few Azerbaijanis are left. The history of Nagorno Karabakh and its conflict is complex and often shows a lack of logic, which make finding a resolution even more difficult. This complexity is exemplified in the name 'Nagorno Karabakh' which is derived from three different languages: Persian (*bag*), Turkish (*kara*), and Russian (*nagorno* and the Russification of *bag* into *bakh*).

Both Armenians and Azerbaijanis claim that the territory of present-day Nagorno Karabakh has always belonged to their ancestors, and both claim to have historical proof of this. According to the Armenian side, the region was part of the Great Armenian kingdom in the fourth century BC, when the Armenian Orontid (Yerevanduni) dynasty created an autonomous entity after the defeat of the Achaemenid Empire by Alexander the Great. However, history cannot fully confirm this claim. It is certain, though, that the region of Mountainous Karabakh was incorporated into Armenia in the first century BC by Tigran the Great. Some sources claim that the region was separated from Armenia and included in Caucasian Albania in AD 387, while others argue that this took place in 428. Arabs conquered Albania in the seventh century, but Nagorno Karabakh was able to retain a form of autonomy which even survived Seljuk, Mongol and Turkmen invasions during the Middle Ages. In the early eighteenth century Mountainous Karabakh became involved in the power struggles between Russia, Persia and the Ottoman Empire. The Ottomans ruled the region from 1728 until 1735, after which it was occupied by the Persian Nadir Shah. Nadir Shah was assassinated in 1747, which led to the fragmentation of his empire into several khanates. At the same time the power of the Armenian elite had greatly diminished as a result of internal conflicts. The Karabakh khanate, with its capital in Shusha, was dominated by a Turkic ruler and had a mixed population, as was the case in most other khanates. As stipulated in both the Treaty of Gulistan (1813) and the Treaty of Turkmenchay (1828), the Karabakh khanate came under the control of Russia, which supported a change in the population mix. This meant that many Azerbaijanis and other Muslims left for Persia or the Ottoman Empire, whereas many Armenians travelled in the opposite direction. As a result, the percentage of Armenians in the Karabakh khanate – not only Nagorno Karabakh but also lower Karabakh – increased from 9 per cent in 1823 to 53 per cent in 1880. These migrations were at their most extensive after the Turkmenchay Treaty and after the Russian–Ottoman wars (1855–6 and 1877–8).

Tensions between the Armenians and Azerbaijanis existed over many generations, but there was never really any violence until 1905, when the first Russian revolution also reached the Caucasus region. Hostilities burst out in Baku, Yerevan and Nakhchivan but quickly extended to Karabakh. The number of casualties ranged from between 3,100 and 10,000, but more Azerbaijanis than Armenians died during these clashes.[2]

After the end of the First World War all short-lived independent South Caucasian republics tried, before the Paris peace conference could settle these conflicts, to gain control over their disputed regions. Several territories were transferred between Armenia and Azerbaijan in the following years. Initially, Armenia tried to impose its rule over Nagorno-Karabakh, Zangezur and Nakhchivan, whereas the British – who replaced the Ottomans – confirmed that these regions fell under Azerbaijani government. But in December 1920 Soviet Azerbaijan was forced by Moscow to issue a statement that Karabakh, Zangezur and Nakhchivan would be brought under Armenian control. A few months later the Soviet Union and Turkey were in the process of establishing more cordial relations. The Turkish president, Kemal Atatürk, favoured a weaker Armenia, and through his influence the Soviet leadership decided that Nakhchivan and Karabakh were to be transferred back to Azerbaijan. In Stalin's presence, the Kavburo (the Caucasian Bureau, i.e. the Caucasian section of the Soviet Communist Party) voted in July 1921 to include Karabakh in the Armenian SSR, but the following day this decision was revoked, and Karabakh received a degree of autonomy under the Azerbaijani SSR.

The Nagorno Karabakh Autonomous Oblast (within the Azerbaijani SSR) was established on 7 July 1923. Its capital moved from Shusha to Khankendi, which was later renamed Stepanakert after the Armenian Bolshevik Stepan Schaumian. Nakhchivan, on the other hand, became an autonomous republic within the Azerbaijani SSR. Thus, although the Armenians had always pledged their allegiance to Russia, the latter chose to cement its friendship with Turkey. Throughout the existence of the Soviet Union, the Armenian leadership tried to reverse this situation and regain Karabakh but never found support from the central authorities. In the 1960s nationalism arose in both Armenia and Nagorno Karabakh, and several protests took place with respect to the case of Nagorno Karabakh. On the other hand, however, the percentage of Armenians in Nagorno Karabakh and Nakhchivan gradually decreased.

The situation became more tense in 1987 and resulted in February 1988 in several waves of Azerbaijani refugees leaving Armenia, mainly for Azerbaijan. On 20 February the soviet of the Nagorno Karabakh Autonomous Oblast requested it be reassigned under the Armenian SSR. A week later disturbances arose in Sumgait, the industrial suburb of Baku, after rumours of unrest in Stepanakert and Askeran. This led to a three-day pogrom where Armenians had to flee Sumgait and the army and troops of the interior ministry were called in but did not interfere. This, combined with the decision of the Supreme Soviet of the USSR that the status of Nagorno Karabakh would remain unchanged, led to the ethnic cleansing of Azerbaijani villages in Armenia, mainly in the Ararat and Zangezur regions. Many Armenians living in Azerbaijan left the country and found protection in Armenia. The demonstrations continued in Nagorno Karabakh, and Moscow replaced the republican leaders of Azerbaijan and Armenia. But the violence persisted, and more and more people fled from both countries. The Azerbaijani population was not only unhappy with the Armenians but also with their own government, because it was unable to exercise any control over Nagorno Karabakh. The earthquake of 7 December 1988, which hit the Armenian city of Leninakan (Gyumri) and killed over 25,000 people, distracted the Armenians and their leadership temporarily from Nagorno Karabakh.

On 12 January 1989 the Soviets established a special government administration in Karabakh. Tensions were initially calmed but no solutions were sought. Consequently hostilities resurfaced and paramilitary groups began to rearm. Less than a year later, on 29 November, direct Soviet rule was abolished and Nagorno Karabakh once again became part of the Azerbaijani SSR, but a few days later the Supreme Soviet of the Armenian SSR officially incorporated Nagorno Karabakh. Riots followed in Azerbaijan and thousands of Soviet troops were moved to Baku and Karabakh. Inspired by the independence declarations of several union republics, the Karabakh Soviet proclaimed independence on 2 September 1991. This decision – which went against those who wished to unify Nagorno Karabakh with Armenia – led to more violence. Azerbaijan gradually lost military and political control over the region, especially after Soviet troops were withdrawn in December.

Total war broke out in February 1992, when several Azerbaijani villages were taken and their population driven out. The most outrageous military activity at that time, in which apparently[3] the last CIS troops that remained in the region participated, was the attack on the Azerbaijani town of Khojaly, where several hundred people were massacred. In the following months many volunteers, including divisions of the Armenian army, took part in the fighting. The conquest of Shusha and Lachin in May created a much needed corridor linking Armenia with Nagorno Karabakh. This not only had a logistical function, for the transport of supplies, it also made political unification of the two countries more realistic. The Azerbaijani counter-offensive which started in June 1992 was successful and resulted in several villages and cities being brought back into Azerbaijani control. However, a new Armenian offensive beginning in February 1993 left a total of around a million Azerbaijani IDPs, and during the summer Azerbaijani land between Nagorno Karabakh and Iran was also conquered. Azerbaijan's less motivated army, its poor leadership and the political chaos in Baku accounts for its weaker position. Colonel Surat Husseynov, who had initially won several military victories for Azerbaijan, but who was later dismissed from his position, started a rebellion against President Elchibey. The new president, Heydar Aliyev, appointed Husseynov his prime minister, but also dismissed him after blaming him for an attempted coup. The ceasefire of July 1993 was broken rapidly, but the new ceasefire announced on 16 May 1994 remains in force, although sporadic shooting occurs. Nagorno Karabakh has become part of Armenia as far as, for example, economic and military issues are concerned, but this is not based on any political settlement.

During the first years of the conflict other countries would not interfere, as the matter was an internal issue for the Soviet Union. With the independence of Armenia and Azerbaijan it became a focus of the entire international community, and several countries offered to mediate. The UN issued Security Council resolutions and gave the CSCE/OSCE a chance to arbitrate. The OSCE Minsk Group, co-chaired by France, Russia and the US, was set up in 1992 in order to encourage a peaceful, negotiated resolution to the conflict.

Finding a solution for the situation is not easy, as this is a war not just between Azerbaijan and Armenia but involves a third party: the unrecognized republic of Nagorno Karabakh. While Armenia does not officially recognize its independence, it supports its right to self-determination. Armenia's army occupies some of the territory of Azerbaijan, and international mediation efforts are concentrated more on talks between these two republics and less on talks with the government of Nagorno Karabakh. These negotiations have been long and inconclusive but have led to several possible solutions: a return to the status quo ante, a renegotiation of autonomy, a territorial swap, joint sovereignty, a guarantee of Armenian influence in Azerbaijani decision-making, or a neutral status for Nagorno Karabakh. However, not everyone is convinced that a diplomatic solution will be reached, and many fear that Azerbaijan may use its revenues from oil to build up a strong army and take the region back by force.

The Georgian–Abkhaz conflict

The Georgian–Abkhaz conflict has been one of the bloodiest and atrocious in post-Soviet history. It has resulted in some 10,000 to 30,000 dead and approximately 250,000 IDPs, and prospects for a mutually agreeable solution do not look very promising. Abkhazia refuses all offers of a large degree of autonomy and wants only full independence. Georgia, for its part, has indicated that the use of force has not been ruled out if diplomacy and political talks do not bring about a favourable outcome, but such a scenario seems less likely since the events of August 2008.

In ancient times the territory of modern-day Abkhazia was part of Kolkha and Egrisi and was ruled by the Romans from the first to the fourth century AD. It then became a principality (*saeristavi*) which fell under the sphere of influence of the Arab caliphate and the Byzantine Empire, and in the early eighth century it became a vassal of Khazaria. In 780 the Abkhaz principality and the province of Imereti were united in the kingdom of Abkhazia, and in 1008 it was incorporated in a unified Georgian kingdom. After the break-up of Georgia, Abkhazia reverted to the status of a principality, led by the Shervashidze dynasty, and in 1578 it became a protectorate of the Ottoman Empire. In the eighteenth century the

Ottomans, who had Islamized part of the population, wanted to subordinate Abkhazia, and the Shervashidzes thus asked for Russian assistance. Abkhazia became a Russian protectorate in 1810, but its self-administration lasted only until 1864. The Abkhaz people revolted in 1866 as a result of land reforms and the taxation system, and during the following eight years there was a mass emigration to Turkey. The number of Abkhaz in Abkhazia not only declined, but because most emigrants were Muslim the majority of those left were Christian.[4] The Soviet Socialist Republic of Abkhazia was proclaimed on 4 March 1921, and thus was independent when the Soviet Union was formed. A few months later Abkhazia and Georgia signed a union treaty and in 1922 they entered the Transcaucasian Federation on an equal basis. However, in 1931 the status of Abkhazia was downgraded to an autonomous republic within the Georgian SSR.

During the Soviet period the Abkhaz complained of a Georgianization and destruction of their culture. One of the reasons for this was that there had been a large influx of Georgians, Russians, Armenians and others. Whereas in 1886 (i.e. after many of them had left for Turkey) ethnic Abkhaz formed 42 per cent of the population, by 1959 this had been reduced to only 15 per cent. Furthermore, schools teaching in Abkhaz were temporarily closed and Abkhaz had been given a Georgian alphabet, while other Caucasian languages adopted a Cyrillic alphabet. As a result there were several disagreements between the Abkhaz and the Georgians (e.g. in 1957 and 1967), but because of the authoritarian system open conflicts were averted. In 1978, after the Soviet leadership had capitulated to demonstrations in Georgia regarding the change of the status of the Georgian language, the Abkhaz saw an opportunity to regain their status of 1921 or to become part of Russia's North Caucasus. A special commission from Moscow assessed the Abkhaz claims and acknowledged that certain of them were legitimate. But nothing very much changed. Tensions rose again in Abkhazia in October 1978, and in 1981 there were demonstrations in Tbilisi against the so-called Abkhazian privileges. Gradually Georgians complained more and more about anti-Georgian policies and their lack of political influence in Abkhazia.

A so-called Abkhazian Letter of 17 June 1988 addressed to the Soviet leadership and the petition of the 'Abkhazian Forum' on 18 March 1989 renewed claims for the status of union republic and thus secession from Georgia. This move, some isolated inter-ethnic clashes, and the growing feeling of nationalism among the Georgians led in April 1989 to demonstrations in Tbilisi, demonstrations that soon called for Georgian independence. On 9 April Soviet troops intervened, killing 19 and leaving many more wounded. But this had the opposite effect from that intended, and led to even greater tensions and anger with the communist government. Paramilitary formations such as the Mkhedrioni (Horsemen) of Jaba Ioseliani emerged. In August 1990 the Supreme Soviet of Abkhazia proclaimed Abkhazia a full union republic. Although it seceded from Georgia, it left the door open for a federation, as had been the case from 1921 to 1931. On 28 October 1990 Gamsakhurdia's 'Round Table – Free Georgia' won in the parliamentary elections after a campaign that paid special attention to the rights of Georgians in

Abkhazia and South Ossetia. Gamsakhurdia's policies of homogenization, Georgianization and Christianization resulted in worsening relations with minorities, who found it impossible to remain within an independent Georgia. The Georgians claimed that the Abkhaz problem, just like the Ossetian one, was instigated by the Russians. No one was willing to compromise. Whereas Georgia did not participate in the 1991 all-union referendum, it declared void the Abkhaz vote in favour of the union treaty. A few weeks later Georgia declared independence.

In June 1992 the Abkhaz president, Vladislav Ardzinba, proposed a solution involving a federation or confederation, but this was refused by the Georgian leadership. One month later Abkhazia restored its 1925 constitution and thus proclaimed its independence again but, as previously, left the possibility for a federation with Georgia. On 14 August 1992 the Georgian National Guard and police were deployed to restore order in Abkhazia. However, that same day war broke out, and Georgian troops, led by Tengiz Kitovani, took Sukhumi and most of Abkhazia in the course of just a few days. The Abkhaz secessionist government fled Sukhumi and moved to Gudauta, a stronghold of Abkhaz separatists. Early in September a ceasefire was reached under the initiative of Boris Yeltsin, but Kitovani refused to retreat from Abkhazia and the ceasefire was violated. Abkhaz forces received support from thousands of volunteers from the North Caucasus, mainly Chechens and Cossacks, and after a few weeks the Georgians were driven back, so that they controlled the region south of the Gumista River – with the exception of the village of Tkvarcheli, which was completely isolated and under a blockade for several months. Apart from Tkvarcheli, the Abkhaz controlled the north of Abkhazia and had their stronghold in Gudauta. The fighting petered out during the winter but recommenced towards the end of February 1993. The Abkhaz launched an assault on Sukhumi in March, which resulted in a large number of casualties and a great deal of destruction.

A new Russian-brokered ceasefire was reached on 15 May, but the Abkhaz continued their attacks in order to regain their territory. Yet another ceasefire came into effect on 27 July 1993 with the Sochi Agreement. This asked for the withdrawal of Georgian troops, the demilitarization of both sides, and the return of a legal government to Abkhazia. However, the withdrawal of Georgian troops was opposed both by the Zviadists, the followers of ousted President Zviad Gamsakhurdia, and parts of the armed forces. Taking advantage of this chaos, the Abkhaz successfully captured Sukhumi at the end of September. Ochamchire and Gali followed soon afterwards, and the remainder of the Georgian population was subject to massacres and looting. Zviadists then took control of a large part of western Georgia and made to attack Tbilisi. Russia successfully used this situation to force Georgia into the CIS and get it to accept Russian troops on its territory. Russia offered its assistance, and soon the Zviadist uprising was put down. Fighting was simultaneously quelled in Abkhazia, with the Abkhaz controlling most of their territory apart from the Kodori gorge and a few places in the Gali district. The latest and most recent ceasefire was concluded in December 1993 and has been largely respected, although there were some significant incidents in 1998. The conflict escalated again in April of that year, when Abkhaz forces entered villages in the Gali district. President Shevardnadze refused – against public opinion – to deploy troops, and a ceasefire agreement was reached on 20 May. However, these renewed hostilities led to hundreds of casualties and 20,000 new IDPs.

During the war the mediation efforts came from both Russia and the UN, but after the peace settlement of 1993 the US, France, Germany and the UK became involved. On 4 April 1994 the Declaration on Measures for a Political Settlement of the Georgian–Abkhaz Conflict was signed, and one month later a CIS peacekeeping force – composed of Russian troops only – was deployed in the disputed region. Later, UNOMIG (the United Nations Organization Mission in Georgia) deployed its observers, mainly in the south of Abkhazia. In July 2006 a resolution demanding the removal of all Russian peacekeeping forces was passed by the Georgian parliament, but the forces are still there.

The August 2008 war between Russia and Georgia focused on Ossetia. Nevertheless, fighting took place in Abkhazia as well, and on 12 August Abkhazian authorities started military operations against the Georgian troops in the Kodori valley. The Georgian forces withdrew the same day.

The Georgian–Ossetian conflict

The Georgian–Ossetian conflict, which erupted in the 1980s and has still not been settled, resulted in the death of more than a thousand people but also forced tens of thousands (both Georgian and Ossetian) to flee their homes.

The Ossetians claim that their ancestors were the Scythians and Alans, who had been living on the territory of South Ossetia as early as 2,700 years ago. The Georgian extremist view claims that the Ossetians are 'guests' who arrived as recently as two or three centuries ago. Georgians see the region as one of the oldest centres of their history and culture, and thus consider that the Ossetians have no right to autonomy there. Zviad Gamsakhurdia, who actually still respected certain rights of the Abkhaz, wanted the Ossetians to go to their 'homeland' in the north. A more reliable and acceptable historical version is that the Ossetians arrived in the South Caucasus during the Mongol invasions in the North Caucasus in the twelfth to thirteenth centuries.

A first major conflict between the two sides occurred during the period 1918–21. When Georgia declared independence on 20 May 1918, the Ossetians did not want to stay within Georgia because they had voluntarily joined Russia in 1774. As a result, South Ossetia declared independence on 8 June 1920. Georgia sent its army to crush this rebellion. According to certain Ossetian sources, some 5,000 Ossetians were killed,[5] but this number is probably overstated. In April 1922 the South Ossetian Autonomous Oblast was created and Tskhinvali was chosen as its capital.

During the late 1980s, when several national popular parties and movements emerged, the Ossetians founded the Ademon Nykhas (Popular Front). At that time the population of South Ossetia consisted of two-thirds Ossetians and less than one-third Georgians. The first signs of a new conflict appeared in spring 1989, when the leader of Ademon Nykhas sent an open letter to the Abkhaz people, expressing his support for their secessionist claims. In the following months there were several rumours of skirmishes between Georgian and Ossetian armed bands. In August, Georgia adopted a new law making Georgian the only official language on its territory. This led to consternation among the Ossetians, because only a minority of them could speak Georgian. Ademon Nykhas therefore sent a petition to the Supreme Soviet of the USSR for the unification of South Ossetia with North Ossetia. In November, the Supreme Council of South Ossetia passed a resolution demanding that Ossetic become the official language, and some groups even called for the status of the autonomous oblast to be changed into that of an autonomous republic. These appeals led to furious reactions from the Georgians, who launched a March to Tskhinvali on 23 November 1989. Whereas the Georgians claimed that this was a peaceful march for reconciliation, the Ossetians saw it as a provocation. The 12,000 to 15,000 participants were prevented from entering the city by Soviet soldiers and Ossetians, and the result was two days of violence. As clashes continued, Gamsakhurdia vowed to drive out all Ossetians. In August 1990 the Georgian Supreme Soviet adopted an election law that made it impossible for parties whose activities were limited to one particular area of Georgia – such as Ademon Nykhas – to participate in the parliamentary elections that October, which were won by the 'Round Table – Free Georgia' coalition led by the nationalist Gamsakhurdia. Motivated by this perceived discrimination, on 20 September 1990 South Ossetian leaders proclaimed their region an independent democratic Soviet republic. That December, elections took place in South Ossetia against the will of Georgia, which in turn abolished the autonomy of South Ossetia and called it Samashablo (Motherland) and Shida Kartli (Heart of Georgia).

Since neither side was willing to compromise, or even to negotiate, the abolition of South Ossetian autonomy turned the conflict into a real ethnic war. After three people were killed in a shoot-out, Georgia introduced a state of emergency in Tskhinvali and Java on 12 December 1990. Russian and Georgian MVD (Ministry of Interior) troops were dispatched, and during the night of 5 January 1991 several thousand Georgian troops entered South Ossetia. The war took place predominantly in Tskhinvali and on the main road to North Ossetia, and the blockade of the city lasted for more than eighteen months. On 7 January 1991, the Soviet president, Mikhail Gorbachev, issued a decree in which he nullified both the South Ossetians' declaration of independence and the Georgians' abolition of South Ossetian autonomy, as these were in contradiction of the Soviet constitution. But the Georgian Supreme Soviet rejected the decree, which it saw as interference in its internal affairs and an attempt to violate its territorial integrity. Concerned about the worsening situation in South Ossetia, on 20 February 1991 the Supreme Soviet of the USSR issued a resolution ordering the expansion of the state of emergency throughout South Ossetia, asking Georgia to provide the population with electricity, fuel, food and medicines, urging negotiations, and requesting protection for refugees in Georgia and North Ossetia. However, Georgia did not wish to comply with this and tried to boycott the all-union referendum in March 1991 – though it took place in South Ossetia and Abkhazia. During a summit on 23 March, Yeltsin and Gamsakhurdia discussed the situation in South Ossetia and signed a protocol aimed at ending the violence. Illegal gangs had to be disarmed, Soviet troops would be moved from South Ossetia to other parts of Georgia, and the refugee problem should be dealt with. In an independence referendum on 31 March, the Georgians decided to secede from the Soviet Union – Ossetia did not take part in this as it no longer considered itself as part of Georgia – and on 9 April (exactly two years after the Soviet army had violently crushed a demonstration in front of the Georgian parliament, killing nineteen people) the Georgian Supreme Soviet issued its declaration of independence. The Georgian–Russian protocol never came into force and the Soviet Union did not recognize Georgian independence. The Georgians in South Ossetia gradually left their homes and many Ossetians living in Georgia proper 'fled' to North Ossetia. Gamsakhurdia had been elected president on 26 May 1991, but was ousted on 8 January 1992 after two weeks of civil war. The violence in Tbilisi led to a calming of the situation in Ossetia, and the expulsion of the extreme nationalistic president also brought new hopes and prospects.

The installation of a new government and especially the appointment of Eduard Shevardnadze the following March resulted in a greater willingness on both sides to find a solution to the conflict. However, when the South Ossetian leadership organized a referendum on 19 January in which a majority of Ossetians supported independence from Georgia and unification with Russia, it was not only Georgia, but also Russia and even North Ossetia, which had enough problems in the Prigorodnyy Rayon, which were displeased. Hostilities and fighting re-emerged in spring 1992, and the killing of 36 Ossetian IDPs in the village of Kekhvi brought about a change in the attitude of North Ossetia, which launched an economic boycott of Georgia.

A fragile ceasefire agreement (the Sochi Agreement, not be confused with the 1993 Sochi Agreement ending the Georgian–Abkhaz War) was reached on 24 June 1992. While it ended the war, it did not tackle the question of the status of South Ossetia. Georgia needed at that time to resolve the situation, as it had new problems with the armed Zviadist rebellion in western Georgia and the first violent incidents in Abkhazia. A joint control commission and peacekeeping force, composed of Russians, Georgians and Ossetians, was set up, but the ceasefire agreement was violated a few times and the peace process was frozen from 1992 until 1995. The Ossetian government controlled the region independently from Tbilisi. Shevardnadze's positive attitude towards minority rights brought the two parties closer together, resulting in the Memorandum on Measures for Providing Security and Joint Confidence of May 1996. In November 1996, Lyudvig Chibirov was elected president of South Ossetia. During the following months there were several high-level meetings between Ossetians and Georgians, and on 14 November 1997 President Shevardnadze visited South Ossetia and signed a joint peace declaration with his South Ossetian counterpart. Relations eased in the following years, but still no agreement could be reached.

Hostilities flared up again in the summer of 2004. In May, the new president of Georgia, Mikheil Saakashvili, had offered humanitarian aid to the region and promised it a high degree of autonomy. But a month later, Georgian police closed down the market in Ergneti, which was a major trading point for tax-free goods from Russia and other smuggling – i.e. of major importance to the South Ossetian economy. Tension between Georgians and Ossetians increased during the following weeks. However, Russia also became involved after Georgian peacekeepers intercepted a Russian convoy with military equipment. Furthermore, the Russian Duma passed a resolution supporting the Ossetian secessionist claims. A ceasefire deal was reached on 13 August but was violated shortly after signature. Three months later a new deal was signed, but the rhetoric from Tbilisi and Tskhinvali did not suggest that either side was prepared to compromise.

In 2006 the South Ossetian authorities organized an independence referendum, which was backed by 99 per cent of voters. The result of this high figure is partly explained by the absence of ethnic Georgians in the region.

Hostilities in South Ossetia escalated once more in June and July 2008. Shooting and shelling started in the first days of August and led to the August War, which unfroze this 'frozen' conflict.

The August 2008 War

Relations with Russia were never really cordial after Georgia declared independence in 1991. They deteriorated after President Saakashvili came to power and reached a historic low in 2008. In March of that year, following Kosovo's declaration of independence, which was supported by a majority in the West, Russia announced it would revise its policy towards self-proclaimed republics. Although Abkhaz and South Ossetian ties with Russia had been very strong and many of the people had already obtained Russian passports, Russia increased its involvement in the region.

There followed a number of security-related incidents between Russia and Georgia, deepening the crisis even further: in April a Georgian drone was shot down above Abkhazia, in May explosions occurred in South Ossetia and Russia captured someone claimed to be working as a spy for the Georgians, in June Russian peacekeepers were detained, and in July several bomb attacks took place.

The war which broke out during the evening of 7 August, at a time when the entire world was watching the opening of the Olympic Games in Beijing, cannot just be called another Georgian–Ossetian war, or even purely a Georgian–Russian war, as it involved Russia, Georgia, South Ossetia and Abkhazia. There is no consensus as to which side initiated hostilities: Georgia claims it was acting in self-defence after South Ossetian attacks, whereas the Ossetians claim that Georgia provoked the war. The course of events and the number of casualties is also highly disputed. Georgia launched an attack on Tskhinvali and claimed to have held it for some time, but did not get much further. Russian troops crossed the border via the Roki tunnel and two days later Russian and South Ossetian troops took back the city. Fighting was not contained solely within the borders of South Ossetia. The Russian air force carried out airstrikes on strategic locations throughout Georgia, targeting several airfields, the port of Poti, navy vessels, a factory producing combat airplanes and tanks. As a result, Georgia's military infrastructure was significantly reduced. The city of Gori, some 25 km from the border of South Ossetia, had been the central rendezvous for the Georgian armed forces, but was occupied by Russian forces from 13 to 22 August. Russian forces advanced as close as 55 km from Tbilisi.

On 10 August, one day after a Georgian naval unit had been sunk by the Black Sea Fleet, and when the Georgian army was already in a weakened position, Abkhazia mobilized its forces to make use of the situation and drove out the 1,000 Georgian troops in the Upper Kodori valley. On 12 August the Georgian military retreated from Kodori, together with hundreds of ethnic Georgians who had been living there. Russian troops based in Abkhazia moved into Georgia proper and occupied Poti on 14 August.

Soon after fighting broke out, the international community called for a ceasefire and a peaceful solution to the conflict. The French president, Nicolas Sarkozy, in his capacity as President-in-Office of the European Council, took a lead and on 12 August agreed with presidents Medvedev and Saakashvili on a six-point peace plan, which was also signed by Eduard Kokoyty of South Ossetia and Sergey Bagapsh of Abkhazia. The withdrawal of Russian troops took longer than foreseen, and it was not until two months later that they had completely retreated from Georgia proper. On 1 October the EU deployed a monitoring mission consisting of 340 field specialists to oversee the implementation of the six-point peace plan.

Kosovo was seen as a precedent, and on 26 August Dmitriy Medvedev signed a decree recognizing Abkhazia and South Ossetia as independent and sovereign states, and called on other states to follow his example. Although the reaction of several countries was positive, only Nicaragua went as far as to formally recognize the break-away republics. Nagorno Karabakh has shown support for this move and silently hopes that its turn for recognition will follow, although Russia has signaled that this is unlikely to happen.

The Tbilisi civil war and Zviadist uprisings in western Georgia

Zviad Gamsakhurdia had become the first president of independent Georgia in 1991, but his autocratic behaviour soon put his position at risk. He made himself unpopular through a series of anti-democratic moves, including the change from locally elected to centrally appointed local government, the ban on the Communist Party after the coup in Moscow in August 1991, and the break-up of an opposition demonstration by police. Towards the end of the year the opposition turned more radical, and on 22 December 1991 the armed forces of warlords

Jaba Ioseliani and Tengiz Kitovani launched an attack against the president. After a two-week civil war in the centre of Tbilisi, Gamsakhurdia was ousted on 8 January 1992 and was granted asylum by Dzhokhar Dudayev in Chechnya. During the ensuing weeks the country was governed by a military council led by Ioseliani and Kitovani. Eduard Shevardnadze, the former minister of foreign affairs of the Soviet Union and of Georgian origin, came back to Tbilisi from Russia in early March and was appointed the new head of state.[6]

Samegrelo remained a loyal stronghold for Gamsakhurdia, mainly because he was Megrelian himself. On several occasions Shevardnadze had to send troops to western Georgia to put down Zviadist uprisings. The largest rebellion took place in the autumn of 1993 – around the same time as Shevardnadze's defeat in Abkhazia – when Gamsakhurdia returned from Chechnya to Samegrelo. After taking control of Samegrelo the insurgents threatened to take Kutaisi and march on to Tbilisi. Georgia suppressed the uprising with the assistance of the paramilitary Mkhedrioni bands and with the covert support of Russia, which claimed to be defending the railways. Soon afterwards Gamsakhurdia died in mysterious circumstances in the village of Jikhashkari in Samegrelo.

Another significant insurrection was the assault on Kutaisi in 1998 led by Colonel Akaki Eliava. Eliava had first joined the National Guard, led by Kitovani (who later overthrew Gamsakhurdia), but during the autumn 1993 revolt he was one of Gamsakhurdia's strongest supporters. After receiving amnesty, Eliava had become a colonel in the Georgian armed forces. In the early morning of 18 October 1998, some 200 soldiers left their barracks in Senaki and marched up to Kutaisi. A few small skirmishes took place with government troops just outside Kutaisi, but the soldiers agreed to return to their barracks. Although many Georgians did not support Eliava as a person, most of them did agree with his demands: the resignation of Shevardnadze and an immediate military solution to the Abkhaz problem.

The Zviadists have also been named in connection with attempts on the life of Shevardnadze. Shevardnadze was finally able to appease the Zviadists by granting them amnesty, and the Zviadist movement lost momentum after the suspicious death of Eliava in 2000. It would be wrong to refer to the civil war and Zviadist uprisings as a 'Megrelian issue', because Gamsakhurdia received support not only in Samegrelo but all over the country. However, due to their proximity, Megrelians are more affected by the unresolved problem in Abkhazia and therefore likely to show their dissatisfaction more openly than those in other parts of the country.

The Ingush–Ossetian conflict over the Prigorodnyy Rayon

The fighting over the Prigorodnyy Rayon, a district within the Republic of North Ossetia of slightly less than 1,000 km², was the first armed conflict on Russian territory after the collapse of the Soviet Union and has its roots in the tsarist

Russian and Soviet divide-and-rule policies. Historically, while the Ossetians and Ingush had never been at war, neither did they have particularly friendly relations. The conflict did not hold the attention of the international community or scholars, but the effects of the dispute, which reached its peak between 30 October and 6 November 1992, are still visible and could flare up again at any time. There remain many IDPs, hatred still exists, and a political settlement for the administrative status of the region has yet to be reached.

Officially, 419 Ingush and 171 Ossetians were killed and between 34,500 and 64,000 Ingush residents were forcibly removed, mainly to Ingushetia. The exact number is hard to determine as the 1989 census counted only the legally registered Ingush in the Prigorodnyy Rayon. Even now, there are several thousands of IDPs living in Ingushetia, and many of the abandoned houses have been taken by refugees from South Ossetia.

Traditionally, most of the right bank of the River Terek was seen as Ingush territory, including the eastern part of the city of Vladikavkaz. In the middle of the nineteenth century the Russians expelled the Ingush from this region and established Cossack settlements instead. The Ossetians, on the other hand, were favoured by the Russians because of their support of the tsarist regime. After the dissolution of the Mountain Republic in 1924, the Ingush and North Ossetian autonomous republics were formed and Vladikavkaz was proclaimed a dual capital. The Cossacks were banished from the region because of their support for the anti-Soviet White forces, while the Ingush had supported the Bolshevik communists. In 1934 the Ingush and Chechen ASSRs were merged, with Groznyy as capital, and Vladikavkaz was left under the sole jurisdiction of North Ossetia. This administrative restructuring was particularly detrimental to the Ingush. Not only did they loose their autonomy, they also lost their capital and the village of Nazran became their main settlement, while the largest part of the Prigorodnyy Rayon remained in the Ingush–Chechen ASSR.

On 23 February 1944 the Ingush and Chechens were deported to Central Asia and two weeks later the Chechen–Ingush ASSR was officially liquidated. The territory was populated by others and the Prigorodnyy Rayon was incorporated in the North Ossetian ASSR. Many people from the South Ossetian Autonomous Oblast were told or forced to move to regions previously inhabited by the Chechens and Ingush, including the Prigorodnyy Rayon. In January 1957 Chechen–Ingush autonomy was reinstated and the Chechens and Ingush were allowed to return to their native lands. However, there was no mechanism for allowing them to resettle in the places they had left, nor could they recover their confiscated properties. The Prigorodnyy Rayon and Novolak Rayon (now in Dagestan) were not returned to the Chechen–Ingush ASSR, though the Kargalin, Shelkov and Naur districts of the bordering Stavropol region were added instead. The Ingush were discouraged by the North Ossetian authorities from returning to the Prigorodnyy Rayon, and those who did faced huge difficulties in obtaining a residence permit, buying a house or finding a job. As a result, many Ingush settled illegally in the region. The relations between the two ethnic groups were tense throughout the 1960s, 1970s and 1980s. In 1973 there was an Ingush demonstration in Groznyy over the Prigorodnyy Region. Eight years later there were Ossetian demonstrations calling for the expulsion of all Ingush after an Ossetian taxi-driver was killed by Ingush passengers. Moscow intervened and, owing to his inability to deal with the situation, replaced the head of the Ossetian republic.

In 1990, at the peak of perestroika, which had led to a growing feeling of national identity, the Ingush demanded the re-establishment of the territorial unit, which had existed until 1934. This had been encouraged by several declarations and resolutions in 1989–91 which had provided for the full rehabilitation of the repressed people and the restoration of territorial integrity. However, these provisions never came into force, and because of the Russian moratorium on border changes the Prigorodnyy Rayon could not be returned.

In September 1989 an Ingush people's congress called for a separate Ingush entity which would include the Prigorodnyy Rayon. Due to their strong pro-Yeltsin attitude, the Ingush initially received support from the central authorities. In March 1990 the Belyakov Commission investigated the claims and concluded that some of them were justifiable. Around the same time the Georgian–Ossetian conflict led to the exodus of tens of thousands of Ossetians from Georgia, mainly to North Ossetia. Many of them settled in the Prigorodnyy Rayon, where it was claimed that they committed several atrocities. In November 1991 the Chechen–Ingush ASSR unilaterally declared independence, but the Ingush wanted their own independence. For several months the Ingush inhabited regions remained in a political vacuum, without any government, without a capital and without fixed borders. Finally, on 4 June 1992, the Ingush Republic was set up.

During 1991–2 both sides armed themselves rapidly and ethnic tensions grew. There was an increasing number of ethnically motivated killings and clashes, culminating at the end of October 1992, when North Ossetian officials blamed the Ingush for blowing up an important gas pipeline and an 11-year-old Ingush girl was run over by an Ossetian armoured vehicle. Several people, both civilians and militiamen, were killed over the following days. The situation escalated, armed Ingush mobs from Ingushetia proper descended on the Prigorodnyy Rayon, and on 30 October the Ingush quarters of two villages were shelled. On the following day some 8,000 Russian troops arrived in Vladikavkaz, but their deployment as peacekeepers on the Ingush–Ossetian border did not begin immediately. The role these forces played is not very clear. Some helped to bring the Ingush safely out of the conflict zone, whereas others did nothing. Yet others assisted the North Ossetian forces to push out the Ingush and loot and destroy the abandoned homes. However, the fact that they were deployed on the border stressed the policy of the Russians that the Prigorodnyy Rayon should remain a part of North Ossetia. On 10 November the Russian troops advanced and occupied Ingushetia, which may have been an attempt to provoke Dudayev. However, Chechnya proclaimed neutrality and blocked its borders.

There was no solution to the conflict and enmity continued. Ingush with a residence permit (*propiska*) have been allowed to return to their homes, but

Ossetians often prevented them from remaining. Those who settled illegally in the region are not allowed to return. Relations between the Ingush and the Ossetians eased a little but have not become friendly, and from time to time hostile messages appear in the media. The hostage-taking at the school in Beslan led to new enmities and fears of a new Ingush–Ossetian war.

Samtskhe–Javakheti

The Georgian administrative-territorial unit of Samtskhe–Javakheti, which because of its harsh climate is often called the Georgian Siberia, is composed of two historically distinct regions. Meskheti, the region around Akhaltsikhe, is the historical homeland of the Meskhetians and is now inhabited by Georgians and Armenians. Javakheti, the region of Akhalkalaki and Ninotsminda, has a population which is 90 per cent Armenian. The Armenians in Samtskhe–Javakheti now constitute one of the biggest Armenian communities in Georgia. They originally lived in the province of Erzurum in the Ottoman Empire and arrived – some forcibly, others voluntarily – in southern Georgia after Russia obtained Samtskhe–Javakheti following the Russian-Ottoman War of 1828–9.

In November–December 1918, Georgia and Armenia fought a short but bloody war over Samtskhe–Javakheti. Georgia had occupied the region after the Turkish army abandoned it at the end of the First World War, but Armenia claimed it was Armenian territory. Samtskhe–Javakheti constitutes the potential for a violent conflict which could lead to a greater Caucasian war, where Armenia, Azerbaijan, and even Russia, Turkey and Iran could be involved. There are many reasons for such a conflict, including socio-economic problems, local Armenian nationalist demands, the repatriation of Meskhetian Turks, and clan struggles in the region. So far there have been no real clashes between the Armenians and Georgians, but frictions do exist and fear for the future is apparent. Ethnic tensions appeared under the nationalist Gamsakhurdia government and led to demands for regional autonomy and even secession. Later, Shevardnadze tried to ease public unrest by encouraging the participation of minorities in the formation of Georgian statehood and civic institutions.

Socio-economic problems are considerable in Samtskhe–Javakheti, the poorest and least advanced region of Georgia, itself in general economically weak. The withdrawal of the Russian base in Akhalkalaki, which used to be the largest employer in the region, has further contributed to the problem. Both the Armenians and the local Georgians suffer from this situation and are equally poor. It is mainly owing to the inability, rather than the unwillingness, to invest in the region that the central government in Tbilisi has not been able to bring prosperity. Furthermore, government institutions are extremely weak because of the highly centralized system, but more importantly because of the rivalries between the different clans. Agriculture is the main source of income and unemployment is soaring. Because of their limited knowledge of the Georgian language, most Armenians have little or no chance of obtaining a good education or of finding a job in Tbilisi or in governmental institutions. Many young men migrated to Russia in search of work and now send money to their families.

In reality, Javakheti in particular is economically and politically closer to Armenia than to Georgia, and several local Armenian political parties defend the rights and opinion of the Armenians there. They strive to establish better minority rights and express concerns about a potential threat from Turkey. The two main parties are Javakhk and Virk. The former is believed to be linked to the (Armenian) Dashnaktsutiun Party, which supports the unification of Javakheti with Armenia but often sends out conciliatory signals to Tbilisi. These unification demands are supported by the Armenian diaspora, but the Armenian government officially backs the territorial integrity of Georgia, and has actually tried to restrain such radical nationalist demands. It realizes that, as its borders with Turkey and Azerbaijan remain closed, any war that were to take place with Georgia would lead to Armenia's almost total isolation.

In April 1999 Georgia agreed to the repatriation of the Meskhetian Turks as a condition of its membership of the Council of Europe. However, both the Georgians and the Armenians in Samtskhe–Javakheti have opposed this 12-year repatriation plan, which in fact has not actually materialized. There is a wide range of fears: claims for autonomy, national consciousness, pan-Turkism, bloodshed between Meskhetians and Georgians or Armenians, shortage of land, religious conflicts, and ambiguity about the number of people who wish to return. There are also potential economic problems, and no money to settle them, which would lead to a competition for land and employment. There are two important Meskhetian movements, and each has its own view on the nationality issue. Vatan (Homeland) is a pro-Turkish organization, while Khsna is aware of its Georgian consciousness.

The Lezgin call for independence

The Lezgin people are split by the Samur River between Dagestan (170,000) and Azerbaijan (205,000), though some sources estimate the total number here as 1.2 million.[7] Their fate is quite similar to that of the Basques, who are divided between France and Spain. Although there has never been an independent and united Lezgin state, there have been calls to create an independent Lezgistan. In 1860 the Russian Empire used the Samur River to reorganize its administrative structure in the Caucasus, a partition that was taken over by the Soviet system. Although the Lezgins were separated according to the borders on the map, they still had close economic and social ties with one another. However, with the collapse of the USSR, they suddenly found that the Samur River was the boundary between two sovereign states, and requests for a 'stability zone' and fewer border formalities were denied.

Although the first calls for Lezgin unification and guarantees of their rights arose as early as 1959, the main political movement fighting for their cause, Sadval (Unity), was created in Dagestan in July 1990. While there was initially no claim of discrimination in Dagestan, they simply wanted the unification of Lezgistan. In December 1991, at the All-National Congress of Lezgins, a declaration was adopted calling for the creation of a unified and independent Lezgistan within the Russian Federation. In Azerbaijan, a more moderate organization called Samur was formed. The Lezgins in Azerbaijan refused to join the Azerbaijani army or fight in Nagorno Karabakh, and in summer 1992 they were afraid they would suffer from the deteriorating relations between Russia and Azerbaijan. Lezgin movements have rarely been violent, even during the rallies and clashes that took place in 1992–4, in both Dagestan and Azerbaijan. Despite this, Sadval has been cited as the cause of the 19 March 1994 bomb blast on the Baku metro, in which 14 people died and 42 were injured. During the trial following the attack, a link was said to be found with Armenia and Nagorno Karabakh. There was evidence that the Armenian Secret Service had cooperated in the establishment of Sadval, provided the Lezgins with funding, training and weapons, and received many visits from its leaders.

Sadval's call for an independent Lezgistan was dropped in April 1996, as it would have created even more ethnic problems. Nevertheless, the potential to destabilize Azerbaijan and Dagestan still exists.

The Talysh call for independence

A Talysh khanate emerged in the seventeenth century and obtained independence in 1747 as a result of the disintegration of Nadir Shah's empire. Because of sustained pressure from Persia, the Talysh khan turned towards Russia, and the khanate became a Russian protectorate in 1802. The Treaty of Turkmenchay of 1828 divided the Talysh nation: the territory north of the Araks River was incorporated into the Russian Empire while that south of the river became part of Persia. At the end of the Second World War the Soviet army invaded Northern Iran, and the country remained under Soviet control for the next two years, until they were forced to retreat under pressure from the Western Allies. During Soviet times there were several attempts to assimilate the Talysh, and they have not been mentioned separately in the population censuses since 1959. But nationalist feelings and resistance towards 'Turkification plans' have led on two occasions to the declaration of an independent Talysh state.

During the summer of 1918 a pro-Russian Mughan dictatorship was established as a counterweight to the independent republic of Azerbaijan, and in May 1919 the Talysh Mughan Socialist Republic was founded (the name Mughan comes from the local geographic region, the Mughan steppe). However, in April 1920 the republic was dissolved and integrated into the Azerbaijani Soviet Socialist Republic.

In 1993, at the height of the war in Karabakh, a popular uprising occurred in the Talysh-Mughan region, partly because the Talysh did not want to serve in the Azerbaijani army against the Karabakhis. The revolt led by Surat Huseynov, leading to the collapse of the government of Abulfaz Elchibey and the rise to power of Heydar Aliyev, and the turmoil and confusion it created in Azerbaijan provided the local military opposition group in Mughan with an additional stimulus. On 20 July 1993 Colonel Alikram Gumbatov declared the Talysh-Mughan Autonomous Republic and proclaimed himself as president, but a month later the Azerbaijani government suppressed the autonomist movement and jailed Gumbatov and his closest supporters. There are theories that this uprising was supported by Moscow and initiated by Ayaz Mutalibov, the first president of independent Azerbaijan, who was replaced by a coup in May 1992. Gumbatov was said to be a supporter of Mutalibov and wanted to see the latter back in office.

The region is still seen as a problem, but there is currently no fear of a similar uprising. Iran has no interest in destabilizing the region, as this might cause more difficulties among its own huge Azerbaijani population.

Adjara

Adjara had been part of Georgia for many years when it was first integrated into the Ottoman Empire in 1614. Most of the Adjars, who feel themselves to be Georgians, adopted Islam between the seventeenth and nineteenth century, and religion is their only distinctive feature. Adjara became part of the Russian Empire after the Russo-Turkish War of 1877–8, and in 1920 the British administration, which had taken control after the end of the First World War, ceded the region to Georgia. The following year, under influence from Turkey, the Soviet government declared the Adjarian Autonomous Soviet Socialist Republic. It was the only autonomy in the Soviet Union based on religion rather than on ethnicity. During the final decades of the existence of the USSR Georgian assimilation attempts took place, but the Adjars remained faithful to Islam.

In 1989 the Adjars wished – like the Abkhazians and South Ossetians – to retain their autonomy, mainly because their local leaders did not want to relinquish power. However, they never desired to secede from Georgia. Two years later there were demonstrations both calling for the preservation of Adjara's autonomy and against the new anti-Islamic practices. Aslan Abashidze, the head of Adjara's supreme council, used the political instability of the early 1990s and his good relations with both Russia and Turkey to achieve his personal goal – the establishment of an authoritarian regime without too much interference from Tbilisi.

Abashidze became quite a popular politician, not only in Adjara but also in the rest of Georgia, but his regime in the small autonomous republic was very autocratic. For example, all elections were characterized by irregularities, Abashidze had close ties with Moscow and promoted the idea of Russian troops in Adjara, opposition was close to non-existent, and the Adjarian leadership refused to transfer taxes and customs duties to the central budget.

Although his relations with the president were extremely bad, and although his Union of Democratic Revival of Georgia formed a large opposition group in Tbilisi, Abashidze was not comfortable with the ousting of Shevardnadze in November 2003. Probably because he rightly understood that he could or would suffer the same fate; he called it a violent coup d'état. The new Georgian president, Mikhail Saakashvili, ordered Abashidze to comply with the Georgian constitution, but the latter refused. Six months after the rose revolution demonstrations took place in Batumi, and on 6 May 2004, following a second rose revolution, Abashidze was forced to step down and leave for Moscow. The Adjar problem was in fact centred on the person of Aslan Abashidze and so it seemed that the problem had been solved. However, some observers say that Adjara's autonomy is currently just nominal and could lead to renewed dissatisfaction.

The Caucasian border disputes

The borders between the Soviet Union and its sovereign neighbors were set efficiently (e.g. the Soviet–Turkish border was demarcated in 1925–6 according to the Treaty of Kars of 13 October 1921). As a result the Turkish and Iranian border with Georgia, Azerbaijan and Armenia is clear-cut and does not give rise to any problems. The situation is completely different as regards the common borders of the successor states of the Soviet Union. Although these were defined in 1921 and changed several times in the following decades, they were not based on the ethnic background of the population of the region nor were they considered to be state borders; their function was purely administrative. The sovereignty of the newly independent states made these administrative borders into state borders, and as a result a matter of crucial importance. The 1921 maps and regulations are ambiguous in some respects, and several borders were changed after the deportations of some of the Caucasian people (e.g. part of Kabardino–Balkaria was part of Georgia for some years). The present border disputes are played down in order to prevent any hostility being created among neighbouring states that might be of strategic importance for the future. Nevertheless, this does not mean these issues are not being discussed.

There are points of the Azerbaijani–Georgian border which could give rise to disputes, but at present relations are friendly. The Armenian–Georgian border is also ambiguous, especially in the Akhalkalaki and Ninotsminda regions (Samtskhe–Javakheti). The problem here is closely related to the issue of the Armenian population in the region. The meandering Azerbaijani–Armenian border with its many enclaves is probably the most difficult of all, as there were agreements that certain areas could be used during winter by Armenia and during summer by Azerbaijan. Furthermore, the borders between Russia on one side and Georgia and Azerbaijan on the other have still not been fully determined. Although this causes potential for conflict, the mountainous and inhospitable character of the region does not make it a burning issue.

The administrative borders between the 83 entities of the Russian Federation are not always distinct, and are often contested in the eastern part of the North Caucasus. First, the dispute between North Ossetia and Ingushetia over the Prigorodnyy Rayon remains unresolved. Second, when Ingushetia separated from Chechnya, which had declared itself independent, no border between the two was clearly defined, but none of the political leaders of the two republics is willing to discuss the issue. Moreover, the Akkin Chechen minority in Dagestan, whose territory had been part of Chechnya before their deportation, clashed with the Laks in the late 1990s in their desire to be part of Chechnya again.

Odd territorial division and the Cossack issue in the North Caucasus

The Northwestern Caucasus has been spared any major conflict in the past few decades. However, the region has a turbulent past, and the current complex territorial division has the potential for civil unrest. The republics of Karachay–Cherkessia and Kabardino–Balkaria, which were created in 1920 as an alternative to autonomies, provide a good example of unusual demographic structure and territorial division. Their asymmetrical division was further complicated by the northern border being drawn further north, which led to the inclusion of many Cossacks, known to be hostile to the Muslim Caucasians. There are also Abazins in Karachay–Cherkessia, and both republics embrace some 10 per cent of other ethnic minorities. The more religious Karachays and Balkars were deported in 1943–4, but following their rehabilitation, in 1957, significant numbers of Balkars were unable to return to their own villages as the Kabardians had taken possession of the lands. Although there have been several requests for a change in status or territorial division, the majority of the population seems to be in favour of a status quo.

Karachay–Cherkessia was re-established in 1957 as an autonomous oblast, and in 1988 the Karachay national movement Jamagat, as part of their quest for full territorial rehabilitation, called for a separate Karachay entity, as had existed from 1926 to 1943. The oblast was not split up, but was upgraded to an ASSR, with approximately 31 per cent Karachays, 10 per cent Cherkess, 7 per cent Abazins, 42 per cent Russians and 10 per cent other minorities. Vladimir Khubiyev was appointed head in 1979 by the central government in Moscow. By 1998 Karachay–Cherkessia was the only republic to have an unelected leader, and following demonstrations the first presidential elections took place in April 1999. In the first round the Cherkess candidate, Stanislav Derev, who also had the support of the Abazins, was considerably ahead of the Karachay candidate, Vladimir Semenov. Semenov won, however, in the second round, which led to discontent among the Cherkess, the Abazins and even some ethnic Russians and Cossacks. In August of that year there was an appeal to President Yeltsin to restore Cherkess autonomy within the Stavropol Kray, which had been the case until 1957. One month later an extraordinary congress in Cherkessia voted in favour of the restoration of this autonomous oblast and designated Derev as its head. While the Russian state Duma would not accept the creation of an independent administrative entity within the Russian Federation, it did not propose a clear solution.

The Balkars, who form a minority in Kabardino–Balkaria (9 per cent Balkars, 48 per cent Kabardians, 32 per cent Russians and 11 per cent others), have also tried to obtain full rehabilitation and regain the lands which were taken by the Kabardians after the deportations of 1944. However, the separatist sentiments that erupted in 1991 were supported by only a small part of the population. The National Council of Balkar People, an independence movement headed by Sufiyan Beppayev, proclaimed Balkar sovereignty on 12 November 1996. However, there was little popular support for this move and, after he had been offered an important governmental position by President Kokov, Beppayev distanced himself from his earlier actions, explaining that the declaration of a separate Balkar Republic was a complete mistake.

The odd territorial divisions are, however, not the only source of tensions. Since perestroika there has been a revival of Cossack identity and several associations to revive Cossack traditions have been set up. The Cossack leadership shifted their focus quite quickly from cultural issues to political matters and has also requested that autonomy should be re-established. Although such autonomy might currently be unrealistic, state subsidies to the Cossacks are increasing and their influence is growing. There have been discussions in Moscow on giving the Cossack paramilitaries some kind of semi-official status in order to secure a strong ally in the North Caucasus. This is especially important on account of the loss of Russian influence in the region from the late 1980s and the parallel increase in national consciousness among the Muslim peoples. For example, there is a full chapter dedicated to the Cossacks in the Charter of the Rostov Oblast. The Cossacks, who tend to be intolerant towards non-Russians, have engaged in clashes with their neighbours – Chechens, Armenians, Jews and other ethnic minorities. In 1991 a congress of Cossack deputies proclaimed the Zelenchuk–Urup Territorial Okrug, which was located in the Karachay–Cherkess Autonomous Oblast, although this autonomy did not last very long. It has also been suggested that Cossacks have assisted the pro-Russian factions in Abkhazia, Transdniestra and the former Yugoslavia.

The role of the Cossacks is also increasing in the Northeastern Caucasus, in their former Terek host (a host being an administrative subdivision in imperial Russia). Nevertheless, they probably took a smaller part in the Chechen wars than might have been the case.

Fragile stability in Dagestan

The complex ethnic composition of Dagestan is characterized by a fragile stability. Many Dagestani ethnic groups have combined their strengths and have violently resisted any Russian advance in the region. Dagestan and many of its ethnic groups played an important role in the Caucasian War, and Dagestan was one of the main centres of the last North Caucasian rebellion, the so-called last *ghazawat* of 1920–22. A hypothesis as to why the Dagestanis were not affected by Stalin's deportations is that this could have led to a new Caucasian war. However, this does not mean there is a strong sense of unity among the Dagestani nations.

Although many analysts expected conflicts in Dagestan after the break-up of the Soviet Union, the region has been spared large-scale violence and the few disagreements that have arisen have been successfully resolved. The Akkin Chechens were deported in 1944, and Laks and Avars were resettled in the Aukhov (renamed into Novolak) district. After their rehabilitation, the Akkin Chechens desired to move back to their native lands and came into conflict with the Laks and Avars, especially in 1991–2. Several Laks agreed to resettle in other parts of Dagestan. Another potentially dangerous situation arose on 7 August 1999, when three villages in the Botlikh district declared it an independent Islamic territory. However, this Islamic republic lasted for only a few days. The previous year a few other Dagestani villages had also proclaimed Islamic rule and renounced Russian authority. In addition, the Kumyk popular front Tenglik has made unclear demands, ranging from some form of local autonomy to the establishment of a sovereign republic.

The legal status of the Caspian

Following the break-up of the Soviet Union, there are five states with coastlines on the Caspian Sea: Russia, Azerbaijan, Iran, Turkmenistan and Kazakhstan. Some of these countries assumed, and unilaterally took, ownership of various oil fields, which led to the emergence of the question of the legal status of the Caspian. The main issue is therefore not one of determination, but about the consequences, of the legal status on the ownership and exploitation rights of the oil fields. In 1992 all five states put forward their own solution, and this led to a polarization in 1994, when Azerbaijan signed 'the deal of the century' with foreign consortia. In 1996 there were some signs of reconciliation, and there have since been several proposals affording compromise, but so far all have been unsuccessful. Azerbaijan in particular holds competing claims with Turkmenistan and Iran over several fields. An important incident took place in July 2001, when an Iranian warship and two jets forced a research vessel working for BP/Amoco to leave what Azerbaijan calls its own sector and to cease exploring a major oil field.

A short historical overview might lead to a better understanding of the policies of certain countries. Russia, which had its first presence there in 913, has exercised a monopoly over the Caspian Sea for many years. The 1723 Treaty of St Petersburg set out the supremacy of Russia and freedom of trade on the Caspian, but was replaced six years later by the Treaty of Resht, giving significant privileges to Persia. Two more important documents dealing with Russian–Persian relations were the treaties of Gulistan and Turkmenchay. These treaties, which acknowledged Russian supremacy and gave the Russians exclusive rights to a military fleet on the Caspian, remained in force for almost a century. The 1921 Friendship Treaty and 1940 Treaty of Commerce and Navigation cancelled all previous treaties and gave equal rights of military and commercial navigation to both countries: while the territorial waters for each extended for 10 miles, the rest of the sea was a zone of common ownership, meaning that neither country had the right of exploitation. In reality, however, Soviet ships also fished in the zone of common ownership, and Iran was unable to do anything about it. This treaty did not make any mention of the legal status of the Caspian or of exploitation rights.

Initially, Russia and Iran wanted to continue applying these rules, but Azerbaijan, Kazakhstan and Turkmenistan considered themselves to be parties outside of these treaties. Gradually, the various countries came up with their own proposals. Azerbaijan, Kazakhstan and Turkmenistan were in favour of dividing the Caspian Sea into sectors based on the median line, thus giving each country a share proportional to the length of its coastline in which it could deal with the resources unilaterally. However, Iran would have ended up with the smallest share, and thus it proposed dividing the sea into five sectors of equal size. Russia from its side argued for a condominium, under which all decisions concerning the exploitation of gas and oil fields would have to be agreed upon by all five countries. Since the late 1990s there have been several diplomatic efforts to reach an agreement, and the opinions of some countries have now begun to merge. Russia, Kazakhstan and Azerbaijan have reached a common agreement about dividing the northern part of the Caspian into sectors with exclusive rights, though Iran does not recognize these agreements and continues bilateral discussions in order to achieve its 20 per cent share. Turkmenistan is in favour of the UN arbitrating the ownership issue.

Racism and anti-Caucasian feelings in Russia

An important conflict-related issue is that of the rise of anti-Caucasian feelings and racism in Russia. In recent years many non-Russians, including several Caucasians, have been beaten up or even killed, purely for racial reasons. This increasing level of xenophobia is apparent not only among the growing groups of ultra-nationalists and neo-Nazis, but also among the Russian intelligentsia, though it is unlikely to be a coordinated government policy. A large proportion of the Russian population cultivates a nationalist, chauvinist and racist mentality in which all darker-skinned people (called *chernye*, or black people) – including Caucasians – are by definition bad. What is perceived in the West as racism is commonly accepted and even promoted in Russia, with the media playing a major role by using the term 'individual of Caucasian nationality' (*litso Kavkazskoy natsionalnosti*). If something bad occurs, a link to the Caucasus, and more specifically to Chechnya or Georgia, is rapidly fabricated. However, most Russians know very little about Caucasians, their history or their culture.

A look at the future: conflicts of the twenty-first century

Whereas some politicians attempt to convince their electorates that they will solve all conflicts quickly and that the Caucasus will be a prosperous place, the future definitely does not look very bright. Mutual alienation among the different ethnic groups will continue, as youth no longer has a common language. Russian used to be the lingua franca that enabled communication among the different nations, but this uniting element is disappearing. Many other potential conflicts are waiting around the corner.

There are many other ethnic minorities in the region that could potentially cause unrest, but most are not likely to fight for autonomy or independence. Many Armenians and Azerbaijanis live in Georgia, and the Ingilo are a Georgian tribe in Azerbaijan. Many of these and other minorities allege discrimination and often have a good reason for their claim.

Resource wars[8] form a second potential for conflict: several parts of the Caucasus suffer from water shortages, the ownership of oil and gas reserves has not been fully determined, and the income generated from these resources is not equally distributed.

Third, there is potential for conflict not only between ethnic groups but also among citizens of one nation. The region has already seen many demonstrations, especially following long electricity cuts or politically motivated illegal arrests. This is because of the huge socio-economic problems in the Caucasus and the unequal treatment of people, often depending on their status. The mass impoverishment and social problems in the Caucasus are caused by such factors as political instability, conflicts, legal uncertainty, bad governance, corruption and tax evasion. While there are a small number of wealthy people, the majority of the population earns little and lives in poor conditions, especially in the South Caucasus. This is aggravated by the large number of IDPs and refugees (e.g. the 750,000 IDPs from Nagorno Karabakh in Azerbaijan, 250,000 from Abkhazia and South Ossetia in Georgia, some 50,000 Meshketians who still did not fully settle, etc.). Furthermore, the emigration of highly qualified people has resulted in a brain drain, and has contributed to economic decline. If the promised economic development, and especially the huge benefits to be obtained from the extraction of oil and gas, turns out not to benefit the general population, civil unrest may arise.

6

INTERNATIONAL POLITICS

As small states surrounded by former superpowers, the three South Caucasian republics have to cope with external pressure and influence while trying to retain their independence and foreign policy priorities. As a result, each has its own distinct foreign policy orientation: Georgia is outspokenly pro-US, Armenia is pro-Russian, and Azerbaijan has a more balanced outlook but with very close ties to Turkey. Russia's external relations are not discussed in much detail in this chapter, as the North Caucasus is not as crucial in foreign policy considerations – mainly because Russia does not want any other third party to interfere in its internal affairs.

Until the end of the Cold War there was a clear bipolar structure in global international relations. The break-up of the Soviet Union dramatically changed this situation, but it also led to the creation of new sovereign states with their own foreign policy orientations. After establishing independence the republics of the South Caucasus, which had only limited experience in international diplomacy, were confronted with a difficult task. Not only did a foreign policy have to be developed, but their Ministry of Foreign Affairs had to be restructured, diplomats had to be trained and embassies had to be set up, and so it was several years before diplomatic relations were fully established.

The attacks of September 11, 2001, resulted in an increased interest in the Caucasus, both as a result of shifting relations between Russia and the United States and because of its proximity to the Middle East and Central Asia. Russia joined the 'War against Terror', but, whereas the focus of the US was on Afghanistan, repackaged its war in Chechnya as part of this. Russia claims the Chechen rebels have links with Al-Qaeda, and as a result rejects the double standards of the West. In 2002 Georgia's Pankisi gorge was bombed by Russian aircraft, as Al-Qaeda was said to be present there.

Until recently the concept of geopolitics has been at the centre of the foreign policy-making of modern states. However, this idea has become outdated and been replaced by the notion of geo-economics, where the emphasis is on the combination of geographical location and economic opportunities.

International relations at the local level

The foreign policy orientations of the South Caucasian states

Armenian foreign policy was shaped soon after Levon Ter-Petrossian was elected president in 1991 and was based primarily on two principles. First, the security of Armenia and its people depends on the normalization of relations with its neighbours and the resolution of the Nagorno Karabakh conflict through peaceful negotiations and the development of regional economic cooperation. This includes improving relations with Turkey. The second principle is that of non-isolation and integration into the world community by participating in international organizations, but without joining any political or military bloc. Almost two decades later these principles still apply, mainly because the conflict over Nagorno Karabakh remains unsettled. There was one potential major change in international relations when Ter-Petrossian seemed to be willing to recognize Azerbaijan's territorial integrity in 1997, which could have led to a breakthrough. However, six months later the president had to resign on account of growing resistance to his policy on Karabakh. The new president, Robert Kocharyan, reverted to a hard stance on this issue but did not alter the country's foreign policy. Although relations with Azerbaijan and Turkey have not been normalized, Armenia has been able to balance its foreign policy quite well, still leaning more towards Russia. While it has cooperated with the US in the 'coalition against terror', it has retained close economic and political links with Russia and has established friendly relations with Iran. In employing the principle of complementarity, Armenia aims to create conditions which overlap rather than contradict the interests of Russia and the West.

From its inception, Azerbaijan's foreign policy has focused specifically on security issues, both at the national and the regional level, the main issue being the resolution of the conflict over Nagorno Karabakh and its outcomes. The position of Azerbaijan in the global economy has gradually gained importance on account of its vast oil and gas resources, and after September 2001 the War against Terror also started to play a role. Initially, relations with Turkey were a priority because of the close ethnic and cultural links between the two countries and because it seemed the most promising avenue for ending the war over Nagorno Karabakh. Furthermore, a pro-Turkish and pro-Western orientation was seen as the best way of securing Azerbaijani independence. At the same time, President Elchibey's support for the autonomy of the Azerbaijanis in northern Iran led to strained relations with their large neighbour to the south. In addition, relations with Russia were at a low ebb. The direction of foreign policy changed considerably when Ilham Aliyev came to power in the summer of 1993. Although Turkey had supported Elchibey during the coup, relations between Aliyev and the Turkish leadership were at the highest level. Aliyev gradually sought to improve relations with Azerbaijan's two big neighbours, Russia and Iran, and the country currently tries to maintain friendly relations with all neighbouring states with the exception of Armenia. In order not to upset anyone and to guarantee its own independence, it attempts to keep a balance between Russia and the West on the one hand and between the US and the Islamic world on the other. An important aspect of its foreign policy is oil diplomacy. First of all, Azerbaijan wishes to attract foreign states and businesses to invest in energy projects. Second, it already has agreements with Russia and Kazakhstan on the division of the Caspian Sea and is still discussing this matter with Iran and Turkmenistan. A third and probably the most important aspect is that Azerbaijan has become more self-confident in international relations. On several occasions the Azerbaijani leadership has pointed out that it might use income from its oil and gas resources to modernize and upgrade its army in order to regain control of Nagorno Karabakh.

Zviad Gamsakhurdia followed an anti-Russian and pro-American line as soon as Georgia declared independence in May 1991 by trying to establish foreign diplomatic relations and break out of his country's isolation. However, because of the continuing existence of the Soviet Union, other states were reluctant to cooperate, and a few weeks after the USSR was officially dissolved Gamsakhurdia was ousted. Things changed completely when Eduard Shevardnadze, the former minister of foreign affairs of the Soviet Union, returned to Tbilisi. Shevardnadze was well known in the West and was even seen as a 'key person in bringing a peaceful end to the Cold War'.[1] Shevardnadze was quite successful in balancing the foreign policy of his country, aiming to seek international support for its position towards the breakaway republics of Abkhazia and South Ossetia. He was a bit more cautiously pro-Russian than his predecessor and tried to maintain friendly relations with his neighbour to the north. However, these ties deteriorated in 1999, when Russia accused Georgia of harbouring Chechen rebels in its Pankisi gorge. As a result Shevardnadze became more and more openly pro-Western, guiding the country into the WTO and even calling for NATO membership. Mikheil Saakashvili, who studied and worked for some time in the US, made an attempt to normalize relations with Russia, but after this proved unsuccessful he began to follow an explicitly pro-Western and anti-Russian policy.

Intra-Caucasian relations

Armenian–Georgian relations have been friendly and, because the two countries are interdependent, several friendship treaties have been signed. Having closed its borders with Azerbaijan and Turkey, Armenia needs Georgia as a vital link to Russia. There are hopes to reopen the railway from Russia to Armenia which runs through Abkhazia, but on account of the conflict over Abkhazia this seems unlikely to happen in the near future. Georgia, on its part, is grateful for Armenia's support for its territorial integrity in regard to the issue of Javakheti and was actually the first country to recognize Armenian independence. On the other hand, relations between the two countries have not always been strong because they have very different foreign policy orientations. Georgia considers

Armenia as a sort of fifth column of Russia, whereas Armenia is not overjoyed about Georgia's good relations with Turkey and Azerbaijan.

Azerbaijani–Georgian relations are very cordial because the two countries are strategic partners, especially when it comes to economic development and the implementation of energy projects. Both Georgia, as the transit country, and Azerbaijan benefit from the export of Azerbaijani oil. These beneficial relations were definitely influenced by the long-standing friendship between Eduard Shevardnadze and Heydar Aliyev, who had similar political careers. The new presidents have tried to continue these friendly relationships, but there is some friction. First of all, Baku does not appreciate the good relations between Armenia and Georgia, but Tbilisi aims at a balanced policy in the South Caucasus. Second, the Azerbaijani–Georgian border is not clearly demarcated and the Azerbaijani minority in Georgia claims of discrimination. There are, however, no real fears of a conflict between the two neighbours, as both realize that it would do a lot more harm than good.

Armenian–Azerbaijani relations have been openly hostile since the independence of the two countries and have resulted in severe social and economic consequences. The mutual distrust and the conflict over Nagorno Karabakh are the key factors in this. Both countries deny responsibility, and Azerbaijan is determined to regain control of the region. There are no diplomatic ties between the two and the border has been closed. While there have been several meetings between Armenian and Azerbaijani politicians, these have been due solely to pressure from third parties. Because it has imposed an embargo on its enemy, Azerbaijan does not want to use Armenia as a transit country for Caspian oil and gas. Allowing Armenia to profit from these resources might make it stronger both economically and militarily.

Towards the end of the 1990s, and especially after the 1999 OSCE summit, there was an escalation in trilateral cooperation initiatives, often supported by another country or an international organization. In most cases, on account of the hostile relations between Armenia and Azerbaijan, Georgia played a central role. Shevardnadze came up with the 'For a Peaceful Caucasus' initiative in 1996, and the Georgian parliament organized meetings with their Armenian and Azeri counterparts. Russia, the US and the Council of Europe set up their own initiatives, and after the 1999 OSCE summit the Caucasian Stability Pact received a lot of attention. Unfortunately, none of these initiatives had any lasting success.

International relations at the regional level

Russia and the CIS

After having ruled over the South Caucasus for almost two centuries,[2] Moscow had to loosen its grip on the region as a result of domestic problems related to the collapse of the USSR. It recognized the independence of these new republics without much reluctance in late 1991 and did not initially try to impose its will on them. Towards the end of 1992, Russia re-emerged on the international scene. The following year a military doctrine was approved which gave special attention to stability in its 'near abroad' (i.e. the regions bordering Russia) and which implied that the Russian sphere of influence corresponded to that of the former USSR. Russia watched the expansion of Turkish, US and Iranian influence in the South Caucasus, and understood that it was losing the region and could lose or see a destabilized North Caucasus as well. The approach to each of the three South Caucasian republics towards Russia was completely different. Armenia welcomed the interest of the Russians, whereas Georgia and Azerbaijan tried to escape their interference and initially refused to join the CIS. From early 1994 until august 1996 Russia was consolidating its influence in the region, after which a gradual retreat took place.[3] At this time it was impossible to identify a 'Russian foreign policy', as the president, the Duma, the Ministry of Foreign Affairs, the Ministry of Defense and the Army, and the FSB all had their own agenda. These different agendas often contradicted each other, and sometimes one actor was not even aware of the actions of the others. One example of this occurred in the early 1990s, when the Russian Ministry of Fuel and Energy sought to cooperate closely with Azerbaijan, but at the same time the Ministry of Defence was supporting the Armenians in the war over Nagorno Karabakh. This situation began to change in the mid-1990s with the appointment of the more pragmatic Yevgeniy Primakov as minister of foreign affairs.

Russia's influence in the Caucasus gained new strength with the election of Vladimir Putin as president and received an additional boost from the increase in gas and oil prices. Russian foreign policy gradually became more coordinated and coherent, and separate agendas were no longer tolerated. But the main principles did not change: Russia still sees the Caucasus as its backyard and part of its rightful sphere of influence, and is irritated by the region's close cooperation with NATO and the West in general.

The year 2008 will go down in history as the year in which the new Russian president, Dmitriy Medvedev, proved to the entire world that Russia could act with impunity in the Caucasus, and that it still held the key to the region's position in the international arena. First, Russia was able to bring Georgia to its knees and to pronounce on the existence of two independent states – Abkhazia and South Ossetia. Second, in November 2008, at a time when nobody had expected it, Medvedev met with the Armenian and Azerbaijani presidents and discussed prospects for peaceful negotiations and confidence-building efforts regarding the 20-year conflict over Nagorno Karabakh.

The main Russian tool for exercising influence over the other newly independent states is the Commonwealth of Independent States (CIS), a regional organization whose members are former Soviet republics.[4] Several statutory bodies meet regularly and deal with politics, economics and military issues, and there are several treaties and cooperation agreements. The CIS Collective Security Treaty (CST) was signed in 1992 by some members, but Azerbaijan and Georgia refrained as they wanted to remain outside the Russian sphere of influence.

However, because of their internal problems they felt obliged to sign the agreement the following year. The treaty expired in 1999, and again Georgia and Azerbaijan refused to sign its renewal. A Collective Security Treaty Organization (CSTO) was founded in 2002 and currently has seven members, including Armenia. Georgia, Ukraine, Azerbaijan and Moldova, in a reaction against the CST, set up the pro-Western GUAM[5] consultative forum in 1997. There are also military cooperation agreements with NATO and its member states.

Through mediation efforts and peacekeeping missions, Russia has attempted to play a leading role in maintaining peace and stability in the South Caucasus. This involvement has not been welcomed on all sides, and there has been speculation about and accusations of direct military support to certain parties in the conflicts. This remains very difficult to prove, especially as military units may have been involved in issues without the leadership in Moscow being aware. One of the most famous examples of direct support of this nature is the case of Russia having provided weaponry with a total value of $US 1 billion to Armenia over the period 1992–7.[6] Some scholars and analysts therefore refer to Russia's policy in the region as one of controlled destabilization.[7]

Russia has shown its discontent at the oil and gas pipelines bypassing its territory and has insisted that oil be transported via a northern route and be shipped through the port of Novorossiysk. This would give it an additional influence in the energy industry and at the same time would make the Caucasus economically more dependent. Furthermore, both Georgia and Armenia are reliant on gas deliveries from Russia, which can use this as leverage to gain influence. Georgia, because of its political differences, has seen the price of gas increase at a rapid pace – from $US 55 to $US110 per 1,000 m^3 in 2006, and to $US 230 in 2007.

Russian–Armenian relations were rather cool at the beginning, as Armenia attempted to prove its self-sufficiency. Immediately after declaring independence the Armenian leadership sought to improve its relations with Turkey, but this turned out to be more challenging than anticipated, and diplomatic relations could not be established. When, in early 1992, total war broke out in Nagorno Karabakh, Armenia reoriented its foreign policy towards Russia, and was the only country in the South Caucasus to join the CIS and the CST of its own free will.

Armenia does not see Russian interests in the region as a threat to its independence. Indeed, they are even seen as providing protection against hostile neighbours. In 1993–4 several treaties were signed giving Russia access to military bases on the border with Iran and Turkey. However, despite speculation and concern in Azerbaijan that Russia would redeploy its troops to Armenia after leaving the four military bases in Georgia, this did not materialize.

Armenian–Russian relations cover several fields, including military cooperation, energy and trade. Armenia is a member of the CSTO, the Russian 102nd military base is stationed on Armenian territory, and Armenian and Russian border troops jointly patrol the border with Iran and Turkey. The military component of the cooperation is important to both parties, as it gives certain leverage to

Russia in the South Caucasus and Armenia feels safer. Most of the energy sector is in Russian hands, Russian GazProm is involved in the construction of the Iran–Armenia gas pipeline, and Armenia buys Russian gas at preferential rates.

Russia has been the main trading partner for Armenia for a considerable period of time, but the negative trend in Georgian–Russian relations has had a tremendous impact. All ground communications between Armenia and Russia pass through Georgia. The closure of the Verkhniy Lars border crossing in July 2006 did not only result in an immense downturn in trade between Georgia and Russia, it also cut off Armenia. As a result, several Armenian businessmen felt obliged to turn towards the West.

In the last years of the existence of the USSR, Moscow sided with Azerbaijan relatively openly on the issue of Nagorno Karabakh,[8] and the Azerbaijani leader, Ayaz Mutalibov, followed an outspoken pro-Soviet and later pro-Russian course. The election of Elchibey in June 1992 resulted in a major change in foreign policy. He did not wish to foster close relations with Russia but instead took a pro-Turkish and pro-Western direction. Russia was seen as a danger to Azerbaijan's independence, as it showed indirect support for Armenia in the conflict over Nagorno Karabakh and because it was associated with communist ideology and the military repression in Baku of January 1990. In 1992 Azerbaijan became the first former Soviet republic to rid itself of Russian military bases on its territory, which did not improve its relations with Russia. A little more than a year later, when Heydar Aliyev took over the leadership of the country, the direction of foreign policy changed again, this time being more balanced in outlook but without showing any willingness to reduce Azerbaijani independence. In September 1993, weakened by the war in Nagorno Karabakh which it was on the verge of losing, Azerbaijan joined the CIS.

Aliyev continued to defend Azerbaijani independence and looked towards the West for direct investment in the oil sector. The famous 'deal of the century' for the development of three major oil fields in the Caspian was a slap in the face for Russia, as it was unable to use Azerbaijani oil to strengthen its own influence on the energy market. However, Russian LukOil took a 10 per cent stake in the deal of the century, and it kept the question on the apportionment of the Caspian Sea open. A thaw in relations occurred after Vladimir Putin came to power. Azerbaijan cut off all support to the Chechens and an agreement on the status of the Caspian Sea was reached. Ilham Aliyev follows the same foreign policy line as his father and has been able to balance relations well.

Nevertheless, there are several disagreements between the two countries. Azerbaijan claims that the Russians incline towards Armenia in the Nagorno Karabakh peace talks. It refuses to allow a Russian peacekeeping force in the disputed region or to see Russian troops patrol its borders. On its part, Russia is not overly enthusiastic about Azerbaijan's policy of laying oil and gas pipelines through other countries, and would prefer to see them all pass through Russian territory to the port of Novorossiysk.

Russian–Georgian relations are not determined solely by the bilateral problems between the two countries.[9] After gaining independence Georgia, under both

Gamsakhardia and Shevardnadze, wished to follow its own path and remain outside the Russian sphere of influence. It showed no interest in the Russian-led CIS, which it perceived as an attempt to reincarnate the Soviet Union, and demanded the withdrawal of Russian troops, while Russia feared the increase of Turkish influence and the loss of control over the Black Sea. There seems to be ampleevidence[10] that Russia sided with the Abkhaz during the conflict, leaving Georgia weakened. Finally, in December 1993 Georgia joined the CIS, but it did not wish either to see a reintegration of the Soviet Union or submit itself fully to Russian authority. Instead, it continued to widen its horizons and make contacts with other actors in the region. In the following years Shevardnadze was fairly successful in balancing foreign policy and establishing good relations with the West without upsetting Russia too much. Shevardnadze was without any doubt more 'obedient' than his Azerbaijani counterpart. Relations sourced again in 1999 and 2000, when Russia accused Georgia of harbouring Chechen terrorists in its Pankisi gorge, which it even bombed in 2002.

The Rose Revolution of autumn 2003 did not cause a major change in relations between Georgia and its northern neighbour – rather these were further aggravated. Russia felt its interests were threatened when the Georgian president, Mikheil Saakashvili, declared his intention to institute closer ties with NATO and the EU and to bring the entire country back under central control. In March 2006 it banned the import of Georgian wines after claiming that heavy metals and pesticides had been found in it. Dissension grew in September 2006, when four Russian officers were arrested on spying charges. Russia immediately pulled out most of its diplomats, deported Georgians from its own territory, closed Georgian businesses in Russia, and closed the common border.

The independence declaration of Kosovo in February 2008 and its wide international support had immense consequences for Russian–Georgian relations. Russia announced that it would review its attitude towards breakaway republics in the former Soviet Union, especially Abkhazia. Two months later a Georgian unmanned plane was shot down above Abkhazia, after which Georgia blamed its northern neighbour of providing military support to the Abkhaz rather than being a neutral guarantor of peace. Tensions rose in the following weeks and months as Russia deployed more troops and heavy armour in Abkhazia and an increasing number of incidents took place between Russian peacekeepers and the Georgian authorities. Attention shifted to South Ossetia in July 2008, when there were several military clashes. This culminated in a war which started on 7 August and continued for five days. The Russian use of military force and its recognition of Abkhaz and South Ossetian independence led to a complete deadlock in relations.

Apart from its peacekeeping forces, Russia had formerly deployed up to 10,000 troops spread over four military bases in Georgia, which it abandoned by September 2007. There were fears that the closure of the four Russian military bases would cause problems, first because they had provided employment for a large number of people. Socio-economic difficulties could arise, especially in the poorer regions such as Samtskhe–Javakheti. Second, there was concern that Russia might leave some weaponry behind, allowing secessionist movements to obtain them.

In February 2006, since it saw its future military cooperation with NATO, Georgia withdrew from the CIS Council of Defence Ministers, and a few months later the government and parliament discussed whether the country was actually benefiting from its CIS membership. On 18 August 2008, following the South Ossetian War, Georgia informed the CIS executive committee that it would withdraw from the CIS on 17 August 2009.

Turkey

Whereas until the early twentieth century the Ottoman Empire had considerable control over some parts of the Caucasus, Turkey exercised only very limited influence in the region during the 70 years of the existence of the Soviet Union. During that time many Turkic nations in the Caucasus and Central Asia were ruled by Moscow and had only restricted contacts with Turkey. With the end of the Cold War and the collapse of the Soviet Union, Turkey faced a power vacuum on its borders and lost its importance as a NATO member – it had been responsible for the organization on the southern flank. On the other hand, the Soviet threat was removed and Turkey could therefore dream of the creation of a Turkic community stretching from Central Asia to Eastern Europe. Thus the early 1990s brought both a challenge and an opportunity, and opened the door to renewed relations with the Caucasus.

In the early 1990s Turkey's ties with the newly independent states focused on cultural, linguistic and religious links, but economic interests soon emerged. Trade expanded and many Turkish companies became active in the region. The West was not unhappy with Turkish influence in the region, as its secular and democratic state model could provide an example for the region and alleviate the fear that fundamentalist Islam would spread among the Muslims of the former Soviet Union. Russia also initially had no objections to the Turkish influence, as it countered Iranian efforts. However, Russia soon became concerned about its own interests in its near abroad. Nevertheless, in the mid-1990s Turkey noticed Russia's relative weakness in the Caucasus and as a result started cooperating militarily with Azerbaijan and Georgia in the NATO framework.

Several factors need to be taken into account when assessing Turkish–Caucasian relations. First of all, the Caucasus forms the geographical link with many Turkic nations and constitutes a cornerstone of pan-Turkic thinking. Relations with Azerbaijan in particular are vital in this respect. Second, the Caucasian diasporas (mainly Azerbaijanis, Cherkess, Abkhaz, Georgians and Chechens) constitute some 10 to 15 per cent of the population of Turkey and thus have a considerable influence on the country's foreign policy. Third, and seen by some observers as the most important of all, Armenia is key because it can block Turkish influence in the region and support Russian influence instead.

Turkey has developed a completely different relationship with all three South Caucasian republics. Azerbaijan is perceived as a smaller brother, relations with Armenia are delicate and officially hostile, and Georgia forms its strategic gateway to the Caucasus and Central Asia.

Turkey was the first to recognize Azerbaijani independence, and the predictions of many analysts that it would develop the best ties with Azerbaijan in the post-Soviet world have proven to be correct. Of course, the importance of the ethnic, cultural, historic and linguistic links should not be underestimated. Azerbaijan's motto in its early years of independence was even 'One Nation – Two States'. Turkey was one of the only two countries – the other being Israel – to express strong support in the war over Nagorno Karabakh. It has attempted to set up a trilateral dialogue,[11] but its own conflict with Armenia prevented this.

Cooperation between the two countries focuses now on shared economic, political and strategic interests, often to the detriment of Russia. This is definitely the case with the export of Azerbaijani oil and gas, and Turkey is Azerbaijan's closest partner in terms of military cooperation.

Whereas Armenians used to hold high positions in the multi-ethnic Ottoman Empire, Turkish–Armenian relations are currently rather hostile. The situation began to change in the nineteenth century, when discriminatory laws were enacted against non-Muslims and when certain Armenian political actors were looking for Armenian independence. The situation deteriorated dramatically towards the end of the nineteenth century, when hundreds of thousands of Armenians died in clashes and massacres. Even more Armenians (but also Turks) died in the period 1915–22, and it is this Armenian genocide that is at the centre of the hostile relations between the two countries. Armenian–Turkish enmity continued during Soviet times.[12]

Turkey was one of the first states to recognize Armenian independence. Both countries were looking at normalizing their relations and even discussed the promotion of cross-border trade, the opening of a highway, and ways to overcome psychological barriers between the two nations. However, Turkey set as a precondition that Armenia should abandon its territorial claims and the allegations of genocide and also find a solution to the conflict over Nagorno Karabakh (which at that time had not turned into a full-scale war). Armenia wanted to establish bilateral relations without preconditions, and as a result nothing happened. In 1993 Turkey closed its border with Armenia and imposed an embargo, as the latter occupied roughly one-fifth of the territory of Azerbaijans's territory. Fifteen years later this situation remains largely unaltered, although there have been some signs of a potential rapprochement in recent years,[13] especially since Tayyip Erdogan became prime minister of Turkey in March 2003. Opening the border between the two countries would have considerable advantages for both sides, as the movement of goods and people would contribute to the economic development of Armenia as well as that of the eastern regions of Turkey. An interesting event took place in September 2008, when the Turkish president, Abdullah Gül, accepted the invitation of his newly elected Armenian counterpart, Serge Sargsian, to watch the World Cup qualifying football match between their countries in Yerevan. Many hope that this 'football diplomacy' might be the start of a thaw in relations. However, although Sargsian's tone may be milder than that of his predecessor, there has as yet been no change in policy.

There have been several supra-governmental and non-governmental efforts to improve Turkish–Armenian relations, but these have all been largely unsuccessful. Some European institutions and EU member states have called for the opening of the border and the recognition of the Armenian genocide, and have mentioned both issues as a hindrance to Turkey's potential membership of the EU. A Turkish–Armenian Reconciliation Commission (TARC), consisting of six Turkish and four Armenian members, was created in 2001 but was not officially supported by the governments of the two states. This commission hoped to improve relations but without discussing historical issues such as the genocide. Recommendations were made to the respective governments in 2004, but no concrete results can be identified. However, a number of organizations, such as the Turkish–Armenian Business Development Council, have been able to bring the two peoples together.

The Turkish stance towards Georgia was initially uneasy, and diplomatic relations were established only after the ousting of Gamsakhurdia. Georgia was seen as anti-Turkish because of its attitude towards the Meskhetians, and the pro-Abkhaz lobby in Turkey exerted pressure on Ankara vis-à-vis the Georgian–Abkhaz conflict. Nevertheless, Ankara has always supported the principle of territorial integrity rather than that of self-determination. This is largely on account of its own internal problem with the Kurdish minority.

Before too long both countries realized that closer ties would be mutually beneficial. Because of its hostile relation with Armenia and the importance of expanding trade links with the Caucasus and Central Asia, Turkey started to put more emphasis on its links with Georgia. This was especially true when exploring realistic routes for the export of Azerbaijani oil and gas. Georgia wished to escape from the Russian dominance of the South Caucasus. A few years later Turkey was its largest trade partner, road connections had been improved, and a strategic relationship between the two countries had begun to develop. Relations had also improved on the political level.

Georgia has been included in several major infrastructure projects to enhance regional trade and exploit the Caspian's gas and oil resources. In 2010 a railway link should be operational between Turkey, Georgia and Azerbaijan,[14] but more importantly Georgia is involved in the Baku–Ceyhan and Baku–Erzurum oil and gas pipeline projects.

Iran

The history of the Caucasus is closely linked to that of the different Persian empires which have existed over the last three millennia. Iran's influence in the region waned completely with the creation of the Soviet Union. Thus the collapse of the USSR raised hopes for renewed influence.

Iran has a wide range of interests in the Caucasus, but its quest for influence has worried many countries, both in the region and the West, on account of its reputation for spreading fundamentalist Islam and supporting revolutionary and radical political movements. Despite all fears and concerns, Iran has been a moderate and pragmatic regional player and has placed economic and security interests above religious and ideological motives. Being internationally isolated and fearing US dominance in the South Caucasus, it has been looking at the region as a new market and for the transit of its own energy resources and other trade goods. Since 9/11 it has understood the need to strengthen its ties even further with Armenia and Azerbaijan in order to counter their support for the global war against terrorism. The Iranian leadership is also aware that conflicts in the Caucasus, such as in Nagorno Karabakh, could create domestic instability, especially in northern Iran, given that more than one-third of its own population is ethnic Azerbaijani and that there is a 300,000 strong Armenian community.

On several occasions, in an attempt to counter Turkish and US influence in the region, Iran has tried – without major success – to mediate in the conflict over Nagorno Karabakh. Because it is the neighbour which would be influenced most directly by both the worsening of and the solution to the conflict, it has attempted to maintain a neutral and balanced stance. During the most critical times Iran has provided energy and other supplies not only to Armenia but also to the population of Nagorno Karabakh, which led to Azeri allegations of it not being a credible guarantor of stability.

Although it would seem logical for Iran to develop its closest ties with Azerbaijan, with whom it shares the same religion, many cultural elements and even to a great extent the same population, this has not been the case. Iranian–Azerbaijani relations are very delicate and have undergone many ups and downs. Iran was one of the first countries to recognize Azerbaijani independence and to establish diplomatic relations, but these initially cordial ties cooled six months later, when Abulfaz Elchibey came to power. Elchibey despised the Iranian government for oppressing its Azerbaijani minority and called for Azerbaijani autonomy in Iran, leading to Iranian fears of uprisings. Being a secular pan-Turkist, Elchibey was also very suspicious of Iran's Islamic influence. He furthermore denounced Iranian peace initiatives for Nagorno Karabakh, claiming they favoured Armenia.

Relations gradually improved under Heydar Aliyev, but reached a new depth in July 2001 when an Iranian warship and two jets attacked an Azerbaijani vessel carrying out exploration in the southern Caspian. Another improvement saw the opening in December 2005 of a gas pipeline from Iran to the isolated Nakhchivan autonomous region. Nevertheless, although bilateral relations currently seem friendly, Iran still fears that one day another leader like Elchibey may come to power in Azerbaijan, which could be detrimental to its interests in the region.

Despite their religious and ideological differences, Iran and Armenia have a strong partnership, as they share a sense of isolation. Iran looks for partners in the international arena and for a link to Russia and Europe. Armenia needs to find other ways of survival as a result of the blockade by Azerbaijan and Turkey. However, Iran remains rather sceptical of Armenia's principle of complementarity and is unhappy with some of its pro-Western policies. Cooperation has focused mainly on energy and other trade goods, but it is possible that there is also some smaller military component.[15] This needs to be put into a greater historical perspective when considering Iranian–Armenian relations. The Armenian lands have been part of the Persian Empire at many times in the past, and the influence on outlook, culture and language should not be underestimated. Furthermore, Iran continues to form a counterweight to the Turkish influence.

As a result of Baku's anti-Iranian attitude and pro-Western orientation, Iran drifted towards closer ties with Armenia in the early 1990s. Of all the newly independent states, Armenia was the most welcoming to Tehran. Iran, which soon became Armenia's largest trading partner, provides energy and goods to Armenia, mitigating the effects of the Azeri–Turkish embargo. Trade between Iran and Armenia grew, and reached its peak in 1997. Thereafter Iran's share gradually diminished, and in 2007 Iran was only Armenia's tenth largest partner for exports and eighth for imports.[16] Iran has been instrumental in aiding Armenian energy security and ending its overreliance on Russia, since the small landlocked country is excluded from all major regional energy plans. A gas pipeline has been operational since 2007, a hydropower station is under construction on the Araks River, and a third high-voltage transmission line is planned.

Georgian–Iranian relations are not much in the public eye as there is no common border between the two countries. Diplomatic relations were set up, high-level meetings took place, but Iran did not exercise much leverage on Georgia. These neutral relations soured when Georgia followed a more open pro-Western course, and the trend continued when Saakashvili came to power and the country's foreign policy towards Iran began to be guided by the US. However, against the wishes of the US administration, Georgia is buying Iranian gas in order to reduce its dependence on Russia.

International relations at the global level

The European Union and its member states

The EU member states have multiple interests in the Caucasus. First of all, through its recent enlargement, the EU's borders have moved eastwards and as a result there is a need to create a 'circle of friends' with whom it can share peaceful and cooperative relations.[17] The conflicts in the Caucasus and the organized crime that are linked to the area might spill over into a problem. Furthermore, since 9/11 the region has been perceived more and more as a potential refuge for terrorist networks. Second, EU member states have increasingly become concerned about the diversification of their energy supplies. The oil and gas reserves of the Caspian Sea form an appealing alternative to the traditional supplies. A third motive is the moral one, for the EU seeks to export its democratic principles and values. The South Caucasian republics also have European aspirations (i.e. they feel themselves to be Europeans, and Georgia would even like to become an EU member), but one of their main aims has been to seek support for their respective views on the conflicts in the region and help bring an end to them.

In the early 1990s, while the Caucasus enjoyed attention from some EU member states, it did not from the EU as a whole. The UK developed close relations with Azerbaijan on account of large investments by some of its oil firms, France built up an understanding with Armenia, and Germany expanded its ties with Georgia and became one of the main European trading partners of Azerbaijan. In 1996 the EU signed Partnership and Cooperation Agreements (PCAs)[18] with the three South Caucasian republics, which came into force in July 1999. These PCAs form the main legal framework for bilateral relations and cooperation in the fields of political dialogue, trade and economy, investment, legislation and culture. As part of their implementation, regular political dialogue takes places through a cooperation council, a parliamentary cooperation committee, and several other specialized subcommittees. This political dialogue gained impetus with the appointment in July 2003 of Heikki Talvitie to the newly created post of EU special representative (EUSR) for the South Caucasus. The mandate of the EUSR, currently held by Peter Semneby, includes assisting the EU in developing a comprehensive policy towards the region and in supporting the conflict-prevention and peace-settlement mechanisms in operation. Through this increasing engagement with the region, the EU also raised its visibility. The European Union, with its highly complex structure, is often poorly understood in the Caucasus: for example, there still seems to be confusion between it and the Council of Europe, of which Armenia, Azerbaijan and Georgia have been members since 1999, but which is not a part of the EU structure.

On 14 June 2004 the European Council decided to incorporate the Caucasus in its European Neighborhood Policy (ENP), an initiative intended to foster closer relations with its immediate neighbours. Five-year action plans have been developed in order to provide assistance to these countries, and are financed through the European Neighbourhood Policy Instrument (ENPI). The European Commission, which prepared the plans in close collaboration with the governments and civil society of the three countries, did not wish to politicize them because their main aim is not to tackle the unresolved conflicts. The Georgian action plan mentions the principle of territorial integrity, but those for Armenia and Azerbaijan do not go much further than expressing support for the OSCE-led peace process.

Armenia, Azerbaijan and Georgia have all been seeking support from the EU and its member states in resolving their territorial conflicts. Georgia in particular has been asking the EU to play a more active role in achieving peace and stability in the region, including through a military mission for South Ossetia and Abkhazia, and it has also tried to push the EU into taking a firmer position against Russia. Until recently Europe was very reluctant to become involved in mediation efforts and would only express its support to the OSCE and UN rather than create yet another vehicle for conflict resolution. But a huge change in policy towards the region took place in August 2008, when the EU, under the leadership of the French president, Nicolas Sarkozy, was able to agree a six-point plan on the establishment of peace with all sides at war in Georgia. An EU monitoring mission was deployed one month later.

The EU has a special partnership with Russia, which is its third largest trading partner, and cooperation takes place in the framework of the EU–Russian Common Spaces. Although minor attempts were made by some EU member states to comment on the security and human rights situation in the North Caucasus, Russia made it clear that it was not looking for any advice in order to solve its internal affairs. Even humanitarian aid to IDPs of the Chechen wars, of which the EU was the largest donor, was not fully appreciated by the authorities of the Russian Federation.[19]

The United States

The United States was one of the first countries to recognize the newly independent republics and to provide them with assistance. The two major factors in its foreign policy towards the Caucasus were its energy policy and the desire to prevent the newly independent states from falling back under the Russian sphere of influence. The interest in the Caucasus grew after 9/11, not only in the fight against terrorism but mainly to counter the spread of Islamic influence in the region. The US saw Azerbaijan initially as its key ally in the Caspian. However, as it has become increasingly crucial as a gateway to the Caspian, since its location is critical to secure the Black Sea region, and because of the uncertainty regarding its future orientation,[20] Georgia's geostrategic importance to Washington gradually intensified.

Azerbaijan formed a major exception in terms of US foreign policy towards the ex-Soviet republics. Section 907 of the US Freedom Support Act hindered bilateral relations with Azerbaijan and made direct governmental aid impossible. It denied humanitarian assistance to refugees and IDPs through Azerbaijani governmental structures, though it did not prohibit technical assistance in the fields of economic, political and social reforms. These sanctions, which Azerbaijan considered as unfair, had been passed through the lobbying efforts of the strong Armenian diaspora in a reaction to the war over Nagorno Karabakh. However, this did not mean the US government did not show any interest in Azerbaijan: an embassy was set up and high-level meetings took place. Several US oil firms, which were not restricted under this Freedom Support Act, were involved in the deal of the century, the largest production sharing agreement in Azerbaijan, which was signed in 1994. The terrorist attacks of 9/11 had a major influence on US foreign policy, including its relations with Azerbaijan, which condemned the attacks and immediately joined the coalition against terror. It also gave the US overflying rights during the wars in Afghanistan and Iraq, sent peacekeeping troops to both countries, arrested some 30 international terrorists and deported many more suspected persons. In return, the US froze the application of Section 907 and initiated strong trade, governance, security and military cooperation. However, although Azerbaijan is a member of the coalition against terror, it has indicated on several occasions that it would not be willing to host bases for any eventual war against Iran.

Armenian–US relations have been extremely complex for several reasons. First, there is a large Armenian diaspora (approximately 1.4 million) in the US, many of whom are politically active and exert a significant influence on American foreign policy. Second, Turkey had been one of the US's main allies during the Cold War and is still seen as a guarantor of stability and security in the region. Third, the hostile relations between the US and Iran have a certain impact. Fourth, the US is very interested in good relations with Azerbaijan because of the access it gives to Caspian oil. As a result, relations between Armenia and the US have been neither bad nor overly good. Armenia has condemned the attacks of 9/11 and opened its airspace to US military planes in their wars in Afghanistan and Iraq. In response, the US has provided military equipment and training in order for Armenia to contribute further in the war against terror. In addition, Armenia is the third largest recipient per capita of United States aid, which shows how strongly it relies on the US for aid and investment.

Relations with Georgia have always been very friendly, as the country turned towards the US as early as 1991. However, because of the continued existence of the Soviet Union, Gamsakhurdia was not able to gain American recognition for Georgian independence. His successor, Eduard Shevardnadze, was able to build a strong relationship with the US, and Georgia became one of the main beneficiaries of US assistance. These cordial relations continued when Saakashvili came to power. As part of Shevardnadze's support for the War on Terror, Georgia profited from a major US-funded Georgian Train and Equipment Program (GTEP), worth $US 64 million. This programme provided equipment and training to the Georgian armed forces to enhance their counter-terrorism capabilities, and was followed by the similar Georgia Sustainment and Stability Operations Program.

The North Atlantic Treaty Organization (NATO)

The Caucasus is of great interest to NATO because of its geopolitical and strategic location, its role in Eurasian security, the vast untapped natural resources of the Caspian, proliferation concerns, and to a certain extent even the wish to keep Russia from gaining strength. The countries of the South Caucasus, especially Azerbaijan and Georgia, are interested in NATO for their stability and security, and see the organization as a way to integrate into the various Euro-Atlantic structures and thus stimulate their economic development.

From its creation until the end of the Cold War, one of the main missions of NATO was to form a military bloc to defend non-communist Europe from the USSR. However, a few years before the dissolution of the Soviet Union there were already some contacts between NATO and the Soviet republics. In 1992 all the South Caucasian republics and Russia joined the North Atlantic Cooperation Council (NACC). This forum was a political institution whose mission was to maintain and strengthen stability, prevent conflicts and manage crises. In its first years in particular, the conflicts of the South Caucasus were often on the agenda. Nevertheless, NATO has never wished to interfere in these conflicts. In January

1994 the Partnership for Peace (PfP) was introduced as NATO's chief engagement tool for practical cooperation with its former enemies. Cooperation takes place in a large variety of spheres, such as political, civil–military relations, military, civil emergency planning, combating organized crime and terrorism, science and technology, and the environment. Azerbaijan, Armenia, Georgia and Russia all signed the PfP framework document in 1994.

Whereas they were not initially very strong, the visit of the secretary-general, Javier Solana, in February 1998 proved to be a real turnaround in NATO–South Caucasian relations. In 1997 the NACC had been replaced by the Euro-Atlantic Partnership Council, which set up a special ad hoc working group on the Caucasus. Its involvement in Kosovo and the events of 9/11 have led to the informal request by certain politicians to instigate NATO participation in the settlement of the various regional conflicts. By making comparisons between their own situation and that of Kosovo, and by using such buzzwords as 'ethnic cleansing' and 'terrorism', they hoped to obtain Western support. NATO, however, remains reluctant and wishes to see a solution within the frameworks of the UN and OSCE.

Armenia tries to balance its foreign policy between Russia and the West, and thus determines how much cooperation it will have with NATO. It tries to use this opportunity to strengthen its relations with its neighbours, but military reforms are almost impossible on account of the Nagorno Karabakh conflict. Armenia's closest partner in the alliance is Greece, but on the other hand relations with NATO are difficult because of another member – Turkey.

From the early years of its independence Azerbaijan was very keen to cooperate with NATO and its members, but there was no significant response. Azerbaijan hoped to part company from Russia and export oil to the West. In May 1994, during a difficult time because of the conflict in Nagorno Karabakh, it joined the PfP. However, it was not interested in NATO membership and preferred to see a larger role for the OSCE. Owing to the failure of the OSCE to reach a settlement in Nagorno Karabakh, Azerbaijan has changed its attitude and has hinted several times at NATO membership, in the hope that the alliance would help restore Azeri territorial integrity.[21] It has good relations with all NATO members, but the allies are reluctant to sell the country modern weapons because a revival of violence cannot be ruled out.

Georgia has a very dynamic relationship with NATO and has taken up a lot of their initiatives. The role of former President Shevardnadze, who was the first ever Soviet official to enter NATO headquarters, should not be underestimated. He tried steadily to increase cooperation with NATO and its members, and officially bid for membership in the alliance at the Prague summit in November 2002. The new Georgian leadership has continued this policy and is attempting to bring its armed forces up to NATO standard. A referendum was held in January 2008, when 77 per cent of the electorate voted in favour of NATO membership. All the signs were that Georgia would join the alliance in 2009, but as a result of the August War some of the other members showed less enthusiasm, and the issue was put on the back burner.

Key to NATO–Caucasus relations is the understanding between Russia and the alliance. The North Caucasus is not an issue for either discussion or cooperation, but Russia is afraid that a too close a partnership with NATO or even membership of the South Caucasian republics would be detrimental to its own security interests. Russia joined the NACC and the PfP, but became involved in a special relationship with NATO in May 1997, when both sides signed the Founding Act on Mutual Relations, Cooperation and Security. This founding act created a NATO–Russia Permanent Joint Council (PJC), whose members could build mutual confidence through consultation and the exchange of information on security and defence-related topics. With the 1999 Kosovo conflict, Russia suspended all consultation and cooperation, but soon afterwards contributed a huge contingent to KFOR (Kosovo Force). When the PJC meetings resumed a few months later, the main item on the agenda was Kosovo. A new stage in relations was achieved in May 2002, when NATO members and Russia signed the Rome Declaration, thereby creating the NATO–Russia Council (NRC). This forum replaces the Permanent Joint Council and goes beyond consultation to envisage joint decisions and joint actions. Georgia's bid for membership and the serious chances of this occurring created a renewed Russian mistrust of the alliance, as it was perceived as an infringement of Russian security interests. The Russia military action against Georgia in August 2008 further cooled relations.

7

ECONOMY

The Caucasian economy in pre-Soviet times

Whereas most of the Western European countries went through their industrial revolutions in the eighteenth and nineteenth centuries, Russia lagged behind, and its industrialization process was confined to only a few cities. The Russian Empire, including the Caucasus, had a mainly agricultural economy and industry was little developed. As an example, 78 per cent of the GDP of the North Caucasus in 1913 came from agriculture and food processing and only 22 per cent from industry.[1] The plains of the North Caucasus were used for grain cultivation, whereas the people who lived in the eastern and mountainous parts focused on animal breeding. In the 25 years before the First World War the amount of land used for agriculture quadrupled, partly because the population increased fourfold in the fifty years before the war.[2] The North Caucasus was one of the most advanced agricultural regions in Russia and the centre of livestock breeding; it also exported a huge amount of cereals to Europe. The situation in the South Caucasus was much the same, but industrialization took place far earlier in Baku on account of the oil industry, which started to boom towards the end of the nineteenth century. The remainder of the Caucasus, and also the entire Russian Empire, saw the industrialization process gather momentum from the 1890s onwards. Foreign investment, mainly from Britain, Germany and France, became a driving force in the economy and railway construction enabled the expansion of industry. Despite this, however, massive industrialization did not begin in the Caucasus until the 1930s.

The Soviet planned economy

The Soviet Union was the world's first centrally planned economy and, from a mainly agrarian society, was transformed into a top manufacturer of capital goods. At its height it was the second largest economic power after the US and produced approximately one-fifth of global industrial output. Over a period of only half a century the Soviet Union became a largely urban society with the majority of its population working in the industrial and service sectors.

When the Russian Empire ceased to exist in 1917, the Russian economy remained underdeveloped and was still focused on agriculture, and a centrally planned economy, guided by a series of five-year plans, was established in order to bring it up to the level of the European countries. GosPlan, the State Planning Commission, was the leading government agency, together with GosBank (the state bank) and GosSnab (State Commission for Materials and Equipment Supply). The centralized system guaranteed stable economic relations between the republics, but made them dependent on Russia and served economic and political goals rather than meeting market demand. The planners had little reliable information, as the planning process was mainly a top-down exercise, and only few people provided negative input or criticism. This resulted in the overproduction of certain goods and the underproduction of others, which was compensated for by a barter system among some factories outside the knowledge of the authorities. The planning took place on a sectoral rather than on a regional basis, which meant that the Soviet republics became interdependent. It also required huge resources for transport and meant that any comparative advantages were lost. In 1967 the USSR was divided into 19 economic regions, including the North Caucasian and Transcaucasian economic regions, but all were heavily dependent on instructions from Moscow.

From the first five-year plan, introduced in 1928, up to the early 1970s, the emphasis was on rapid industrialization and modernization of the Soviet Union through the production of capital goods (metallurgy, machinery, chemicals, energy, building materials, etc.). Consumer goods did not receive much attention, often leading to severe shortages and the creation of a black market. Nevertheless, their production gained importance after Stalin's death in 1953: the economy witnessed explosive growth and the Soviet Union became the world's leading producer of oil, coal, iron ore and cement. Growth rates and productivity slowed down after 1970 and even stagnated under Brezhnev. One of the main reasons for this was that the planned economy had not adapted to the demands of a more complex modern economy. The cumbersome bureaucratic administration, corruption, data massaging to 'meet' quotas and ignorance of market mechanisms all reduced its effectiveness.

Companies were not only providing employment, but were also responsible for a wide range of social welfare purposes, such as housing, health, education and recreational facilities. As the economy grew, social services and living standards improved: vaccination campaigns were instigated and health facilities improved, which resulted in a decrease in infant mortality rates. The highest living standards were achieved in the 1970s and 1980s.

The transition to market economies

Corruption and the rigid planned system led to such a crisis in the economy that, in the late 1980s, GDP fell. After the dissolution of the Soviet Union the economic ties between the republics were broken. However, their interdependence remained, and was now difficult to deal with as administrative borders had suddenly become state borders. Nor could the newly independent markets compete with international competition, which resulted in a rapid reduction in production and exports as well as imports. The crisis was further aggravated by hyperinflation and affected all sectors of the economy. Certain industries died out completely and led to a sharp decrease in living standards.

The three independent republics of the South Caucasus and the regions of the North Caucasus reacted in different ways to this new reality. Although the 1990s were marked by a huge decline in industry and a return to agriculture, each region followed its own path. For example, Ingushetia and Chechnya focused on oil extraction and refining, while Kabardino–Balkaria and North Ossetia specialized in non-ferrous metals. Today the North Caucasus is again one of Russia's main agricultural regions and a centre of food processing. Armenia and Georgia also concentrated on agriculture, but they simultaneously tried to revive other industries. Azerbaijan turned its attention on the extraction of oil and gas.

An important aspect of the transition to a market economy was privatization, aimed at reducing state interference in the economy and at increasing profitability. During the Soviet era, most means of production (i.e. land and enterprises) had been collective. Privatization, which had already begun in some areas during the last years of the Soviet era (e.g. housing), was carried out via different schemes, such as distributing shares and vouchers to employees, holding auctions or going out to tender. Armenia was one of the leaders in the privatization process, especially in terms of agriculture. But privatization of agricultural land or of small and medium-sized enterprises was of only limited success, as it was generally the previous employees who took them over. Privatization of the larger companies was unpopular among the public, since only the elite was able to benefit. A common feature of all privatizations was corruption, patronage, a lack of transparency, and the absence of a stock market.

Macro-economic indicators

Gross domestic product

After the break-up of the USSR all successor states faced a severe economic decline, experiencing a decrease in GDP of up to 60 per cent. The biggest drop was in 1992 and the lowest levels were reached around 1993–5. The violent conflicts in the region aggravated the already dire economic situation. The situation for Armenia was even worse, as the 1988 earthquake had long-lasting consequences, and the blockade imposed by two of its neighbours still has a strong adverse effect on the economy today. This blockade has had a positive consequence for Georgia, though, as all transit routes run through the country. Around 1994–5 the economy began to grow again. A common feature of the time was that industrial output fell sharply and agriculture, which had been the basis for the economy in pre-Soviet times, regained its importance once more.

The Russian Federation went through a financial crisis in 1998, with the result that GDP dropped by 5.3 per cent. This was felt throughout most of the North

Caucasus – the fall in Ingushetia was as much as 21.5 per cent – though some republics managed to see a small amount of growth (e.g. 2 per cent in North Ossetia), and the three South Caucasian republics did not seem to suffer as much. Fifteen years later real GDP has grown in the entire Caucasus, which seems to have recovered from the consequences of the break-up of the Soviet Union. Only the Republic of Ingushetia forms an exception, as its GDP in 2006 was 1 per cent lower than that in 1997.

When comparing GDP per capita at PPP figures for 2005 there are huge regional differences, especially in the North Caucasus. Azerbaijan stood at $US 4,648, Armenia at $US 3,903 and Georgia at $US 3,505.[3] Regions such as Ingushetia ($US 1,443) and Chechnya ($US 1,871) achieved only 10 to 15 per cent of the GDP of Russia ($US 11,861) and therefore constitute the poorest regions in the entire Russian Federation. The Rostov Oblast and the Krasnodar Kray realized 50 per cent of the country-wide average.[4]

Whereas agriculture and construction are currently the main economic sectors of the Armenian economy, they constitute only a minor part of Georgian and Azerbaijani GDP. Mining and quarrying provide over half of Azerbaijani GDP, mainly through the development of oil fields. Georgia obtains most of its GDP from the service sector. There are huge variations across the different territorial entities of the North Caucasus, though all of them have a developed agricultural sector, and with shares ranging from 10 to 25 per cent of GDP are much above the country-wide percentage of 5 per cent. Industry is very well developed outside the unstable regions. Both Chechnya and Ingushetia benefit from the extraction of oil, while the transport and communication sector has flourished in the Rostov Oblast, the Stavropol Kray and especially the Krasnodar Kray. This is largely because 40 per cent of Russian foreign trade passes through the ports of the Krasnodar Kray.

Remittances from Russia and to a lesser extent from the US are high in all three South Caucasian republics. According to official data, the level of remittances in 2006 stood at 18.3 per cent of GDP in Armenia, 6.4 per cent in Georgia and 4 per cent in Azerbaijan.[5] In reality, however, these figures are probably even higher.

Monetary policy

During the era of the Soviet Union the rouble was the only currency allowed in the Caucasus. The rouble had been made non-convertible in 1932, and selling or buying foreign currency was forbidden by law. Monetary policy was controlled by GosBank, the state bank. When free conversion of the rouble was made legal, it lost 90 per cent of its official value.

In the early years, some newly independent republics continued to use the rouble (e.g. Armenia), while others issued their own currency in order to control their own economies and to demonstrate their independence from Moscow (e.g. Azerbaijan). However, it was only a matter of a few years before all had adopted their own currency and set up their own national banks. In 1992 Azerbaijan issued

Table 7.1 GDP growth rates

	1993	1994	1995	1996	1997	1998	1999	2000	2001	2002	2003	2004	2005	2006	2007
Republic of Armenia	-14.1	5.4	6.9	5.9	3.3	7.3	3.3	6.0	9.6	13.2	14.0	10.5	14.0	13.3	13.8
Republic of Azerbaijan	-23.1	-19.7	-13.0	2.5	8.9	6.0	11.4	6.2	6.5	8.1	10.5	10.4	24.3	30.6	23.4
Georgia	–	–	2.6	10.5	10.6	2.9	3.0	1.9	4.7	5.5	11.1	5.9	9.6	9.4	12.4
Russian Federation	-8.7	-12.7	-4.1	-3.6	1.4	-5.3	6.4	10.0	5.1	4.7	7.3	7.2	6.4	7.4	8.1
Republic of Adygea	–	–	–	–	–	-3.7	4.7	5.6	0.7	1.2	3.9	11.5	7.9	7.0	–
Republic of Dagestan	–	–	–	–	–	-8.3	1.8	14.9	19.0	11.1	13.9	15.9	8.8	15.2	–
Republic of Ingushetia	–	–	–	–	–	-21.5	-6.1	25.1	18.3	-20.2	5.5	6.0	2.0	-0.1	–
Kabardino–Balkar Republic	–	–	–	–	–	0.6	9.1	18.2	15.0	5.6	4.5	6.2	7.8	4.8	–
Karachay–Cherkess Republic	–	–	–	–	–	0.4	-2.8	12.4	13.2	7.4	1.8	7.5	7.2	13.5	–
Republic of North Ossetia	–	–	–	–	–	2.2	12.0	13.6	9.9	12.8	3.1	5.8	5.5	12.4	–
Chechen Republic	–	–	–	–	–	–	–	–	–	–	–	–	–	11.9	–
Krasnodar Kray	–	–	–	–	–	-5.2	16.5	10.6	-1.9	8.5	2.0	9.3	6.1	10.7	–
Stavropol Kray	–	–	–	–	–	-5.5	4.2	6.5	10.1	6.5	5.4	13.2	8.3	8.2	–
Rostov Oblast	–	–	–	–	–	-3.2	9.2	11.0	16.0	4.2	6.4	13.2	6.9	12.2	–

Sources: IMF 2008 World Economic Outlook and Federal State Statistics Service of the Russian Federation.

Table 7.2 Origin of GDP

All data are for 2006, except for Georgia, which are for 2007	Agriculture, forestry and fishery	Electricity, gas and water supply, and other industry	Extraction industries	Construction	Trade and repair services	Transport and communication	Other service activities
Republic of Armenia	19.0	18.6	3.2	19.6	11.4	6.0	22.2
Republic of Azerbaijan	7.1	6.4	50.9	7.7	5.4	6.6	15.9
Georgia	9.4	10.9	1.0	6.7	13.2	10.8	48.0
Russian Federation	5.2	22.8	11.9	5.8	22.2	10.5	21.6
Rep. of Adygea	14.1	16.4	1.2	5.5	19.6	10.0	33.2
Rep. of Dagestan	21.0	7.2	1.1	13.2	22.8	14.1	20.6
Rep. of Ingushetia	20.4	4.5	7.3	8.0	19.7	5.8	34.3
Kabardino–Balkar Republic	25.2	16.2	0.2	6.4	19.7	8.0	24.3
Karachay–Cherkess Republic	22.8	16.1	2.1	8.2	16.5	5.4	28.9
Rep. of North Ossetia	15.3	25.3	0.2	6.5	18.8	8.2	25.7
Chechen Rep.	10.2	6.4	9.8	13.9	12.2	8.0	39.5
Krasnodar Kray	14.8	15.1	1.7	8.6	17.4	20.3	22.1
Stavropol Kray	14.0	21.4	2.8	7.2	17.8	13.3	23.5
Rostov Oblast	11.6	23.5	1.3	7.8	22.5	10.2	23.1

Sources: National Statistical Service of the Republic of Armenia, State Statistical Committee of the Republic of Azerbaijan, Department of Statistics of Georgia, Federal State Statistics Service of the Russian Federation.

the manat (subdivided into gopik). The following year Georgia used the interim coupon, before introducing the lari (subdivided into tetri) in 1995, and Armenia started printing its own dram (subdivided into luma).

Inflation reached its peak in 1994, with rates of up to 15,000 per cent. In 2007 it stood at 4.4 per cent in Armenia, 9.3 per cent in Georgia, 16.7 per cent in Azerbaijan and 9 per cent in Russia.[6]

The main economic sectors

Agriculture, forestry and fisheries

Archaeological evidence hints at the existence of agricultural activity in the Caucasus some six to seven millennia ago. First different types of cereals were grown and later domesticated animals were reared as well. Agriculture remained the basis of society, and even during the Soviet era, when a lot of attention was given to industry, it remained a cornerstone of the economy. At that time agriculture was organized into a system of collective farms (*kolkhozy*) and state farms (*sovkhozy*), all of which possessed immense land resources and a huge workforce. Irrigation and drainage had been common practice for several centuries, but it was only in the early Soviet period that real networks were set up. Also fertilizers, chemicals and heavy machinery were introduced. Despite all of this, Soviet agriculture remained relatively unproductive: worker productivity was poor as a result of collectivization. In addition, because of all the innovations and intensive industry, many plants and animal species disappeared and both water and soil became polluted.

After the collapse of the USSR the structure of agriculture changed. Its share in GDP rose up rapidly, as the industry sector had broken down and labour was redirected to the fields. Despite this, there was a decrease in productivity as less fertilizer and pesticide was used, and so shortages began to occur. Those countries that lacked arable lands, in particular Georgia and Armenia, suffered most. As a result there was a shift from the production of crops for export to those which could be sold on the domestic market. For example, many tea plantations were turned into pasture lands and cornfields.

Even now, agriculture remains one of the major economic sectors in the Caucasus, providing employment for a large part of the population. The diverse climatic conditions and the various types of fertile soil lead to a huge variety of crops. The plains of the North Caucasus, with their black earth, produce mainly cereals, sunflower seeds, sugar beet, vegetables and fruits. In the valleys and mountain areas of both North and South Caucasus, animal breeding and fodder crops dominate. The Caucasus, and more particularly the Black Sea coastal region, used to provide the entire Soviet Union with subtropical produce such as citrus fruit, tea and tobacco. Even now, almost half of the grapes and almost all rice, tea and citrus fruit grown in Russia come from the Black Sea region of the Krasnodar Kray, and other subtropical crops are exported to Russia from

Abkhazia and Adjara. The excess agricultural output in Soviet times formed the basis for an immense food industry: winemaking, canned vegetables and fruits, vegetable oil production, dried fruits, etc.

During the nineteenth century, many foreign owners of forests in the Caucasus exported timber, and massive deforestation took place in the first half of the twentieth century. Commercial logging decreased in the 1970s and 1980s on account of the import of cheaper timber from Siberia. This trend continued even further after the break-up of the USSR. Nevertheless, many people cut down trees in order to obtain firewood during the socio-economic crisis following the collapse of the Soviet system, and such illegal cutting became commonplace as a result of the inefficiency of law enforcement bodies and soaring corruption. However, the mountain regions remained largely untouched, commercial logging is banned in many Caucasian areas and special attention has been paid to replanting. Despite this, deforestation continues on account of higher timber prices in neighbouring countries. Some 46 per cent of the necessary timber supply comes from the North Caucasus, 40 per cent from Georgia and only 10 per cent and 4 per cent from Azerbaijan and Armenia respectively.[7] Non-sustainable methods have not supported the regeneration of these forests, and as a consequence landslides have become frequent.

The Black, Caspian and Azov seas have provided fish for many centuries, and fishing provided work and income for significant parts of the population. A huge industry developed in the early nineteenth century especially in the lower reaches of the Don River and the area around the Azov Sea. Sturgeon from the Caspian Sea is renowned for producing the best black caviar in the world, but its harvest and sale are restricted. Over the course of the past 30 years the amount of commercial fish produce has decreased as the result of the destruction of habitats, natural breeding grounds and migration routes following from new settlements, water pollution, the dumping of waste, the building of hydropower facilities, overfishing and poaching. Illegal fishing affects particularly sturgeon, salmon and trout.

Electricity, gas and water supply, and other industry

As previously mentioned, industrialization in the Caucasus began in the late nineteenth century and was centred in only a few locations. It was not until the 1930s, and even after the end of the Second World War, that this industrialization began to expand on a large scale. During the war many factories were relocated to the South Caucasus in order to provide both weaponry and food products, and the excessive industry of the 1970s to 1990s led to an overutilization of natural resources and extensive pollution. This industry had a wide scope, for example machinery construction, food processing, light manufacturing, oil and gas refining, metallurgy, chemicals, cement and building materials, and wood processing.

With the collapse of the USSR there was a huge decline in industrial output, partly because of the resulting energy crisis and the disappearance of economic ties among the successor states. As a result, industry was the worst hit sector and its recovery has been slow, particularly in Dagestan, North Ossetia and Kabardino–Balkaria.[8] Light industry has started up again but most heavy industries are still not functioning.

There were 11 unified energy production and distribution systems in the USSR, including those in the North Caucasus and the Transcaucasus. Towards the end of the 1980s there was an increase in consumption but a decrease in power generation. This led ultimately to power cuts, which paralysed all economic activities in some parts of the region.

The disintegration of the Soviet Union and the resulting armed conflicts led to the break-up of the Transcaucasian energy production and distribution system. Both Armenia and Georgia became net importers. Electricity comes mainly from hydropower, and also from fossil fuels and a small amount of nuclear power. The only nuclear power plant in the Caucasus is located in Medzamor in Armenia, and its two reactors have a combined capacity of 815 megawatts. The plant was closed down for safety reasons a few months after the 1988 earthquake, but one reactor resumed operation in 1995 after the country faced a major energy crisis as the result of the economic blockade. The international community, and more specifically the EU, has been encouraging the Armenian leadership to close the plant, as the region is prone to seismic activity and they wish to avoid a Chernobyl-like catastrophe. However, before doing so, Armenia wants to secure sufficient electricity from other sources.

The North Caucasian unified energy production and distribution system still exists, and the republics of Kabardino–Balkaria and Karachay–Cherkessia import almost all their electricity. Electricity is generated primarily from stations powered by coal, oil or natural gas and also from hydropower plants, such as that on the Sulak River.

Extraction of oil and gas

The oil and gas reserves of the Caspian region, and also to a lesser extent those of the North Caucasus plain, form one of the greatest assets of the region. At the beginning of the twentieth century the oil industry boomed and the Absheron peninsula was the largest oil extracting region in the world, accounting for almost half of global production. The district around Groznyy produced almost all the rest of Russian oil, and as time went on oil deposits were found in the regions of Maykop and Malgobek. The industry was initially owned by Russian companies, but following a change in government policy foreign capital – mainly British – was allowed in and started to dominate the sector. At the end of the First World War foreign powers struggled for control over the Absheron peninsula. Securing the oilfields of the Caucasus was also one of the motives behind Hitler's invasion of the Soviet Union, as these would have been a huge asset to the German war machine. After the Second World War, the USSR understood that it had become overdependent on Caucasian oil and directed its major investments towards Siberia. Oil production in the Caucasus therefore decreased, in relative as well as in absolute terms, a trend which continued until the mid-1990s.

At the dissolution of the Soviet Union foreign oil companies were attracted to the region, and after declaring independence Azerbaijan hoped to revive its oil industry in order to bring stability and prove its self-sufficiency. By early 2009, 27 production sharing agreements had been signed, the most important being the 1994 'deal of the century', which will tap reserves from the Azeri–Chirag–Guneshli deepwater oilfields. This contract involves an investment of $US 13 billion for the extraction of up to 6 billion barrels through a consortium of 11 companies called the AIOC – Azerbaijan International Operating Company. Chechen and Ingush oil reserves, on the other hand, have diminished tremendously and may last for only another decade.

Although much exploratory work remains to be done, it is already clear that the Caspian seabed holds approximately 3 per cent of the world's energy supplies. Most of these are located in the deeper southern section. Proven oil reserves for the entire Caspian Sea region are between 17.2 and 49.7 billion barrels, with possible reserves of some 186 billion barrels. Azerbaijan holds 7 billion barrels of proven reserves and 32 billion of possible reserves. The Russian section holds only 0.7 billion barrels of proven reserves and 7 billion of possible reserves. The Caspian also holds 232 trillion cubic feet of proven gas reserves and 328 trillion cubic feet of possible reserves, out of which respectively 30 and 35 trillion cubic feet are on Azerbaijani territory.[9] This unequal distribution has increased the importance of solving the legal status of the Caspian Sea, as it has huge implications for the ownership of the resources beneath it. The proven reserves of the North Caucasian deposits are 184 million tons of oil and 313 billion cubic metres of gas – i.e. only enough for local consumption for just a few more decades.

Armenia has no oil or gas reserves at all, and is therefore reliant on imports, a situation which is further complicated by the blockade by Turkey and Azerbaijan. Georgia has only 35 million barrels of proven oil reserves and 300 billion cubic feet of gas reserves,[10] which makes it also a net importer of both commodities.

The extraction of oil and gas could bring prosperity to Azerbaijan and some of the North Caucasian republics and krays. Nevertheless, experience has shown that most oil-rich countries have difficulty in redistributing the wealth that comes from such resources and that social inequalities increase. In the case of Azerbaijan there is a real fear that the finances gained from selling these reserves may be used to increase spending on defence, and indeed politicians have already hinted that they will be used to regain the country's occupied territories. A special State Oil Fund was created in Azerbaijan in 1999 in order to preserve economic stability and financial reserves for the future, and to finance major national-scale projects to support socio-economic progress.

There is some extraction of coal in the Rostov Oblast and Georgia, which is destined mainly for electricity generating plants.

Construction

Construction works were interrupted with the fall of the Soviet Union and the accompanying economic decline, and uncompleted apartment blocks still exist throughout the entire former Soviet Union. The economic growth of recent years has given new life to the construction sector, which has formed a major source of GDP in some regions. For example, in 2006 it accounted for one-fifth of Armenian GDP. The figure is also high in Chechnya, on account of reconstruction works after the war.

Transport and communications

As the bridge between east and west and also between north and south, the Caucasus has an important geo-economical location. During the Soviet era, however, the region was considered to be only peripheral to the USSR and remained isolated from the rest of the world. Freight transfer, primarily by rail and waterways, occurred mostly between sister republics but increased steadily during the 1970s and 1980s. The main commodities were oil, oil products, manganese, coal, metals, chemical products, timber and grain. From 1990 onwards, hand in hand with the weakening economic links, freight transfer dropped drastically and in 1996 reached its lowest point. Breaking the railway connections between the North and South Caucasus definitely had a negative impact on this process.

After the dismantling of the Soviet Union, hopes arose that the Caucasus, and more specifically the South Caucasian republics, could become stable and wealthy with the creation of transport corridors and the transport of oil and gas. Indeed, a positive trend has been noticeable but the early optimism has not been realized. The unresolved conflicts and the various blockades have continued the isolation which the region suffered during the Soviet era.

One of the main problems is the delivery of oil and gas to the European markets, though this does provide an additional source of income for the transit countries. A large network of pipelines has been set up, the most important being the 1,760-km Baku–Tbilisi–Ceyhan pipeline which began operations in 2005 and has a capacity of up to 1 million barrels of crude oil per day. Over time, Groznyy had become a key hub for the oil and gas industry, as the city housed huge petrochemical operations (refineries, the production of lubricants and paraffin, etc.) for North Caucasian and other Soviet consumers. The two Chechen wars, however, have led to the republic being bypassed and the use of pipelines further to the north. The shortest option would have been to transport Caspian oil through Iran, thus also providing direct access to Asian markets, but US foreign policy concerns meant that this was unacceptable.

The transport and communications sector is very well developed in the Krasnodar Kray and also in the Stavropol Kray and the Rostov Oblast. There is a huge network of roads and railways across the region which are connected to the main sea ports on the Black Sea coast. Novorossiysk is not only the main port for the export of oil, it is also the biggest commercial port in the entire Russian Federation. Tuapse, only 120 km southeast of Novorossiysk, is the third largest in the country. Some 40 per cent of Russian foreign trade passes through the Krasnodar Kray, which therefore constitutes a major hub for Russian foreign trade.

Trade

The Caucasus held a key role in the trade routes between eastern China and Europe in ancient times. It was part of the Silk Road, which linked the different empires of the Eurasian continent as early as the second century BC. Apart from goods, religion, science and new technologies also travelled along this route. Logically, control of the trade routes was of major importance and partially explains why the regional powers fought for influence in the Caucasus. Its importance gradually grew, but around 1400 it disintegrated because the empires along the Silk Road became economically separate.

During the Soviet era, foreign trade was not very significant and accounted for only a few per cent of GDP, but trade among the different Soviet republics was extensive. With the collapse of the Soviet Union, trade between the Caucasus and the other republics was reduced to a minimum.

The emergence of independent republics led to the creation of foreign trade. Georgia's main export products are copper ore and concentrates, and ferrous metals; Azerbaijan's exports are related to the oil and gas industry; and Armenia exports precious stones and metals. Their main trading partners are their immediate neighbours Turkey and Russia (except for Georgia), but also the EU (especially Germany) and the US.

Tourism

The beautiful beaches of the Black and Caspian seas, the mountains of the Greater and Lesser Caucasus, the spas in the region of Mineralnye Vody and the multitude of archaeological sites, fortresses and churches have all attracted many visitors, but the astonishing potential for tourism is currently not fully exploited. A huge infrastructure was set up in the twentieth century and millions of people spent their holidays in the Caucasus, which developed into one of the main resort areas and one of the principal centres for tourism and alpinism in the Soviet Union. The disintegration of the USSR, the decrease in living standards and the emergence of violent conflicts resulted in the collapse of this flourishing industry. Although the infrastructure is in need of renovation, for which huge amounts of capital are needed, the tourism industry has begun to revive and specialized firms have mushroomed in the past decade. The North Caucasus has again become a major recreational zone, and many thousands of Russians spend their summer holidays on the Caucasian Riviera. Many others go skiing or mountain climbing in the North Caucasus. The South Caucasian states have tried to attract foreign tourists as well, but so far only small groups of more adventurous-minded people have come to the region, as the infrastructure is not up to international standards and many feel uncomfortable with the political tensions. Hence the region is not yet competitive in the global tourism market.

8

CULTURE AND TRADITIONS

Caucasian traditions and values

With its great diversity of ethnic groups, it is no wonder that the Caucasus possesses a rich spectrum of different traditions, customs, songs and literature. The local culture of the early Caucasian tribes was influenced by that of invading Turkic and Alan tribes, migrating tribes from Asia, and other nations that had a political influence in the region (e.g. Greek, Roman, Byzantine and Persian). Influences from Western civilizations can be found in religion and literature, while more Eastern facets are present in the clan structure, the importance of family and the central role of older people in society. The intrusion of Soviet customs is also apparent, and the Soviet socialist ideology and structure of society have modified many old customs.

Caucasians – though this can probably be generalized to almost all nations worldwide – have a very ethnocentric and nationalist point of view when it comes to cultural pride. Every ethnic group puts itself at the centre of Caucasian culture and claims that all the region's cultural values stem from them and were spread to the other peoples. Their own ethnic group or tribe is the most heroic, civilized, cultured and belligerent of all Caucasian nations. This cultural pride has been crucial for the survival of each of these nations. Although each nation claims to be different, many traditions, values and cultural traits are the same across geographical and ethnolinguistic borders. Even warring nations, such as the Armenians and Azerbaijanis, have numerous common cultural traits. All the same, every aspect will always be perceived as 'theirs' – for example, shashlik is the typical national food of every nation and the duduk is the 'national' instrument of most Caucasian peoples.

Some particularly important or remarkable aspects of these values and traditions are the family and its honour, hospitality, courage and freedom. Family is one of the cornerstones of life, and several generations often live together under one roof. The honour, name and image of the family and clan are extremely important and thus many Caucasians fear shame and attach greater value to the honour of the family than to their own lives (or that of their relatives.) There have been several instances of young women being killed by their own family for not being virgins at the time of their marriage. Hospitality is an important principle in the entire Caucasus and guests are said to be sent from God. Therefore a guest cannot be sent away and should receive support and protection from his host.

Names

Until the administrative reforms of the Russian Empire in the late nineteenth century, when the structure of names became the same in the entire Caucasus, each nation had its own way of constructing names. All individuals have a first name, a patronymic based on the name of their father, and a family name. In addressing a friend one uses the first name or often a diminutive. The use of first name and patronymic together shows respect and is used professionally, but also with older people or people one does not know well. Family names were not commonly used during the Soviet era. However, since the 1990s the form of Mr or Mrs combined with a family name, which was used in tsarist times, has resurfaced. Georgia is a special case, where *batono/kalbatono* and the first name are the form of respect.

In many cases the first name of a person can give an indication of their ethnic background, though this is a bit more difficult among Muslim ethnic groups, where many names are inspired by Arabic ones.

The patronymic, or *otchestvo*, consists of the father's first name and the suffix -vich or -evich for a male and -ovna or -evna for a female – for example, Ivanovich, Alekseyevich, Ivanovna, Alekseyevna.

A person's name can reveal a great deal about their roots as well as their ethnic background. Russian family names have separate endings depending on the gender of the person, ending mostly in -ov, -ev or -in for males and -ova, -eva or -ina for females (e.g. Chekhov, Chekhova). Most Armenian family names end in -ian, -yan or -uni, though there are some exceptions, especially in Turkey, where some families have added the suffix -oghlu to their names in order to avoid drawing attention to themselves in the event of any anti-Armenian feelings. Some Russified their family names during the years of the Russian Empire and the Soviet Union – for example, the family name Artutyunyan became Arutyunov. Most Azerbaijani family names end with the suffix -ogly, -bay, -bey, -beg, -bek, -bekov, -bayov ,-li, -beyli or -zade. Georgian family names often divulge information about the historic region where their ancestors lived: -dze (Kartli, Imereti and Guria), -shvili (Kartli and Kakheti), -ia (Samegrelo), -iani (Svaneti), -uri (east Georgia), -va (Abkhazia and Adjara), -ua (Samegrelo and Georgians from Abkhazia). The suffix -eli mostly indicates a name based on a city – for example, Rustaveli (from the city Rustavi). Abkhaz family names mainly end in -ba or -iya.

Food and drink

There is a huge variety of food in the Caucasus, including delicate sauces and sharp spices, and a wide range of ingredients is employed. Every nation has its own specialities, although there are also many dishes that can be found throughout the

region but whose origins are obscure. These can even cause quarrels among different ethnic groups as, for example, the Georgians claim they invented the cheese-
bread (*khachapuri*) whereas Ossetians argue their *ualibakh* is the original.
Caucasian food is famous not only in the Caucasus itself: one can find Georgian and
Armenian restaurants in all the former Soviet republics.

Caucasians also consume a wide range of drinks. After a meal, tea or small
cups of extremely strong coffee are the order of the day. Georgia is famous for its
wines (Kindzmarauli, Tsinandali, Mukuzani, Khvanchkara, etc.), which are sold
all over the former Soviet Union. However, most of these so-called Georgian
wines are produced in Russia or Moldova. Vodka is drunk as well, even by
Muslim nations.

However, it is not only the food and drink that is important. Eating with others
is seen as a major social event and sometimes takes on the nature of a theatrical
performance. Probably the most infamous of these Caucasian table cultures is the
Georgian *supra*, a formal dinner where the plates can be stacked three or four
deep by the end of the evening. The event is almost always led by a *tamada*, who
should be eloquent and philosophical, have a good sense of humour, but also be
able to be serious. This master of ceremonies is responsible for the evening's pro-
ceedings and the well-being of the guests: he brings the people together, enter-
tains them and leads the toasts. The many toasts to a specific theme or person are
spontaneous, the speeches often lasting up to ten minutes, and take place in a
strict hierarchy of the importance of the guests. Glasses are raised, for example,
to the guests, distant friends and relatives, women, peace, the departed, children,
the motherland, memories and the future. No one is allowed to eat, drink or talk
during a toast. After the *tamada* has finished speaking, each person at the table
may complete and interpret the toast before drinking. In general, all kinds of alco-
hol is drunk, though in Georgia it is seen as a curse to toast with beer.

Literature

Literature is loved throughout the Caucasus, and most people know their national
poets and writers very well. The need to have read widely as a precondition for
being an educated and cultured person is a Soviet heritage. Only the Georgians
and the Armenians have a literary tradition which goes back to the first centuries
of Christianity.

The literature of the Caucasus can be divided into several historical stages, and
is in most cases directly linked to the political situation in the region. Popular
myths and legends (e.g. the Armenian hero Hayk) were initially transmitted orally
and only written down later, after alphabets were developed for some languages
(Georgian, Armenian, old Albanian). Early writings were almost all purely religious in character, though gradually historical works and books containing
proverbs and riddles appeared. The political stability in the South Caucasus from
the eleventh to early thirteenth century resulted in a golden age of culture, including literature. This was the time when poetry gained importance. The Azerbaijanis

and some other smaller ethnic groups developed their literature from the fifteenth century onwards. With the conquest of the Caucasus by Russia, a larger Western influence became evident. Most of the small ethnic groups set down their stories and poetry after an alphabet had been created for their language, and especially after the October Revolution. During Stalin's regime, as elsewhere in the Soviet Union, many writers and artists were victims of a great purge, being either exiled or executed.

An important fact to be noted is that many Caucasian authors did not write in their own language. The most substantial example is that of Azerbaijani literature, where Persian was the language until the sixteenth century. Avars, Tats and Lezgins also wrote in Persian and even Arabic. More recently, many authors have been writing in Russian, both out of choice and as a result of intense Russification. Traditional themes in literature are love for a woman (both the sweet, tender maiden and the wife who takes care of the family when their husbands are away from home, at work or at war), love of the fatherland, heroes, mountains, water sources, the fireside and Caucasian hospitality.

Georgian literature

The oldest surviving Georgian text can be dated to between 476 and 484 and is *The Martyrdom of the Holy Shushanik*, by Iakob Tsurtaveli. The ninth and tenth century witnessed a particular flourishing of Christian theology, though coupled with an ever stronger sense of national identity among Georgians. A good example of this is *Praise and Glory to the Georgian Tongue*, by Ioane-Zosime, a tenth-century monk.

The eleventh to thirteenth century, following King David the Builder's unification of the country, was a time of great Georgian political and military strength and a golden age for culture. Christian literature was heavily influenced by the Byzantines, and many Byzantine works were translated into Georgian. Several Georgians were active in philosophy, and historiography took an important place. It was also at this time that Georgian secular literature first appeared, which was obviously influenced by Georgian folklore as well as by Persian (and Arabic) literary traditions, heroic epics, stories of chivalrous love and knightly adventures. Poetry was the major literary genre, and it was not until the mid-nineteenth century that prose gained importance. The peak in medieval literature was reached during the reign of Queen Tamar, with the epic poem *The Knight in the Panther's Skin (vepkhistqaosani)* of Shota Rustaveli. This describes the adventures of Avtandil, who is sent by his beloved Queen Tinatin to find the knight in a panther's skin. The latter turns out to be the Indian prince Tariel, who grieves about the disappearance of Nestan-Darejan, daughter of the king of India. Together they free the princess and the story ends with the double wedding of Avtandil to Tinatin and Tariel to Nesta-Darejan.

The political division of Georgia and the foreign invasions following the reign of Queen Tamar led to a cultural decline. The seventeenth and eighteenth centuries brought kings who were also very active in the literary field, the main representatives being Teimuraz I and Archil II. Probably the most famous work of that time is the *Book of Wisdom and Lies*, from the hand of the diplomat-writer Sulkhan-Saba Orbeliani. David Guramishvili and Bessarion (Besiki) Gabashvili should also be mentioned from this period. Among the main themes were those of the oppressed motherland, sorrow and grief. Despite their oppression by the Persians, most authors seemingly admired and were influenced by the Persian language and poetry.

At the beginning of the nineteenth century, when Georgia was gradually incorporated into the Russian Empire and the idea of national independence grew, Georgian literature entered its Western stage of development and Romanticism became the leading style. The greatest poets were Aleksandre Chavchavadze, Grigol Orbeliani and Nikolos Baratashvili. The next generation, who reached a new literary height, was dominated by the Tergdaleulebi ('those who drank from the Terek River'), a movement for public, educational and political reform led by Georgians who had studied in Russia. Realism became more important, and there was an orientation towards Russian and Western European literature as well as a growth in nationalism. The four most illustrious authors of that time were Ilia Chavchavadze, Akaki Tsereteli, Alexandre Kazbegi and the novelist-dramatist Vazha Pshavela. The first quarter of the twentieth century saw a huge expansion in the number of authors and styles that was further stimulated by the 1917 revolution and lasted until the Stalinist purges of the 1930s. At that time, many writers who did not wish to conform to a more socialist realistic approach were killed or committed suicide. The city of Kutaisi became a literary centre, guided by the symbolist group the Blue Horns, which included Titian Tabidze, Galaktion Tabidze, Paolo Iashvili and their supporter but non-member Grigol Robakidze. The greatest writers of prose in the twentieth century were undoubtedly Micheil Javakhishvili, Konstantine Gamsakhurdia and Nodar Dumbadze.

Armenian literature

The oldest known Armenian literary work is the *De Deo*, written by Eznik of Kolb around AD 445, some 40 years after the creation of the Armenian alphabet. The fifth century is notable for a high degree of perfection in translations of the Bible, some early Christian works and also a few historical works. Whereas the fifth century was a time of bloom in literature, in the following centuries works became more erudite and consequently rather dry. Quantity of translations in the so-called Hellenistic style rather than quality was what seemed to be important. The first poetry made an appearance during Arab rule, but religious literature was still the most important form of literature at that time.

The golden age of Armenian literature lasted from 1095 till 1344 and took the fifth century as inspiration. St Nerses Klayetsi, nicknamed Shnorhali (the Gracious), wrote religious works, as well as lyric poems, proverbs, fables and riddles, and the prayers and *sharakans* (hymns) of this catholicos are still in use today. Love poetry originated during this period and continued to develop in the following centuries, which were marked by a cultural decline.

The nineteenth century marked a literary revival, which was strongly influenced by Armenians who had studied in Europe. Many new genres were introduced, but the themes remained the same – Armenia, its customs, freedom. Khatchatour Abovian is seen as the creator of modern Armenian literature, mainly because he abandoned Grabar, the classical language, and used modern Armenian instead. The main Romanticist of that time was Hakop Melik-Hakopian, who is better known under his pseudonym Raffi. The revival continued during the twentieth century, when the genocide became a significant source of inspiration. However, it faltered under the restriction of freedom of expression during the Stalinist era. Eghishe Charents, who died in a Stalinist purge, is seen as the main poet of the twentieth century.

Azerbaijani literature

Literature written in the Azerbaijani language has a relatively short history. Until the fifteenth and sixteenth centuries most literature in the region which is now populated by Azerbaijanis (both Azerbaijan and northern Iran) was in Persian and Arabic, and in some cases in Turkish. Most works were written in the language of the political rulers of the time. While these consist mainly of poetry, their authors were also great philosophical thinkers who influenced a great deal of later Azerbaijani literature.

The first remarkable writers (e.g. Gatran Tabrizi) appeared in the eleventh century, which was also when the famous national heroic folk epic *The Book of my Grandfather Gorgud* (*Kitabi Dede Gorgud*) appeared. The twelfth century was a period when literature flourished throughout the region on account of the many caravans passing along the ancient Silk Road. Poetry reached a high point, with Nizami Ganjavi becoming the most famous of all Azerbaijani poets, celebrated for his *Pentalogue (Khamsa)* and *Leyli and Majnun*, one of the best-known legends of the Orient.

Imadeddin Nasimi, who lived from the end of the fourteenth to the beginning of the fifteenth century, was one of the first poets to write some of his texts in Azerbaijani and is seen as a great example of heroism and courage. He lived in the times of Tamerlane and adopted the doctrine of Hurufism, which holds that God is in the heart of the individual rather than existing as a separate physical entity. In the sixteenth century Azerbaijani was used increasingly in literature, partly through the statesman and poet Shah Ismail I, better known under his poetic pen name Khatai, under whose reign (Saffavid dynasty) Azerbaijani became the official state language. At that time many Azerbaijanis were living in Iraq, having fled their homeland during the stormy years of invasions and foreign rulers. However, they retained both their roots and the Azerbaijani traditions. Perhaps the most famous is Mehmed Fuzuli, who is seen as the father of Azerbaijani poetry and who influenced the writers of the seventeenth and eighteenth centuries. Fuzuli also rewrote *Leyli and Majnun*.

In the nineteenth century, after Azerbaijan had been annexed by Russia, some authors started to follow a Western style and Western themes such as calls against religious fundamentalism, social oppression, violence and despotism. Best known from this period is Mirza Fatali Akhundov, who initiated the trend towards realism, democratic ideas and dramatic genre in Azerbaijani literature, and is also responsible for some linguistic reforms. Towards the beginning of the twentieth century there were several progressive satirists, such as Dzhalil Mamedkulizade and Mirza Sabir. Other well-known twentieth-century writers were Samed Vurgun and Rasul Rza.

Literature in other Caucasian languages

Some of the minority languages started developing their own literature after receiving an alphabet, but real growth took place after the October Revolution. However, as early as the fourteenth and fifteenth centuries, writers from ethnic minorities (e.g. Avar, Lak, Tabasaran, Kumyk) wrote in Arabic or in their own language using an Arabic alphabet. Towards the end of the eighteenth century their literature was well developed and poetry became very popular. Prose flourished mainly after the October Revolution. The deportation of several Caucasian peoples (1940s–1957) hindered their cultural expression, but from the 1960s onwards a new advance in their literature can be noticed. Important writers, many of whom are world famous, are the Avars Gamzat Tsadassa, his son Rasul Gamzatov, and Fazu Aliyeva; the Chechens Abusar Aydamirov and Raissa Akhmatova; the Ingush Idris Bazorkin; and the Abkhaz Darmit Gulia.

The Nart sagas, which form the basis of the mythology of the North Caucasian tribes, play an important cultural role, especially for those living in the western region. There are also reminiscences of this epic among the Svans, Georgian mountain tribes and Dagestani nations. The Narts were a tribe of heroes that came after the giants, whom they exterminated, and before the human race. They were the sons of Satanaya, a beautiful, wise and immortal young woman. The central theme of the sagas, which were handed down orally by bards and written down only from the middle of the nineteenth century onwards, is the heroic activities of the warriors, who fought, hunted, feasted and debated. Several theories claim that they had a strong influence on the cycle of Arthur and the Knights of the Round Table as well as on Greek mythology. Prometheus, just like the Nart Sosriko, stole fire from the Gods and gave it to mankind, for which his punishment was to be chained to a rock in the Caucasus and have his liver eaten daily by an eagle.

Many eighteenth- and nineteenth-century Russian authors participated in the military conquest of the Caucasus and described the beauty but also the peculiarities of the region in their literary works. The most famous of these are Pushkin's poem *Captive of the Caucasus*, Lermontov's novel *A Hero of our Time*, and

Tolstoy's novels *The Cossacks* and *Hadji Murad*. However, many other writers, such as Griboyedov and Belinskiy, also wrote about the Caucasus.

Music

Music plays an important role in the life of Caucasians and many people actively play an instrument. A piano can be found in most homes. Whereas all kinds of music can be heard in the Caucasus, the native styles consist of an interesting mix of Western and Oriental influences. The oldest indigenous forms are to be found in Armenian and Georgian church music, which has remained largely unchanged since the fifth century.

Most folk music has only a melodic voice, but Georgian folk music usually involves three-part harmony. In Eastern Georgia, the music has a relatively quiet pace with a leading upper voice and a second parallel one over a third bourdon-like bass. Dissonance is normal in western Georgian music, where singers perform independently from one another. A form of yodelling appears in folk music in many parts of the Caucasus. In Armenia there were many *ashoughs*, travelling musicians, who improvised songs mainly about love. In Azerbaijan, where these bards were known as *ashiqs*, there was also another musical tradition – *mugham* – a combination of poetry and instrumental interludes.

A classical music tradition has developed in the Caucasus since the nineteenth century. Most of the local composers gained their education in Moscow or St Petersburg with masters such as Rimsky-Korsakov and Taneyev. One of the most famous is the Armenian Aram Khachaturian, whose best-known works are probably the ballets *Gayane*, which includes the renowned Sabre Dance, and *Spartacus*. Another is Comitas (the pseudonym of Soghomon Soghomonian), who wrote *Telo*, a dramatic piece of music commemorating the deaths of Armenians killed by the Turks in the early 1900s. The first major figure in Georgia is Zakaria Paliashvili, whose operas *Abesalom and Eteri* and *Daisi* are known throughout world. A major contemporary composer is Gia Kancheli, who has a large international following and has composed much important theatrical music. Although he is not famous in the West, Azerbaijan's favourite composer is Uzeyir Hajibeyov, who wrote an opera on Fuzuli's *Leyli and Majnun*.

While contemporary Caucasian music is written mainly for the instruments that are commonly known in the West, there is a wide variety of folk music instrument specific to the region. None is particular to any ethnic group, and their names often differ from nation to nation. The most famous are probably the duduk (a woodwind instrument with a double reed; it is played by the internationally known Armenian artist Djivan Gasparjan) and the kamancha (a three- or four-stringed fiddle). There are also many types of flutes, string instruments and drums.

Cinematography

The first film screening in the Caucasus took place in Georgia in 1896, only one year after the Lumière brothers showed the first ever motion pictures. The region became one of the early centres of cinematography, and the productions of Georgia and Armenia in particular were notable in the history of Soviet film.

The earliest films were short documentaries showing scenes of daily life and such activities as oil extraction. In 1915, when the first real movies were produced in the Caucasus, the Pirone brothers established film distribution offices in Baku, Tbilisi and Yerevan. Film studies were later set up in these three main cities of the South Caucasus. The Bolsheviks promoted cinematography, and therefore central themes for most of the films of the 1920s were the revolution, the Civil War, the rights of women and the struggle against ignorance and illiteracy. However, films also based on literary works and plays or daily events were produced. Directors were ruled by Soviet ideology and often had to make use of symbols and metaphors to express themselves artistically. One of the most famous directors of that time was the Georgian Nikolai Shengelaia, who was married to Nato Vachnadze, the first major Georgian film star.

The production of films with sound started in 1935 and the film industry expanded after the Great Patriotic War. One of the most important movies of that era is *The Cranes are Flying* (1957), by the Georgian Mikhail Kalatozov, which was the only Soviet film to win a Palme d'Or at the Cannes Film Festival. In the following years a new generation of film-makers emerged and many famous movies were made. Although the Armenian film producer Sergey Parajanov was shunned for not following the prescribed style of Soviet realist art and did not receive official support, he created several notable films (e.g. *The Colour of Pomegranates*) that gained him respect among Italian film producers and directors in 1960s, such as Fellini and Antonioni. In the 1970s and 1980s, Caucasian film-makers were among the first to satirize life in the Soviet Union, and many of these movies are still extremely popular in the former Soviet republics. A number of Georgian and Armenian actors, such as Vakhtang Kikabidze and Frunzik Mkrtchyan, have become famous.

Movie production fell after the break-up of the Soviet Union, but the film industry has gradually recovered and is still growing. And, of course, with the end of communist ideology, the style and structure of movies has changed.

APPENDIX I: CONFUSING
TERMS

Some terms associated with the Caucasus also have another meaning or are similar to other words.

<u>Identical words with different meanings</u>

Albania: 1. Country in the Balkans.
2. Caucasian Albania: state that existed from the third century BC to the seventh century AD on the territory of present-day Azerbaijan and south Dagestan.

Armavir: 1. City in the Krasnodar Kray.
2. Province (*marz*) and its administrative centre in Armenia.

Arran: 1. Name used in early medieval times to define some parts of what is now the Republic of Azerbaijan as well as parts of the Republic of Armenia.
2. Scottish island, famous for its whisky.

Avars: 1. Nomadic people of Eurasia who established a state in Eastern Europe in the early sixth century (Avary in Russian).
2. Modern Caucasian people, mainly from Dagestan, where they are the predominant group (Avartsy in Russian).

Azerbaijan: 1. Historical name for the region of Media Minor or Atropatena, i.e. lands south of the Araks River.
2. The region covering the northern provinces of Iran: east Azerbaijan, west Azerbaijan, Ardabil and Zanjan. This territory, largely corresponding to the ancient Azerbaijan, is better known by the Soviet term 'South Azerbaijan'.
3. Contemporary republic in the South Caucasus.

Caucasian: 1. Adjective denoting 'from the Caucasus'.
2. An anthropological term denoting a person of a major physical type characterized by a light skin pigmentation. The term was coined by the German anthropologist Friedrich Blumenbach,

who considered the people of the Caucasus to be archetypical of this grouping.

Digor:
1. One of the two sub-ethnic groups of the Ossetians.
2. District in the Kars Province in Turkey, at the border of Armenia.

Ganja:
1. Second largest city in the Azerbaijan Republic.
2. Popular Sanskrit term for cannabis or marijuana.

Georgia:
1. Independent country in the South Caucasus.
2. State in the southeastern part of the United States.

Iberia:
1. Ancient region in the South Caucasus on the territory of modern-day Georgia.
2. Iberian peninsula, which includes Spain and Portugal.

Java:
1. City in South Ossetia.
2. An island of Indonesia.
3. Object-oriented computer programming language.

Kuban:
1. One of the main rivers in the Northern Caucasus.
2. Another name for the region of the Krasnodar Kray.

Kura:
1. One of the main rivers in the Southern Caucasus, originating in Turkey and flowing through Georgia and Azerbaijan.
2. Small river (150 km) flowing through Kabardino–Balkaria and the Stavropol Kray.
3. Test range for intercontinental ballistic missiles in the Kamchatka Kray in northeastern Russia.

Magas:
1. Capital of the Republic of Ingushetia.
2. Also Meget, capital of the state of Alania (tenth to early thirteenth century). There is no archaeological evidence of the exact location of the old Magas.

Sevastopol:
1. Roman name for the former Greek city of Dioskuria or modern-day Sukhumi.
2. City in Ukraine, home to the Black Sea fleet.

Sochi Agreement:
1. Agreement reached on 24 June 1992, ending the war between Georgia and South Ossetia.
2. Ceasefire agreement reached on 27 July 1993, leading to a short break in the Georgian–Abkhaz war.

<u>Similar words with different meanings</u>

Absheron: The Absheron (also Apsheron) peninsula extends into the Caspian Sea and is rich in oil and gas fields.

Apsheronsk: City in Krasnodar Kray at the border with Adygea.

209

Artashesian:	Also Artaxiad; Armenian dynasty, from 189 BC to AD 12.
Arshakid:	Also Arsakid; dynasties in different countries of the Caucasus and surrounding region (i.e. Parthia, Armenia, Kartli and Albania.)
Aryan:	A person who spoke one of the Indo-European languages, but no longer in technical use. In Nazism and neo-Nazism, someone supposedly a member of a master race.
Ayran:	Drink made of yoghurt and water, and very popular in Turkey, Armenia, Azerbaijan and the Middle East.
Ataman:	Noun: a chief of the Cossacks.
Ottoman:	Adjective: relating to the Ottoman Empire, its people, culture, etc.
Balkar:	Turkic people in the North Caucasus, the titular population of Kabardino–Balkaria.
Balkhar:	Lak village in Dagestan which is a centre of ceramic art.
Bulgarians:	Southern Slavic people living mainly in Bulgaria.
Bulgars:	Also Bolgars: Turkic tribe that moved into the Caucasus in the fourth century AD.
Chobanid:	Also Chupanid: Mongol clan that ruled over most of contemporary Azerbaijan and Armenia in the early fourteenth century.
Shaibanid:	Uzbek dynasty in Bukhara (Central Asia) in the sixteenth century.
Cossacks:	Members of a Slavic people living in southern European Russia and Ukraine and adjacent parts of Asia and noted for their horsemanship and military skill; they formed an elite cavalry corps in tsarist Russia.
Kazakhs:	Member of the Turkic ethnic group inhabiting Kazakhstan.
Kazakh District:	District in contemporary Azerbaijan.
Cuba:	Island country in the Caribbean Sea.
Cuman:	Also known as Polovtsy or Kipchaks: a powerful alliance of Turkic-speaking people in the eleventh to fourteenth centuries which, among others, occupied the steppes of the North Caucasus.
Koban:	Aul (village) in North Ossetia where an ancient burial mound was found; this led to the term 'Koban Culture'.
Kubachi:	Ethnic group in Dagestan, famous for their art.
Kuban:	1. One of the main rivers in the North Caucasus.
	2. Another name for the region of the Krasnodar Kray.
Quba:	City in Azerbaijan.
Elbrus:	Highest mountain in Europe, located in the border region of Kabardino–Balkaria, Karachay–Cherkessia and Georgia.

Elburz:	Mountain range in northern Iran.
Iran:	Country in Southwest Asia.
Iron:	One of the two sub-ethnic groups of the Ossetians.
Khagan:	Great khan or emperor; khan of khans.
Khan:	Sovereign or ruler of a monarchy.
Khazar:	Adjective from Khazaria, the kingdom in the North Caucasus from 650 to 1019.
Qajar:	Iranian dynasty, from 1794 to 1925, which threatened the Caucasus in the last decade of the eighteenth century.
Krasnodar:	City in the North Caucasus.
Krasnoyarsk:	City in Siberia.
Kumukh:	Village which was part of the Kazi–Kumukh khanate and inhabited by Laks (i.e. there was no link with the Kumyk ethnic group).
Kumyk:	Turkic language spoken by the Kumyks in Dagestan.
Kvareli:	Town in northeastern Georgia.
Tkvarcheli:	Town in western Georgia (Abkhazia).
Mahajir:	Someone who migrated (often forced) from the Northwest Caucasus (and Abkhazia) to Turkey and the Middle East. The term is derived from the Islamic word *hijra*, designating population movement triggered by the occupation by non-Muslims of Muslim territories and the unwillingness of Muslim communities to live under non-Muslim rule.
Mohajir:	Community descended from Muslim immigrants and refugees from North India who settled in present-day Pakistan around 1947. There is a large concentration of Mohajirs in the port city of Karachi.
Majahid:	Somebody who engages in an Islamic holy war (Mujahid in Arabic).
Mughal:	Muslim rulers of India who claimed to be descended from Genghiz Khan and the Mongols.
Mugham:	Highly complex form of art music in Azerbaijan.
Mughan:	Region in the south of Azerbaijan.
Narzan:	Famous healing mineral water which can be found in many parts of the North Caucasus.
Nazran:	Largest city and former capital of the Republic of Ingushetia.
Safavid:	Iranian dynasty from Azerbaijan that ruled from 1501 to 1736, and which established Shia Islam as the official religion of Persia and united its provinces under a single Persian sovereign.

Salafi: Adherent of a contemporary movement in Sunni Islam that is sometimes called Salafism.

Shusha: City in Nagorno-Karabakh which was the capital of the Karabakh khanate.

Susa: Old city in contemporary Iran; one of the capitals of the Achaemenid Empire and Parthia.

Turkic: In ethnolinguistic terms a subfamily of Altaic, which also includes Turkish.

Turkish: Related to Turkey, its people, its language and culture.

APPENDIX II: POPULATION STATISTICS BY ETHNIC GROUP

Appendix II **Population statistics by ethnic group**

	Total	Republic of Armenia	Republic of Azerbaijan	Georgia**	North Caucasus (Russian Federation)	Republic of Adygea	Republic of Dagestan	Republic of Ingushetia	Kabardino–Balkar Republic	Karachay–Cherkess Republic	Republic of North Ossetia–Alania	Chechen Republic	Krasnodar Kray	Stavropol Kray	Rostov Oblast
Total	34,722,194	3,213,011	7,953,400	4,645,551	18,910,232	447,109	2,576,531	467,294	901,494	439,470	710,275	1,103,686	5,125,221	2,735,139	4,404,013
Slavonic (Indo-European)															
Russian	11,844,885	14,660	141,700	91,068	11,597,457	288,280	120,875	5,559	226,620	147,878	164,734	40,645	4,436,272	2,231,759	3,934,835
Ukrainian	364,718	1,633	29,000	8,834	325,251	9,091	2,869	189	7,592	3,331	5,198	829	131,774	45,892	118,486
Belorussian	70,404	–	–	542	69,862	1934	547	23	1,194	733	1,002	222	26,260	11,343	26,604
Polish	7,754	–	–	870	6,884	211	99	8	247	64	232	22	2,958	1,262	1,781
Bulgarian	6,061	–	–	138	5,923	129	43	0	332	82	336	9	3,138	780	1,074
Other Indo-European															
Armenian	4,140,805	3,145,354	120,700	293,798	580,953	15,268	5,702	64	5,342	3,197	17,147	424	274,566	149,249	109,994
Ossetian	556,754	–	–	82,028	474,726	413	897	106	9,845	3,333	445,310	230	4,133	7,772	2,687
Greek	87,528	1,176	–	16,652	69,700	1,726	184	8	304	1,349	2,332	25	26,540	34,078	3,154
Yezidi	67,536	40,620	–	18,329	8,587	56	9	0	5	9	19	0	4,441	2,417	1,631
German	39,727	–	–	651	39,076	1,204	311	45	2,525	486	964	185	18,469	8,047	6,840
Moldovan	18,340	–	–	864	17,476	303	182	110	270	116	184	63	6,537	2,112	7,599
Kurd	28,147	1,519	13,100	2,514	11,014	3,631	45	9	301	89	84	12	5,022	1,259	562
Tajik	3,886	–	–	15	3,871	143	230	13	141	178	425	57	1,179	607	898
Iranian	1,720	–	–	46	1,674	23	719	0	511	51	81	5	113	115	56
Tat	12,198	–	10,900	–	1,298	3	825	1	98	5	6	0	70	253	37
Talysh	76,868	–	76,800	–	68	1	0	0	5	8	0	0	14	12	28
Romani	52,295	–	–	472	51,823	1,850	93	44	2,357	804	1,553	11	10,873	19,094	15,144
Turkic															
Azeri	7,652,910	–	7,205,500	284,761	162,649	1,399	111,656	123	2,281	1,024	2,429	226	11,944	15,069	16,498
Kumyk	396,255	–	–	42	396,213	103	365,804	136	713	244	12,659	8,883	586	5,744	1,341
Karachay	187,128	–	–	–	187,128	64	65	9	1,273	169,198	58	15	784	15,146	516
Balkar	106,689	–	–	–	106,689	18	32	9	104,951	476	117	72	142	783	89
Nogay	78,337	–	–	–	78,337	15	38,168	1	409	14,873	194	3,572	219	20,680	206
Tatar	103,726	–	30,000	455	73,271	2,904	4,659	151	2,851	2,021	2,108	2,134	25,589	12,988	17,866

Appendix II (Continued)

	Total	Republic of Armenia	Republic of Azerbaijan	Georgia**	North Caucasus (Russian Federation)	Republic of Adygea	Republic of Dagestan	Republic of Ingushetia	Kabardino–Balkar Republic	Karachay–Cherkess Republic	Republic of North Ossetia–Alania	Chechen Republic	Krasnodar Kray	Stavropol Kray	Rostov Oblast
Turkish	64,843	–	–	441	64,402	103	181	903	8,770	683	2,835	1,662	13,496	7,484	28,285
Meskhetian Turk	46,248	–	43,400	53	2,795	1	2	8	2,283	0	11	8	116	39	327
Turkmen	15,783	–	–	74	15,709	109	160	1	123	155	114	40	635	13,937	435
Kazakh	8,220	–	–	70	8,150	94	619	38	285	248	265	470	1,331	1,779	3,021
Uzbek	6,688	–	–	81	6,607	187	245	7	290	193	361	84	2,210	1,210	1,820
Crimean Tatar	2,951	–	–	15	2,936	15	45	1	112	4	6	1	2,609	66	77
Kalmyk	2,338	–	–	0	2,338	22	105	98	40	23	88	148	294	584	936
Hamito Semitic															
Arab	1,873	–	–	44	1,829	40	110	68	73	20	107	44	669	254	444
Assyrian	13,901	3,409	–	3,299	7,193	173	28	0	73	59	182	2	3,764	872	2,040
Jew	26,911	–	8,900	3,772	14,239	184	1,478	17	1,088	81	513	24	2,945	2,925	4,984
Mountain Jew	1,527	–	–	–	1,527	2	1,066	24	198	4	3	1	44	137	48
South Caucasian															
Georgian	3,731,395	–	14,900	3,712,616	55,322	925	876	323	1,731	556	10,803	208	20,500	8,764	10,636
Northeast Caucasus															
Kabardian	511,189	–	–	23	511,166	309	233	35	498,702	915	2,902	133	727	6,619	591
Adyghe	128,838	–	–	–	128,838	108,123	68	20	585	309	81	17	19,034	209	392
Cherkess	57,855	–	–	22	57,833	642	47	26	725	49,591	83	13	4,446	2,097	163
Abaz	36,551	–	–	–	36,551	71	20	0	514	32,346	21	7	196	3,300	76
Abkhaz	101,839	–	–	98,124	3,715	310	13	2	114	364	36	1	1,988	198	689
Northeast Caucasian															
Chechen	1,265,342	–	–	8,381	1,256,961	1,122	87,867	95,403	4,241	1,757	3,383	1,031,647	2,864	13,208	15,469
Avar	829,570	–	50,900	1,996	776,674	133	758,438	102	386	207	610	4,133	1,460	7,167	4,038
Lezgin	531,406	–	178,000	44	353,362	300	336,698	40	867	444	848	196	3,752	6,558	3,659

(Continued)

Appendix II (Continued)

	Total	Republic of Armenia	Republic of Azerbaijan	Georgia**	North Caucasus (Russian Federation)	Republic of Adygea	Republic of Dagestan	Republic of Ingushetia	Kabardino–Balkar Republic	Karachay–Cherkess Republic	Republic of North Ossetia–Alania	Chechen Republic	Krasnodar Kray	Stavropol Kray	Rostov Oblast
Dargi	475,373	–	–	–	475,373	108	425,526	35	504	290	401	696	860	40,218	6,735
Ingush	390,862	–	–	9	390,853	151	272	361,057	1,236	173	21,442	2,914	723	1,751	1,134
Lak	147,280	–	–	210	147,070	103	139,732	50	1,800	349	685	245	915	2,561	630
Tabasaran	119,916	–	–	–	119,916	165	110,152	2	135	58	237	128	1,331	5,477	2,231
Rutul	26,735	–	–	–	26,735	14	24,298	2	0	21	18	21	510	937	914
Agul	25,558	–	–	–	25,558	27	23,314	26	18	28	26	16	357	1,476	270
Tsakhur	24,659	–	15,900	–	8,759	4	8,168	0	2	0	6	4	139	197	239
Udi	7,036	–	4,100	203	2,733	1	1	9	3	1	0	0	809	336	1,573
Others															
Korean	29,866	–	–	22	29,844	820	302	22	4,722	51	1,841	33	3,289	7,095	11,669
Mordovian	11,778	–	–	19	11,759	378	148	23	490	102	207	157	4,861	1,946	3,447
Chuvash	10,251	–	–	28	10,223	349	294	38	197	81	330	372	4,141	1,404	3,017
Udmurt	9,115	–	–	13	9,102	311	123	6	87	67	155	157	3,425	1,141	3,630
Mari	7,003	–	–	–	7,003	184	88	4	81	62	168	171	2,733	760	2,752
Bashkir	5,934	–	–	36	5,898	214	383	51	192	134	315	594	2,061	812	1,142
Komi-Permyak	3,367	–	–	–	3,367	75	8	0	25	39	22	13	1,095	279	1,811
Lithuanian	2,419	–	–	134	2,285	80	35	2	55	32	55	20	990	355	661
Estonian	2,600	–	–	505	2,095	52	10	0	44	65	44	7	1,138	472	263
Vietnamese	2,067	–	–	–	2,067	1	1	3	0	0	12	0	293	1,315	442
Others ***	75,397	4,640	9,600	9,642	51,515	2,438	1,363	2,240	536	409	3,887	1,658	20,848	2,739	15,397

Notes

* Nagorno Karabakh did not participate in the 1999 Azerbaijan census, but is still included in the official data: the number of Armenians in Nagorno Karabakh at the time of the 1989 census was copied.

** There are no recent full population statistics for the entire territory of Georgia. The figures here are an aggregate of the 2002 Georgia census (which did not include the Abkhaz and Ossetian-controlled territories), the 2003 Abkhazia census (which is disputed by Georgia, claiming that some figures are beefed up), and a rough estimate for South Ossetia in the absence of any recent census. The population of South Ossetia (including the Georgian zone of South Ossetia that was included in the 2002 census) is commonly estimated to be 70,000 people, out of which 45,000 are Ossetians and 17,500 Georgians. As a result, the figures for Georgia are not reliable completely.

*** The censuses of Armenia, Azerbaijan and Georgia do not list as many ethnic groups as the Russian one. The fact that the number of Nogay or Adyghe is not mentioned does not mean there are none at all in the South Caucasus. Therefore, the total number of 'other' ethnic groups may not be fully accurate.

NOTES

1 GEOGRAPHY

1 The Georgian myth of Amirani and the Armenian myth of Artavazd (this time at Mount Ararat) are very similar to the one of Prometheus.
2 The glaciers of the Caucasus and their retreat over the last decades are described in C. Stokes, S. Gurney, M. Shahgedanova and V. Popovnin, 'Late-twentieth-century changes in glacier extent in the Caucasus Mountains, Russia/Georgia', *Journal of Glaciology*, 52, 176 (2006), pp. 99–109.
3 GRID-Tbilisi, *Caucasus Environment Outlook (CEO) 2002*, Tbilisi: UNEP, 2003, p. 15.
4 V. Krever, N. Zazanashvili, H. Jungius, L. Williams and D. Petelin (eds), *Biodiversity in the Caucasus Ecoregion: An Analysis of Biodiversity and Current Threats and Initial Investment Portfolio*, Baku, Yerevan, Gland, Moscow and Tbilisi: WWF, 2001, p. 18.
5 Ibid., pp. 13–14.
6 Ibid., p. 13.
7 GRID-Tbilisi, *Caucasus Environment Outlook (CEO) 2002*, Tbilisi: UNEP, 2003, p. 25.
8 Ibid., p. 32.
9 Ibid., p. 7.
10 A. Mekhtiev and A. Gul, 'Ecological problems of the Caspian Sea and perspectives on possible solutions', in M. Glantz and I. Zonn (eds), *Scientific, Environmental and Political Issues in the Circum-Caspian Region*, Dordrecht: Kluwer Acadamic Publishers, 1997, p. 82.
11 T. Mkrtchyan, 'The prospects of "physical" border-spanning at the neighbours of Europe (the case of South Caucasus) and the role of NATO in that process', in *Expanding Borders: Communities and Identities*, Riga: University of Latvia, 2005, p. 219.
12 This theory of Samuel P. Huntington was formulated in the article "The clash of civilisations?" in the journal *Foreign Affairs* in 1993 as a reaction to Francis Fukuyama's 1992 book *The End of History and the Last Man*; it was further elaborated in *The Clash of Civilisations and the Remaking of World Order* (1996). The theory explained that future conflicts would be based on culture and religion, and not on economy or ideology.

2 TERRITORIAL DIVISION, GOVERNMENT AND ADMINISTRATION

1 Robert Kocharyan was allowed to run for president despite article 50 of the constitution, which stipulates that all candidates should have been resident in Armenia for the previous ten years.
2 International Institute for Strategic Studies, *The Military Balance 2008*, London: Routledge, 2008, pp. 165–6.

3 Ibid., p. 166.
4 Ibid., pp. 167–8.
5 Irakli Okruashvili, born in Tskhinvali (the Georgian spelling of the name; Tskhinval in Ossetian), had been an ally of Saakashvili but turned into an enemy of the Georgian leadership after being dismissed in November 2006. Thereafter he created his own opposition party.
6 International Institute for Strategic Studies, *The Military Balance 2008*, London: Routledge, 2008, pp. 176–7. Furthermore, Jared Feinberg's *The Armed Forces in Georgia* (Washington, DC: Center for Defense Information, 1999) gives a very detailed overview of the armed forces and foreign military presence in Georgia at the end of the twentieth century.
7 There were approximately 1,500 peacekeepers in 2007, but in spring and summer 2008 Russia radically increased this number. The 1994 Moscow Agreement stipulates a ceiling of 3,000, but there is no official ceiling for South Ossetia.
8 The territorial division into districts is not the same in the Georgian and Abkhaz constitutions. The Georgian constitution mentions the Ochamchire district, whereas the Abkhaz constitution (not accepted by the Georgians) subdivides this area into two distinct districts – Ochamchira and Tkvarchal.
9 Anonymous, *Ossetian War article*, http://www.militaryphotos.net/forums/showthread. php?t=140546 (accessed 24 December 2008).
10 This has been reported frequently in the press, e.g. by Interfax on 16 June 2005 and by RIA Novosti on 20 May 2008.
11 Anonymous, *Ossetian War article*, http://www.militaryphotos.net/forums/showthread. php?t=140546 (accessed 24 December 2008).
12 When the constitution was adopted in 1993 it listed 89 subjects, but later some of them were merged.
13 There is one exception, though – the Jewish Autonomous Oblast, which was not elevated to the status of a republic but remained an autonomous oblast.
14 Initially, the president could serve for a period of five years, but this was reduced to four years in the 1993 constitution. In December 2008 a constitutional amendment was approved, prolonging the presidential term to six years as of the next elections.
15 According to the 2008 military balance, they numbered 1,027,000 in 2007.
16 This Caspian flotilla was divided among Russia, Azerbaijan, Kazakhstan and Turkmenistan after the collapse of the USSR, but is operated jointly under Russian command.
17 Russia withdrew from its bases in Batumi and Akhalkalaki in 2007, but it is still guarding the Armenian–Turkish border.
18 The official figure is 396 dead, but the real number is probably much higher.
19 The investigation carried out after the school siege was flawed and left many questions unanswered. Survivors of the drama and family members of the victims, who believe that the authorities are responsible for the deaths, have called for a full inquiry.
20 From August 1987 until April 1990 he was chairman of the Presidium of the Supreme Soviet of the Dagestan ASSR, from April 1990 until July 1994 he was the chairman of the Supreme Soviet of the Dagestan ASSR, and from July 1994 until his resignation he was chairman of the State Council of the Republic of Dagestan.

3 POPULATION AND SOCIETY

1 Data come from the State Statistical Committee of the Republic of Azerbaijan.
2 Most of these emigrants were from the Ashkara tribe, who fought against the Russian forces. The Tapantas mainly fought alongside the tsarist army and so stayed in their homeland.

3 The Adyges consist of four groups: the Abadzekhs, the Bzhedugs, the Temirgoyevs and the Shapsugs. The Shapsugs are sometimes seen as a distinct ethnic group and were even mentioned separately in the 2002 census.

4 M. Kolga, *The Red Book of the Peoples of the Russian Empire*, Tallinn: NGO Red Book, 2001; available at http://www.eki.ee/books/redbook/

5 G. Ibragimov, *Tsakhurskij jazyk*, Moscow: Nauka, 1990, p. 11.

6 M. Kolga, *The Red Book of the Peoples of the Russian Empire*, Tallinn: NGO Red Book, 2001; available at http://www.eki.ee/books/redbook/

7 Ibid.

8 Abkhaz used a Cyrillic script from 1862 to 1928, a Latin script from 1928 to 1938 and a Georgian script from 1938 to 1954, and reverted to a Cyrillic script in 1954. Abaz used a Latin script from 1932 to 1938 and then changed to a Cyrillic script. Kabardino–Cherkess used an Arabic script from 1920 to 1923 and a Latin script from 1923 to 1936, when it also took on a Cyrillic script. Adyge used an Arabic script from 1918 to 1927 and a Latin script from 1927 to 1938, since when it has used a Cyrillic script. Ubykh never existed in a written form.

9 Chechen and Ingush used an Arabic script sporadically in the nineteenth century, but this became more official from 1918 onwards. Ingush changed to a Latin script in 1923 and Chechen followed two years later. In 1938 both languages took on a Cyrillic alphabet.

10 All these languages used the Arabic script sporadically during the Middle Ages but made this script official only in 1918. From 1928 onwards a Latin script was used and since 1938 they have taken up a Cyrillic alphabet.

11 The terms are used interchangeably, as there is no agreement in the English language as to which of them is correct.

12 Jassic, a third dialect, was spoken by a nomadic tribe which settled in Hungary in the thirteenth century. Two centuries later most of them had been assimilated into the Hungarian population and the language disappeared.

13 The clearest example is that of the excommunicated Georgian priest Basil Mkalavishvili, who masterminded and carried out attacks against Jehovah's Witnesses and Baptist Evangelists and burnt their religious literature in Tbilisi in 2002. Still, the Georgian Orthodox Church has always distanced itself from Mkalavishvili's actions.

14 Tengri, the sky god of the ancient Turkic people, is known as Teyri by the Karachay–Balkars or as Tengiri by the Kumyks.

15 I. Saffron, 'The Mountain Jews of Guba', *Philadelphia Inquirer*, 21 July 1997, p. 1.

16 From 224 Armenia was threatened by the Sassanid Persian Empire, and as a result the Armenian kings sought an alliance with Rome. It is thus unlikely that the Armenian king would have proclaimed Christianity the state religion before 313.

17 The Georgian Church claims that this miracle actually took place in the year 326. According to the legend, King Mirian was in a forest but suddenly darkness fell. The king prayed to his idols but nothing happened. After he prayed to the God of Nino it became light again and he could find his way out.

18 This Fourth Ecumenical Council was held from 8 October to 1 November 451 in Chalcedon (in modern-day Turkey) and dealt mainly with settling theological disputes about the person of Jesus Christ. Several churches had been following the position that Christ had only one nature, which was divine, and the legates of Pope Leo I argued that Christ had two natures (diophysite: one divine and one human) in one person. This led to a schism, with those churches rejecting the Confession of Chalcedon forming the Oriental Orthodoxy.

19 These reforms, which called for purification of the Russian Orthodox faith, were leading towards a centralization of the Church and a strengthening of Nikon's own authority.
20 At that time, the Doukhobors were led by Illarion Pobirokin, the father-in-law of Semeon Uklein.

4 HISTORY

1 Some theories claim that they were Indo-European or at least had a ruling Iranian class, whereas others link them to the Celts and the Gauls.
2 Some scholars claim the name Crimea is derived from Cimmeria.
3 However, there is no clarity as to when the Roman Empire actually became the Byzantine Empire; some claim this was in the third century, others that it was as late as 476. As a result, the names are interchangeable during those centuries.
4 The word Megrelian is derived from Egrisi.
5 Allahverdi Khan, a Georgian, was the army's commander-in-chief for 18 years. Several other Georgians became governors, and many shahs had Georgian wives.
6 J. McCarthy, 'The population of the Ottoman Armenians', in *The Armenians in the Late Ottoman Period*, Ankara: Turkish Historical Society for the Council of Culture, Arts and Publications of the Grand National Assembly of Turkey, 2001, p. 73.

5 CONFLICTS

1 From 14 to 19 June 1995, some 50 fighters led by Shamil Basayev stormed the city of Budennovsk in the Stavropol Kray and held around 1,800 people hostage in the local hospital. Some 120 were killed and approximately 400 others were wounded during this incident.
2 S. E. Cornell, *Small Nations and Great Powers: A Study of Ethnopolitical Conflict in the Caucasus*, Richmond: Curzon Press, 2001, p. 69.
3 Ibid., p. 96.
4 During the Georgian–Abkhaz war, and in the following years, several Abkhaz families migrated back from Turkey to the land of their ancestors.
5 International Crisis Group, *Georgia: Avoiding War in South Ossetia*, Brussels: ICG, 2004, p. 3.
6 Shevardnadze was appointed acting chairman of the Georgian State Council in March 1992 and was elected in November 1995, when the presidency was restored.
7 J. Minahan, *One Europe, Many Nations: A Historical Dictionary of European National Groups*, Westport, CT: Greenwood Press, 2000, p. 410.
8 Conflict based on the scarcity of water and other natural resources is described in Michael T. Klare's *Resource Wars: The New Landscape of Global Conflict*, New York: Metropolitan Books, 2001.

6 INTERNATIONAL POLITICS

1 Speech by President Bill Clinton during Shevardnadze's visit to the US in 1994.
2 With exception of 1918–20, when the three South Caucasian republics enjoyed a short-lived period of independence.
3 S. Cornell, *Small Nations and Great Powers: A Study of Ethnopolitical Conflict in the Caucasus*, Richmond: Curzon Press, 2001, p. 341.
4 Of the 15 former Soviet republics, the three Baltic states did not join the CIS, Ukraine signed and ratified the creation agreement but never ratified the CIS charter (i.e. it is a founding country but not a member), and Turkmenistan signed and ratified the creation agreement but only became an associate member.

5 Between 1999 and 2005 Uzbekistan was part of the then GUUAM group.
6 S. Cornell, *Small Nations and Great Powers*, p. 364.
7 K. Kasim, 'Russian–Armenian relations: a strategic partnership or hegemonic domination', *Review of Armenian Studies*, 1/2 (2003), p. 29.
8 S. Cornell, *Small Nations and Great Powers*, p. 353.
9 I. Indans, 'Relations of Russia and Georgia: development and future prospects', *Baltic Security & Defence Review*, 9 (2007), p. 131.
10 S. Cornell, *Small Nations and Great Powers*, pp. 347–52.
11 The foreign ministers of Turkey, Armenia and Azerbaijan met in Reykjavik in 2002 and in Istanbul in 2004.
12 From 1975 to 1991 the Marxist–Leninist guerrilla diaspora organization ASALA (Armenian Secret Army for the Liberation of Armenia) carried out an assassination and bombing campaign against Turkish diplomats all over the world, killing almost 50 people. The Armenian Revolutionary Army, a similar organization, also carried out several killings.
13 In April 2005, two weeks before the commemoration of the 90th anniversary of the Armenian genocide, Erdogan sent a letter to his Armenian counterpart suggesting the setting up of a 'joint group of historians and other experts'. In his answer, President Kocharyan called for the establishment of normal relations without preconditions.
14 When Turkey closed its border with Armenia in 1993, the Kars–Gyumri–Tbilisi railway was blocked as well. The Kars–Akhalkalaki–Tbilisi–Baku railway, bypassing Armenia, should be in operation by 2010.
15 This military component would deal only with logistics, but would demonstrate the level of friendly relations between the two countries.
16 *Statistical yearbook of Armenia*, Yerevan: National Statistical Service of the Republic of Armenia, 2008, p. 460.
17 Commission of the European Communities, Wider Europe – Neighbourhood: A New Framework for Relations with our Eastern and Southern Neighbours, Brussels: EU, 2003. Available online at http://www.ec.europa.eu/world/enp/pdf/com03_104_en.pdf
18 These PCAs replace the 1990 Trade and Cooperation Agreement (TCA) between the EU and the Soviet Union and add a political component.
19 Assistance from the European Commission came mainly through ECHO, the EC Humanitarian Aid Office. Although aid to the value of some €220 million was distributed through NGOs and UN agencies, ECHO was not allowed to open an office in the North Caucasus, and many of its implementing agencies were hampered in their work.
20 R. D. Asmus, *Next Steps in Forging a Euroatlantic Strategy for the Wider Black Sea*, Washington, DC: German Marshall Fund, 2006, p. 35.
21 T. Mkrtchyan, 'The prospects of "physical" border-spanning at the neighbours of Europe (the case of South Caucasus) and the role of NATO in that process', *Expanding Borders: Communities and Identities*, Riga: University of Latvia, 2005, p. 219.

7 ECONOMY

1 O. Konstantinov, *Severnyy Kavkaz*, Moscow, 1930, p. 12.
2 A. Kozlov, 'Ekonomika Dona i Severnoga Kavkaza v nachale XX veka', in *Rostovskaya Elektronnaya Gazeta*, no. 23[29] (1999). Available online at http://www.relga.rsu.ru/n29/don29.htm (accessed 14 January 2009).
3 Data from IMF, *World Economic Outlook: Financial Stress, Downturns, and Recoveries*, Washington, DC: IMF, 2008. Available at http://www.imf.org/external/pubs/ft/weo/2008/02/pdf/text.pdf
4 GDP per capita in $US at PPP figures for 2005 are Ingushetia: 1,443 (83rd); Chechnya: 1,871 (82nd); Dagestan 3,235 (81st); Adygea: 3,613 (78th); Karachay–Cherkessia: 3,636

(77th); Kabardino–Balkaria: 3,872 (75th); North Ossetia: 4,173 (73rd); Stavropol Kray: 5,083 (65th); Rostov Oblast: 5,373 (58th); Krasnodar Kray: 6,885 (56th). Figures are taken directly or based on data from the Federal State Statistics Service of the Russian Federation; the number in parenthese is the ranking among the federation's 83 entities.

5 Data come from World Bank, *Migration and Remittances Factbook*, Washington, DC: World Bank, 2008.

6 Economist Intelligence Unit, country reports for Armenia, Azerbaijan, Georgia and Russia, June 2008.

7 GRID-Tbilisi, *Caucasus Environment Outlook (CEO) 2002*, Tbilisi: UNEP, 2003, p. 32.

8 I. G. Kosikov and L. S. Kosikova, *Severnyy Kavkaz (Sotsialno-ekonomicheskij spravochnik*, Moscow: Eksklyuziv-press, 1999.

9 Data come from the July 2006 Survey of Key Oil and Gas Statistics and Forecasts for the Caspian Sea Region produced by the US government's Energy Information Administration (www.eia.doe.gov). Proven reserves are defined by the EIA as those volumes of oil and gas that geological and engineering data show with reasonable certainty; possible reserves are less precisely quantified and are defined here to include other reserves found through extensions, divisions and new discoveries.

10 Energy Information Administration, World Proved Reserves of Oil and Natural Gas, 2008. Available online at http://www.eia.doe.gov/emeu/international/reserves.html

SUGGESTED READING

General books on the Caucasus

Abdulatipov, R. G., Khamchiev, V. V. and Khapsirokov, K.-G.-Kh. (eds) (2007) *Kavkaz: istoriya, narody, kultura, religii*, Moscow: Vostochnaya literatura.

Avioutskii, V. (2005) *Géopolitique du Caucase*, Paris: Colin.

Beroutchachvili, N. and Radvanyi, J. (1996) *Atlas géopolitique du Caucase*, Paris: Inalco.

Cornell, S. E. (2001) *Small Nations and Great Powers: A Study of Ethnopolitical Conflict in the Caucasus*, Richmond: Curzon Press.

Gachechiladze, R. (1995) *The New Georgia: Space, Society, Politics*, London: University College of London Press.

GRID-Tbilisi (2003) *Caucasus Environment Outlook (CEO) 2002*, Tbilisi: UNEP.

Gumppenberg, M.-C. Von and Steinbach, U. (eds) (2008) *Der Kaukasus: Geschichte, Kultur, Politik*, Munich: C. H. Beck.

Herzig, E. (1999) *The New Caucasus: Armenia, Azerbaijan and Georgia*, London: Royal Institute of International Affairs.

Karny, Y. (2000) *Highlanders: A Journey to the Caucasus in Quest of Memory*, New York: Farrar, Straus & Giroux.

Kaufmann, R. (2000) *Kaukasus: Georgien, Armenien, Aserbaidschan*, Munich: Prestel.

Medvenko, L. and Oganyan, R. (2007) *Moskva – Kavkaz: Rossiya 'kavkazskoy natsionalnosti'*, Moscow: Grifon.

Nuriyev, E. (2007) *The South Caucasus at the Crossroads: Conflicts, Caspian Oil and Great Power Politics*, Berlin: LIT.

Rosen, R. (1999) *Georgia: A Sovereign Country of the Caucasus*, Hong Kong: Odyssey.

Shnirelman, V. A. (2001) *The Value of the Past: Myths, Identity and Politics in Transcaucasia*, Senri Enthological Studies no.57, Osaka: National Museum of Ethnology.

Suny, R.G. (ed.) (1983) *Transcaucasia: Nationalism and Social Change*, Ann Arbor: University of Michigan Press.

Tishkov, V. (ed.) (2007) *Rossiyskiy Kavkaz: kniga dlya politikov*, Moscow: Rosinformagrotekh.

van der Leew, C. (2000) *Azerbaijan: A Quest for Identity: A Short History*, New York: St Martin's Press.

Journals

Eurasian Geography and Economics, Palm Beach, FL: V. H. Winston.

Central Asia and the Caucasus, Luleå, Sweden: Central Asia and the Caucasus Information and Analytical Centre.

Caucasian Review of International Affairs, available online on http://www.cria-online.org/
The Caucasus & Globalization, Luleå, Sweden: CA&CC Press.
Caucasus Context: Washington, DC: World Security Institute.

Geography

Beruchashvili, N. L. (1995) *Kavkaz: landshafty, modely, eksperimenty*, Tbilisi: Tbilisskiy Gossudarstvenniy Universitet.

Bolshaya Rossiyskaya Entsiklopediya (1998) *Geografiya Rossii: Entsiklopedicheskiy Slovar*, Moscow: Izdatelstvo Bolshaya Rossiyskaya Entsiklopediya.

GRID-Tbilisi (2003) *Caucasus Environment Outlook (CEO) 2002*, Tbilisi: UNEP.

Krever, V., Zazanashvili, N., Jungius, H., Williams, L. and Petelin, D. (eds) (2001) *Biodiversity of the Caucasus Ecoregion: An Analysis of Biodiversity and Current Threats and Initial Investment Portfolio*, Moscow: WWF.

Levine, R. M. and Wallace, G. J. (2000) 'The mineral industry of the Commonwealth of Independent States', in *Minerals Yearbook 2000*, Washington, DC: US Geological Survey.

Lurye, P. M. (2002) *Vodnye resoursy i vodnyy balans Kavkaza*, St Petersburg: Gidrometeoizdat.

Lyayster, A. F. and Chursin G. F. (1929) *Geografiya Zakavkazja: Ocherki po fizicheskoy geografii i etnografii ZSFSR*, Moscow: Zakkniga.

Mangott, G. (1999) *Brennpunkt Südkaukasus*, Vienna: Braumüller.

Sokolov, V. E. and Siroyechkovskiy, E. E. (eds) (1990) *Zapovedniki Kavkaza*, Moscow: Mysl.

Territorial division, government and administration

Arakelian, A. and Nodia, G. (2005) *Protsess konstitutsionno-politicheskoy reformy v Gruzii, v Armeni i v Azerbaydzhane: politicheskaya elita i golos naroda*, Tbilisi: Mezhdunarodnyy institut demokratii i sodeystviya vyboram.

Arashidze, I. (2007) *Democracy and Autocracy in Eurasia: Georgia in Transition*, East Lansing: Michigan State University Press.

Babak, V. (ed.) (2004) *Political Organization in Central Asia and Azerbaijan: Sources and Documents*, London: Frank Cass.

Bailes, A. (2003) *Armament and Disarmament in the Caucasus and Central Asia*, Solna, Sweden: Stockholm International Peace Research Institute.

Bochorishvili, T., Sweet, W. and Ahern, D. (eds) (2005) *Politics, Ethics and Challenges to Democracy in 'New Independent States'*, Washington, DC: Council for Research in Values and Philosophy.

Coppieters, B. and Legvold, R. (eds) (2005) *Georgia after the Rose Revolution*, Cambridge, MA: MIT Press.

Gammer, M. (ed.) (2008) *Ethno-Nationalism, Islam and the State in the Caucasus*, London: Routledge.

International Institute for Strategic Studies (2008) *The Military Balance 2008*, London: Routledge.

Ishkanian, A. (2008) *Democracy Building and Civil Society in Post-Soviet Armenia*, London: Routledge.

Masih, J. and Krikorian, R. (1999) *Armenia: At the Crossroads*, Amsterdam: Harwood Academic.

Matveeva, A. and Hiscock, D. (eds) (2003) *The Caucasus: Armed and Divided*, London: Saferworld.

Misrokov, Z. (2002) *Adat i shariat v rossiyskoy pravovoy sisteme: istoricheskiye sudby yuridicheskogo plyuralizma na Severnom Kavkaze*, Moscow: Izdatelstvo Moskovskogo Universiteta.

Katz, R. (2006) *The Georgian Regime Crisis of 2003–2004: A Case Study in Post-Soviet Media Representation of Politics, Crime and Corruption*, Stuttgart: Ibidem.

Kozhokin, E. M. (1998) *Armeniya: problemy nezavisimogo razvitiya*, Moscow: Rossiyskiy Institut Strategicheskikh Issledovaniy.

Libaridian, G. (1999) *The Challenge of Statehood: Armenian Political Thinking since Independence*, Watertown, MA: Blue Crane Books.

Magamarov, E. M. (2007) *Sovremennaya geopoliticheskaya situatsiya na Severnom Kavkaze: problemy regionalnoy geostrategii Rossii*, Rostov-na-Donu: Severo-Kavkazskiy Nauchnyy Tsentr Vysshey Shkoly.

Mekhtiev, R. E. (2007) *Na puti k demokratii: razmyshleniya o nasledii*, Baku: Sarq-Qarb.

Minassian, G. (2005) *Géopolitique de l'Arménie*, Paris: Ellipses.

Ó Beacháin, D. (2009) 'Georgia's Rose Revolution', in I. Ness (ed.), *The World Encyclopaedia of Protest and Revolution: 1600 to Present*, Oxford: Blackwell.

Rau, J. (2002) *Politik und Islam in Nordkaukasien: Skizzen über Tschetschenien, Dagestan und Adygea*, Vienna: Braumüller.

Scholtbach, A. P. and Nodia, G. (2007) *The Political Landscape of Georgia: Political Parties: Achievements, Challenges, and Prospects*, Delft: Eburon.

Serrano, S. (2007) *Géorgie: sortie d'Empire*, Paris: CNRS.

van der Leeuw, C. (2000) *Azerbaijan: A Quest for Identity*, New York: St Martin's Press.

Waters, C. (2005) *The State of Law in the South Caucasus*, Basingstoke: Palgrave Macmillan.

Wheatley, J. (2005) *Georgia from National Awakening to Rose Revolution: Delayed Transition in the Former Soviet Union*, London: Ashgate.

Population and society

Alikberov, A. (2003) *Epokha klassicheskogo islama na Kavkaze: Abu Bakr ad-Darbandi i ego suficheskaya entsiklopediya 'Raykhan al-Khaka-ik'*, Moscow: RAN.

Arakelov, V. and Asatrian, G. (2002) *The Ethnic Minorities of Armenia*, Yerevan: Human Rights in Armenia.

Balci, B. (2007) *Religion et politique dans le Caucase post-soviétique*, Paris: Maisonneuve & Larose.

Baykal, M. (2005) *Evreyskiy mir Kavkaza: traditsii i tsennosti*, Baku: Qanun.

Breyfogle, N. B. (2005) *Heretics and Colonizers: Forging Russia's Empire in the South Caucasus*, Ithaca, NY: Cornell University Press.

Chenciner, R. (1997) *Daghestan: Tradition & Survival*, Richmond: Curzon Press.

Chernous, V. V. (ed.) (2001) *Islam i politika na severnom Kavkaze*, Rostov-na-Donu: Severo-Kavkazskiy Nauchnyy Tsentr Vysshey Shkoly.

Funch, L. and Krag, H. (1994) *The North Caucasus: Minorities at a Crossroads*, London: Minority Rights Group.

Fyodorov, Y. A. (1983) *Istoricheskaya etnografiya Severnogo Kavkaza: Uchebnoye posobiye*, Moscow: Izdatelstvo Moskovskogo Universiteta.

Gammer, M. (ed.) (2008) *Ethno-Nationalism, Islam and the State in the Caucasus: Post-Soviet Disorder*, London: Routledge.

Gardanov, V. A. (ed.) (1962) *Narody Kavkaza*, Tom II, Moscow: Izdatelstvo Akademii Nauk SSSR.

Guchinova, E.-B. M. (2006), *The Kalmyks: A Handbook*, Richmond: Curzon Press.

Hahn, G. (2007) *Russia's Islamic Threat*, New Haven, CT: Yale University Press.

Herzig, E. and Kurkchiyan, M. (eds) (2005) *The Armenians: Past and Present in the Making of National Identity*, London: RoutledgeCurzon.

Hewitt, G. (ed.) (1999) *The Abkhazians: A Handbook*, Richmond: Curzon Press.

Hewitt, G. (2004) *Introduction to the Study of the Languages of the Caucasus*, Munich: Lincom Europa.

Ibragimov, G. K. (1990) *Tsakhurskiy yazyk*, Moscow: Nauka.

Jaimoukha, A. (2001) *The Circassians: A Handbook*, Richmond: Curzon Press.

Jaimoukha, A. (2005) *The Chechens: A Handbook*, Abingdon: RoutledgeCurzon.

Karpov, Y. (2001) *Zhenskoye prostranstvo v kulture narodov Kavkaza*, St Petersburg: Peterburgskoye Vostokovedeniye.

Kolga, M. (2001) *The Red Book of the Peoples of the Russian Empire*, Tallinn: NGO Red Book.

Kosven, M. O. (ed.) (1960) *Narody Kavkaza*, Tom I, Moscow: Izdatelstvo Akademii Nauk SSSR.

Kreyenbroek, F. G. (1995) *Yezidism: Its Background, Observances and Textual Tradition*, Lewiston, NY: Edwin Mellen Press.

Kuznetsov, V. (2002) *Khristianstvo na Severnom Kavkaze do XV v*, Vladikavkaz: Ir.

Lavrov, L. I. (1982) *Etnografiya Kavkaza*, Leningrad: Izdatelstvo Nauk.

Malashenko A. (2001) *Islamskiye orientiry Severnogo Kavkaza*, Moscow: Gendalf.

Malashenko A. and Brill Olcott M. (eds) (2001) *Islam na postsovetskom prostranstve: vzglyad iznutri*, Moscow: Moskovskiy Tsentr Karnegi.

Mchedlov, M. P. (ed.) (1999; 2nd edn, 2002) *Religii narodov sovremennoy Rossii: Slovar*, Moscow: Respublika.

Menon, R. (ed.) (1999) *Russia, the Caucasus and Central Asia: The Twenty-First Century Security Environment*, Armonk, NY: M. E. Sharpe.

Mgaloblishvili, T. (1998) *Ancient Christianity in the Caucasus*, Richmond: Curzon Press.

Ro'i, Y. (2001) *Islam in the CIS: A Threat to Stability*, London: Royal Institute of International Affairs.

Seibt, W. (ed.) (2002) *The Christianization of Caucasus (Armenia, Georgia, Albania)*, Vienna: Austrian Academy of Sciences Press.

Semenov, I. Y. (2001) *Istoriya zakavkazkikh molokan i dukhoborov*, Yerevan.

Todua, Z. (2006) *Ekspansiya islamistov na Kavkaze i Tsentralnoy Azii*, Moscow: In-Oktavo.

History

Allen, W. E. D. (1971) *A History of the Georgian People*, New York: Routledge & Kegan Paul.

Allen, W. E. D. and Muratoff, P. (1953) *Caucasian Battlefields: A History of the Wars on the Turko-Caucasian Frontier (1828–1921)*, New York: Cambridge University Press.

Baddeley, J. F. (1908) *The Russian Conquest of the Caucasus*, London: Longmans, Green.

Barrett, T. M. (1999) *At the Edge of Empire: The Terek Cossacks and the North Caucasus Frontier, 1700–1860*, Boulder, CO: Westview Press.

Bayev, K. (1979) *Vosstaniya na Severnom Kavkaze v kontse 1920-go goda*, Paris: PIUF.

Bechhofer, C. E. (1971) *In Denikin's Russia and the Caucasus, 1919–1920*, New York: Arno Press.

Beroutchachvili, N. and Radvanyi, J. (1996) *Atlas géopolitique du Caucase*, Paris: Inalco.

Braund, D. (1996) *Georgia in Antiquity: A History of Colchis and Transcaucasian Iberia 550 BC–AD 562*, Oxford: Oxford University Press.

Brook, K. A. (1999) *The Jews of Khazaria*, Northvale, NJ: Jason Aronson.

Bryer, A. (1988) *Peoples and Settlement in Anatolia and the Caucasus, 800–1900*, London: Ashgate.

Davis-Kimball, J., Bashilov, V. A. and Yablonsky, L. T. (eds) (1995) *Nomads of the Eurasian Steppes in the Early Iron Age*, Berkeley, CA: Zinat Press.

Dédéyan, G. (ed.) (2007) *Histoire du peuple arménien*, Toulouse: privately published.

Dunlop, D. M. (1967) *The History of Jewish Khazars*, New York: Schocken Books.

Gammer, M. (1994) *Muslim Resistance to the Tsar: Shamil and the Conquest of Chechnia and Daghestan*, London: Frank Cass.

Grechko, A. (2001) *Battle for the Caucasus*, Honolulu: University Press of the Pacific.

Jones, S. F. (2005) *Socialism in Georgian Colors: The European Road to Social Democracy, 1883–1917*, Cambridge, MA: Harvard University Press.

Kazanski, M. and Mastykova, A. (2003) *Les peuples du Caucase du Nord: le début de l'histoire (Ier–VIIe s. apr. J.-C.)*, Paris: Errance.

Kazemzadeh, F. (1951, repr. 1981) *The Struggle for Transcaucasia (1917–1921)*, Westport, CT: Greenwood Press.

King, C. (2008) *The Ghost of Freedom: A History of the Caucasus*, Oxford: Oxford University Press.

Koestler, A. (1976) *The Thirteenth Tribe: The Khazar Empire and its Heritage*, New York: Random House.

Kushnareva, K. (1997) *The Southern Caucasus in Prehistory: Stages of Cultural and Socioeconomic Development from the Eighth to the Second Millenium BC*, Philadelphia: University of Pennsylvania Museum.

Lionnet, B. (ed.) (2007) *Les cultures du Caucase: (VIe–IIIe millénaires avant notre ère): leurs relations avec le Proche-Orient*, Paris: CNRS.

Lordkipanidze, M. and Hewitt, G. (eds) (1987) *Georgia in the XI–XII centuries*, Tbilisi: Ganatleba.

Lybin, V. and Belyayeva, E. (2006) *Rannyaya preistoriya Kavkaza*, St Petersburg: Peterburgskoye Vostokovedeniye.

Minorsky, V. (1978) *The Turks, Iran and the Caucasus in the Middle Ages*, London: Variorum Reprints.

Mostashari, F. (2006) *On the Religious Frontier: Tsarist Russia and Islam in the Caucasus*, London: Taurus.

Motika, M. (ed.) (2000) *Caucasia between the Ottoman Empire and Iran, 1555–1914*, Wiesbaden: Reichert.

Novoseltsev, A. P. (1990) *Khazarskoye gosudarstvo i ego rol v istorii Vostochnoy Evropy i Kavkaza*, Moscow: Nauka.

Pliyeva, Z. (2006) *Myuridizm: ideologiya Kavkazskoy voyny*, Vladikavkaz: SOGU.

Suny, R. G. (1983) *Armenia in the Twentieth Century*, Chico, CA: Scholars Press.

Suny, R. G. (1993) *Looking Toward Ararat: Armenia in Modern History*, Bloomington: Indiana University Press.

Suny, R. G. (1994) *The Making of the Georgian Nation*, 2nd edn, Bloomington: Indiana University Press.

Thieke, W. (1995) *The Caucasus and the Oil: The German–Soviet War in the Caucasus 1942/43*, Winnipeg: J. J. Fedorowicz.
Tsutsiyev, A. A. (2006) *Atlas etnopoliticheskoy istorii Kavkaza (1774–2004)*, Moscow: Evropa.
Zelkina, A. (2000) *In Quest for God and Freedom: The Sufi Response to the Russian Advance in the North Caucasus*, New York: New York University Press.

Conflicts

Bayev, P. K. and Berthelsen, O. (1996) *Conflicts in the Caucasus*, Oslo: Institutt for Fredsforskning.
Beissinger, M. R. (2002) *Nationalist Mobilization and the Collapse of the Soviet State*, Cambridge: Cambridge University Press.
Chorbajian, L., Donabedian P. and Mutafian C. (1994) *The Caucasian Knot: The History and Geopolitics of Nagorno-Karabagh*, Atlantic Highlands, NJ: Zed Books.
Croissant, M. (1998) *The Armenia–Azerbaijan Conflict: Causes and Implications*, London: Praeger.
Dehdashti, R. (2000) *Internationale Organisationen als Vermittler in innerstaatlichen Konflikten: Die OSZE und der Berg-Karabach-Konflikt (1992–1998)*, Frankfurt am Main: Campus.
de Waal, T. (2003) *Black Garden: Armenia and Azerbaijan through Peace and War*, New York: New York University Press.
Ebel, R. E. and Menon, R. (eds) (2000) *Energy and Conflict in Central Asia and the Caucasus*, Lanham, MD: Rowman & Littlefield.
Evangelista, M. (2002) *The Chechen Wars: Will Russia Go the Way of the Soviet Union?*, Washington, DC: Brookings Institution.
Farrell, W. B., Kay, B., Philips, A. and Robertson, L. (2002) *Georgia Conflict Assessment*, Washington, DC: ARD.
Gall, C. and de Waal, T. (1998) *Chechnya: Calamity in the Caucasus*, New York: New York University Press.
Halbach, U. and Kappeler, A. (eds) (1995) *Krisenherd Kaukasus*, Baden-Baden: Nomos.
Hughes, J. and Sasse, C. (2002) *Ethnicity and Territory in the Former Soviet Union*, London: Frank Cass.
Lieven, A. (1998) *Chechnya: Tombstone of Russian Power*, New Haven, CT: Yale University Press.
Lynch, D. (1998) *The Conflict in Abkhazia: Dilemmas in Russian 'Peacekeeping' Policy*, London: Royal Institute of International Affairs.
Mangott, G. (ed.) (1999) *Brennpunkt Südkaukasus: Aufbruch trotz Krieg, Vertreibung und Willkürherrschaft?*, Vienna: Braumüller.
Matveeva, A. (1999) *The North Caucasus: Russia's Fragile Borderland*, London: Royal Institute of International Affairs.
Politkovskaya, A. (2001) *A Dirty War: A Russian Reporter in Chechnya*, London: Harvill Press.
Souleimanov, E. (2007) *An Endless War: The Russian–Chechen Conflict in Perspective*, Frankfurt am Main: Lang.
Trenin, D. V. *et al.* (2004) *Russia's Restless Frontier: The Chechnya Factor in Post-Soviet Russia*, Washington, DC: Carnegie Endowment for International Peace.

Vitkovskaya, G. and Malashenko, A. (eds) (1998) *Vozrozhdeniye kazachestva: nadezhdy i opaseniya*, Moscow: Moskovskiy Tsentr Karnegi.

Zürcher, C. (2007) *The Post-Soviet Wars: Rebellion, Ethnic Conflict, and Nationhood in the Caucasus*, New York: New York University Press.

Zürcher, C. and Koehler, J. (eds) (2003) *Potentials of Disorder: Explaining Conflict and Stability in the Caucasus and in the Former Yugoslavia*, Manchester: Manchester University Press.

International politics

Abdullayev, E. (2007) *Azerbaydzhan na puti demokraticheskogo razvitiya*, Baku: Takhsil.

Akiner, S. (ed.) (2004) *The Caspian: Politics, Energy and Security*, Abingdon: RoutledgeCurzon.

Amirahmadi, H. (ed.) (2000) *The Caspian Region at a Crossroad: Challenges of a New Frontier of Energy and Development*, Basingstoke: Macmillan.

Aphrasidze, D. (2003) *Die Außen- und Sicherheitspolitik Georgiens: zur Rolle kleiner und schwacher Staaten in der neuen europäischen Friedensordnung*, Baden-Baden: Nomos.

Asmus, R. D. (ed.) (2006) *Next Steps in Forging a Euroatlantic Strategy for the Wider Black Sea*, Washington, DC: German Marshall Fund.

Bayev, P. (1997) *Russia's Policies in the Caucasus*, London: Royal Institute for International Affairs.

Bertsch, G. K., Craft, C. B. and Jones S. A. (eds) (1999) *Crossroads and Conflict: Security and Foreign Policy in the Caucasus and Central Asia*, New York: Routledge.

Coene, F. (2003) *NATO i yuzhnyy Kavkaz*, Tbilisi: CIPDD.

Eyvazov, D. (2004) *Bezopasnost Kavkaza i stabilnost razvitiya Azerbaydzhanskoy Respubliki*, Baku: Nurlan.

Geistlinger, M. (ed.) (2008) *Security Identity and the Southern Caucasus: The Role of the EU, the US and Russia*, Vienna: Neuer Wissenschaftlicher Verlag.

Karagiannis, E. (2002) *Energy and Security in the Caucasus*, London: RoutledgeCurzon.

Krylov, A. B. (2006) *Nagornyy Karabakh v geopoliticheskom kontekste XXI veka*, Moscow: Akademiya Gumanitarnykh Issledovaniy.

Lynch, D. (ed.) (2003) *The South Caucasus: A Challenge for the EU*, Paris: European Union Institute for Security Studies.

Mayer, S. (2006) *Die Europäische Union im Südkaukasus: Interessen und Institutionen in der auswärtige Politikgestaltung*, Baden-Baden: Nomos.

Melvin, N. (2007) *Building Stability in the North Caucasus: Ways Forward for Russia and the European Union*, Solna, Sweden: Stockholm International Peace Research Institute.

Menon, R. and Nodia, G. (eds) (1999) *Russia, the Caucasus, and Central Asia: The Twenty-First Century Security Environment*, New York: M. E. Sharpe.

Minassian, G. (2007) *Caucase du Sud, la nouvelle guerre froide: Arménie, Azerbaïdjan, Géorgie*, Paris: Autrement.

Muradyan, I. M. (2001) *Geoekonomicheskiye factory razvitiya politicheskix protsessov v kavkazsko-kaspiyskom regione*, Yerevan: Antares.

Nation, R. C. (2007) *Russia, the United States, and the Caucasus*, Carlisle, PA: Strategic Studies Institute.

Nygren, B. (2008) *The Rebuilding of Greater Russia: Putin's Foreign Policy towards the CIS Countries*, London: Routledge.

Rau, J. (2005) *Russland – Georgien – Tschetschenien: der Konflikt um das Pankisi-Tal (1997–2003), ein Handbuch*, Berlin: Köster.

Rybkin, I. P. (1998) *Consent in Chechnya, Consent in Russia*, London: Lytten Trading.

Shakirzade, N. (2007) *Sodruzhestvo Nezavisimykh Gosudarstv (SNG): Azerbaydzhanskaya Respublika vo vneshnopoliticheskikh i vneshneekonomicheskikh protsessakh (1991–2006 gg.)*, Baku: Sada.

Soghomonyan, V. (2007) *Europäische Integration und Hegemonie im Südkaukasus: Armenien, Aserbaidschan und Georgien auf dem Weg nach Europa*, Baden-Baden: Nomos.

Svarants, A. (2002) *Pantyurkizm v geostrategii Turtsii na Kavkaze*, Moscow: Akademia Gumanitarnykh Issledovaniy.

Winrow, G. (2001) *Turkey and the Caucasus: Domestic Interests and Security Concerns*, Washington, DC: Brookings Institution.

Wright, J. (ed.) (1996) *Transcaucasian Boundaries*, London: School of Oriental and African Studies.

Economy

Alirzayev, A.G. and Kurbanova, F.A. (2007) *Transformatsii ekonomiki stran perekhodnogo perioda v usloviyakh integratsii*, Baku: Igtisad Universiteti.

Ardillier-Carras, F. (2004) *L'Arménie des campagnes: la transition post-soviétique dans un pays du Caucase*, Paris: Harmattan.

Auty, R. M. and de Soysa, I. (eds) (2006) *Energy, Wealth and Governance in the Caucasus and Central Asia: Lessons Not Learned*, London: Routledge.

Champain, P., Klein, D. and Mirimanova, N. (eds) (2004) *From War Economies to Peace Economies in the South Caucasus*, London: International Alert.

Efendiyev, O. (2007) *Vneshneekonomicheskaya deyatelnost sovremennogo Azerbaydzhana: uchebnoye posbiye*, Baku: Zardabi.

Gregory, P. (2004) *Before Command: An Economic History of Russia from Emancipation to the First Five-Year Plan*, Princeton, NJ: Princeton University Press.

Gurbanov, T. (2007) *Le pétrole de la Caspienne et la politique extérieure de l'Azerbaïdjan*, Paris: Harmattan.

Henning, J. (2000) *Georgien: Institutioneller Wandel und wirtschaftliche Entwicklung*, Cottbus: BTU.

Ismailov, E. (2007) *Tsentralnyy kavkaz: istoriya, politika, ekonomika*, Moscow: Mysl.

Ismailov, E. and Papava, V. (2006) *The Central Caucasus: Essays on Geopolitical Economy*, Stockholm: CA & CC Press.

Jeffreys, I. (2003) *The Caucasus and Central Asian Republics at the Turn of the Twenty-First Century: A Guide to Economics in Transition*, London: Routledge.

Kosikov, I. G. and Kosikova, L. S (1999) *Severnyy Kavkaz (Sotsialno-ekonomicheskij spravochnik)*, Moscow: Eksklyuziv-press.

Lerman, Z. and Mirzakhanian, A. (2001) *Private Agriculture in Armenia*, Lanham, MD: Lexington Books.

Melloni, N. (2006) *Market without Economy: The 1998 Russian Financial Crisis*, Stuttgart: Ibidem.

Mir-Babayev, M. F. (2004) *Brief Chronology of the History of Azerbaijan's Oil Business*, Baku: Sabah.

Najman, B., Pomfret, R. and Raballand, G. (eds) (2007) *The Economics and Politics of Oil in the Caspian Basin: The Redistribution of Oil Revenues in Azerbaijan and Central Asia*, New York: Routledge.

Papava, V. G. (2005) Necroeconomics: The Political Economy of Post-Communist Capitalism: Lessons from Georgia, New York: iUniverse.

Sutela, P. (2004) *The Russian Market Economy*, 3rd edn, Helsinki: Aleksanteri Institute.

van der Leeuw, C. (2000) *Oil and Gas in the Caucasus & Caspian: A History*, Richmond: Curzon Press.

Vinogradov, V. A. (2003) *Privatizatsiya v Rossii i drugikh stranakh SNG*, Moscow: Rossiyskaya Akademiya Nauk.

Yazykova, A. A. (ed.) (2008) *Severnyy Kavkaz: problemy ekonomiki i politiki*, Moscow: LKI.

Yuzbasheva, G. (1997) *Strukturnaya perestroyka ekonomiki Azerbaydzhana na sovremennom etape razvitiya*, Baku: Sada.

Culture and traditions

Abrahamian, L. and Sweezy, N. (eds) (2001) *Armenian Folk Arts, Culture, and Identity*, Bloomington: Indiana University Press.

Chotiwari-Jünger, S. (2003) *Die Literaturen der Völker Kaukasiens*, Wiesbaden: Reichert.

Colarusso, J. (2002) *Nart Sagas from the Caucasus: Myths and Legends from the Circassians, Abazas, Abkhaz, and Ubykhs*, Princeton, NJ: Princeton University Press.

Fähnrich, H. (1993) *Georgische Literatur*, Aachen: Shaker.

Gogiberidze, G. M. (ed.) (2004) *Literatura narodov Severnogo Kavkaza*, Stavropol: Izdatelsko-poligraficheskaya firma 'Stavropole'.

Layton, S. (1994) *Russian Literature and Empire: Conquest of the Caucasus from Pushkin to Tolstoy*, Cambridge: Cambridge University Press.

Mühlfried, F. (2006) *Postsowjetische Feiern: das georgische Bankett im Wandel*, Stuttgart: Ibidem.

Nasymth, P. (1998) *Georgia: In the Mountains of Poetry*, New York: St Martin's Press.

Nooter, R., Koshoridze, I. and Tatikyan, V. (2004) *Flat-Woven Rugs & Textiles from the Caucasus*, Atglen, PA: Schiffer.

Roudik, P. (2008) *Culture and Customs of the Caucasus*, Westport, CT: Greenwood Press.

Wright, R. E. and Wertime J. T. (1995) *Caucasian Carpets & Covers: The Weaving Culture*, London: Hali.

Literary works

Brecht, B., *The Caucasian Chalk Circle*

Dumas, A., *Tales of the Caucasus: The Ball of Snow and Sultanetta*

Lermontov, M., *A Hero of our Time*

Lermontov, M., *Izmail-Bey*

Lermontov, M., *The Novice (Mtsyri)*

Pushkin, A., *A journey to Erzurum*

Rustaveli, S., *The Knight in the Panther's Skin*

Said, K., *Ali and Nino: A Love Story*

Tolstoy, L., *A Captive of the Caucasus*

Tolstoy, L., *Hadji Murat: A Tale of the Caucasus*

Tolstoy, L., *The Cossacks*

INDEX

Note: Page numbers for illustrations appear in **bold**.